ABSOLUTE BEGINNER GUIDE

TO

Microsoft® Office
Outlook® 2003

Ken Slovak

800 East 96th Street,
Indianapolis, Indiana 46240

Absolute Beginner's Guide to Microsoft® Office Outlook® 2003

International Standard Book Number: 0-789-72968-7

Library of Congress Catalog Card Number: 2003103667

Printed in the United States of America

First Printing: September 2003

06   05   04   03   4   3   2   1

Trademarks

All terms mentioned in this book that are known to be trademarks or service marks have been appropriately capitalized. Que Publishing cannot attest to the accuracy of this information. Use of a term in this book should not be regarded as affecting the validity of any trademark or service mark.

Warning and Disclaimer

Every effort has been made to make this book as complete and as accurate as possible, but no warranty or fitness is implied. The information provided is on an "as is" basis. The author and the publisher shall have neither liability nor responsibility to any person or entity with respect to any loss or damages arising from the information contained in this book.

Bulk Sales

Que Publishing offers excellent discounts on this book when ordered in quantity for bulk purchases or special sales. For more information, please contact

U.S. Corporate and Government Sales
1-800-382-3419
corpsales@pearsontechgroup.com

For sales outside of the U.S., please contact

International Sales
1-317-428-3341
international@pearsontechgroup.com

Associate Publisher
Greg Wiegand

Acquisitions Editor
Stephanie J. McComb

Development Editor
Laura Norman

Managing Editor
Charlotte Clapp

Project Editor
Sheila Schroeder

Copy Editor
Chuck Hutchinson

Indexer
Mandie Frank

Proofreader
Suzanne Thomas

Technical Editor
Vince Averello
Milly Staples

Team Coordinator
Sharry Lee Gregory

Interior Designer
Anne Jones

Cover Designer
Dan Armstrong

Page Layout
Stacey DeRome
Michelle Mitchell
Ron Wise

Graphics
Tammy Graham

Contents at a Glance

Table of Contents

About the Author

Ken Slovak is President of Slovak Technical Services, a company specializing in Outlook, Exchange, SQL Server, and Office custom development and consulting. He has been an Outlook MVP since 1998. He co-authored *Programming Microsoft Outlook 2000*, *Professional Programming Outlook 2000*, and *Beginning Visual Basic 6 Application Development;* has contributed material to other Outlook books; and has written numerous magazine articles about Outlook. He makes his home in central Florida with his wife and dog and enjoys swimming, boating, fishing, cooking, and chasing squirrels for the dog.

Dedication

This book is dedicated to my beloved wife, Susie, for her patience in putting up with the long hours of writing and for just being there, and to my dog, Casey, for keeping me company while I was writing this book.

Acknowledgments

A book like this is a team effort, and even though only the author's name is on the cover, everyone on the team makes valuable contributions. I'd like to thank the editors at Que for all their work on the book, which I appreciate more than I can ever express. Stephanie McComb has been a patient acquisitions editor, guiding the book from beginning to end; Laura Norman is the best development editor I've worked with; Sheila Schroeder, the project editor, and Chuck Hutchinson, the copy editor, and everyone else at Que have been great to work with. The technical editors, Milly Staples and Vince Averello, both Outlook MVPs, are responsible for everything that's correct in the book and nothing that's incorrect.

I constantly learn more about Outlook from my fellow MVPs Sue Mosher, Diane Poremsky, Randy Byrne, Jessie Louise McClennan, Vince Averello, Russ Valentine, Patricia Cardoza, Ben Schorr, Steve Moede, Milly Staples, Dmitry Streblechenko, Robert Crayk, Jay Harlow, Hollis Paul, Bill Rodgers, Jocelyn Fiorello, Nikki Peterson, Patrick Reed, Thomas Wenzl, and Peter Raddatz. There is no better group of MVPs and people, and I appreciate being included in their company.

The Outlook team at Microsoft led by Marc Olsen and Jensen Harris and including Jeff Stephenson and many others is outstanding, and the best and most open product group I've ever worked with. The Outlook MVP Leads John Eddy and Brandon Hoff are always helpful, as are Bill Jacob and Folke Kiesler of PSS. Finally, as always, Ronna Pinkerton has been our guiding light and deserves the description "everyone loves Ronna."

We Want to Hear from You!

As the reader of this book, *you* are our most important critic and commentator. We value your opinion and want to know what we're doing right, what we could do better, what areas you'd like to see us publish in, and any other words of wisdom you're willing to pass our way.

As an associate publisher for Que Publishing, I welcome your comments. You can email or write me directly to let me know what you did or didn't like about this book—as well as what we can do to make our books better.

Please note that I cannot help you with technical problems related to the topic of this book. We do have a User Services group, however, where I will forward specific technical questions related to the book.

When you write, please be sure to include this book's title and author as well as your name, email address, and phone number. I will carefully review your comments and share them with the author and editors who worked on the book.

Email: feedback@quepublishing.com

Mail: Greg Wiegand
             Associate Publisher
             Que Publishing
             800 East 96th Street
             Indianapolis, IN 46240 USA

For more information about this book or another Que Publishing title, visit our Web site at www.quepublishing.com. Type the ISBN (excluding hyphens) or the title of a book in the Search field to find the page you're looking for.

Introduction

Microsoft Office Outlook 2003 (referred to throughout the book as Outlook 2003) is not only Microsoft's premier e-mail client but is also a powerful Personal Information Manager and a tool for collaborating with workgroups in a corporate setting. I've worked with Outlook since the first version, Outlook 97, and Outlook 2003 is already my favorite version of Outlook.

Using Outlook 2003, you can manage your calendar, appointments, and meetings; manage contacts and e-mail address books; organize tasks and to-do lists; keep notes and a journal; manage and control junk e-mails; share information with other people in a workgroup setting utilizing Microsoft Exchange Server; and use Outlook with other Microsoft Office applications for mail merging and data import and export.

Outlook's power does you little good, however, until you know how to navigate Outlook and exploit its many features. This *Absolute Beginner's Guide to Microsoft Office Outlook 2003* provides you with all the instructions you need in an easy-to-follow, fully illustrated format. This book begins with a general overview of Outlook and shows you how to set up Outlook initially; it then leads you step by step through the tasks you perform as you use Outlook every day.

A Book for the True Beginner

The *Absolute Beginner's Guide to Microsoft Office Outlook 2003* is for novice Outlook users, those who have little or no experience with Outlook. Whether you must learn Outlook for work, school, or home, this is the book for you. This book also provides complete information about all the new features added to Outlook 2003. If you have used previous versions of Outlook and want to get up to speed quickly on using all the new features of Outlook 2003, this book is for you.

With its no-frills approach, the *Absolute Beginner's Guide to Microsoft Office Outlook 2003* provides instructions on how to master the most basic tasks and then goes on to teach you to take advantage of the most powerful features that Outlook 2003 has to offer.

How This Book Is Organized

The overall structure of this book is designed to feed you information as you're ready for it. The book begins by providing a basic explanation of Outlook as Microsoft's premier e-mail client and as a Personal Information Manager (PIM) for managing personal as well as corporate and collaborative information. Later chapters show you how to set up Outlook profiles, e-mail accounts, and data store files and how to work with Outlook's items, folders, and the many Outlook functions and features. You will learn how to navigate Outlook and customize Outlook's features and user interface, with tips on making the best use of that area of Outlook.

In addition to progressing from the basics to more advanced techniques, this book is divided into five parts to help you easily locate the information you need.

Part 1: Outlook Basics

Consider this part to be Outlook 101, the starting point for those who have no experience with Outlook. You will learn how Outlook is organized, how it stores your data, and what happens the first time you run Outlook. Learning how to set up Outlook to connect to the Internet and get your e-mail is next on the agenda, followed by the basics of using folders and moving around in Outlook. This part concludes with a section that teaches you how to set preferences for the way Outlook works.

Part 2: Working with E-mail

As soon as you understand the basics of Outlook, you're ready to learn about working with e-mail in depth. Here, you learn how to receive e-mail and work with the Reading Pane, Outlook 2003's way to quickly read information without actually opening items. You also learn how to reply to e-mails, create new e-mails, and use Outlook's e-mail editors and formats. Next are advanced e-mail topics such as custom signatures, using stationery, attachments, junk e-mail (spam) filtering, and e-mail links to the Web.

Finally, you learn about Outlook 2003's brilliant new feature, Search Folders. Search Folders give you a whole new way to organize and work with your data that previous generations of Outlook users never had available.

Part 3: Managing Information in Outlook

In this part, you learn about the many other things Outlook can do in addition to sending and receiving your e-mail. You will learn about contact records and address books, managing a calendar and setting up appointments, using tasks to create a to-do list, keeping a journal, and taking notes in Outlook. This part begins to reveal why Outlook is such a powerful application.

Part 4: Making Outlook Work for You

Part 4 is the place where you learn how to manage Outlook information. You will learn how to add and organize folders; customize the Navigation Pane; find things; archive data; customize views; and print, export, and import Outlook information. When you finish this part, you will have graduated as an advanced Outlook user.

Part 5: Advanced Outlook Topics

In this part, you learn how Outlook interfaces with Word to perform mail merges and sends and receives secure e-mails. You also learn how to design custom Outlook forms and create and use Outlook rules that help automate Outlook's functionality.

If you use Outlook at work and your company uses Microsoft Exchange Server to send and receive e-mail, you are actually using an advanced workplace collaboration platform. Outlook and Exchange together provide public folders that can host discussion areas, common document storage, and advanced meeting planning. You learn how to use all these features as well as how to use shared folders, work with delegated folders, and ensure privacy in a workgroup environment.

Appendixes

The appendixes, which can be found on the book's web site (www.quepublishing.com), show how to install Outlook 2003 and the installation options available for Outlook 2003 and how to get help with Outlook problems. They also provide solutions to the most common problems Outlook users face and provide information about Outlook add-ins that extend Outlook's functionality and synchronize Outlook with a Personal Digital Assistant (PDA).

Conventions Used in This Book

This book explains the essential concepts and tasks in an easily digestible format. At the beginning of each chapter is a bulleted list of "In This Chapter" highlights that provides you with a framework for what you are about to learn. At the end of each chapter, under the heading "The Absolute Minimum," you can review the main points covered in the chapter.

In addition, several boxes appear throughout the book to direct your attention to a *note* that provides more detailed information, a *tip* that can help you perform a step more efficiently, or a *caution* to help you steer clear of a potential problem. Following is a brief description of each box:

Notes provide additional information about the subject matter covered in a particular section. You can safely skip these notes and still learn the basics.

Tips provide an insider's guide to a particular concept or task. Look for the tip icon to learn useful shortcuts that show you how to perform a task more efficiently.

caution

Cautions point out common user errors and problem areas, so you can avoid the problems that hundreds of other users already have made. To avoid trouble and stay on the right track, read the cautions.

Assumptions in This Book

In this book, all the illustrations show full Outlook menus and assume that all Outlook features are installed on your hard drive. Outlook is also shown in full-screen mode to show the maximum amount of detail for illustrations. This book also assumes that Outlook is installed as part of Microsoft Office 2003 and was not purchased as a separate application.

Outlook Menus

Outlook menus show a subset of the available menu commands when you first start using Outlook. As you use Outlook, the menus are personalized to show the commands you use most frequently and to hide the commands you use less often. If you leave a personalized menu open for a while, the full menu is displayed, and you also can display a full menu by hovering the mouse cursor over the double down arrow at the bottom of the personalized menu. Figure I.1 shows the Outlook Tools menu using personalized menus.

FIGURE I.1

Personalized menus show the commands you use most often and hide less frequently used commands.

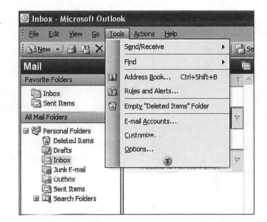

Outlook can be configured to show full menus instead of personalized menus. This book shows full menus in all illustrations that contain menus. Figure I.2 shows the Outlook Tools menu with Outlook configured to show full menus.

FIGURE I.2

Full menus show every menu command in the menu.

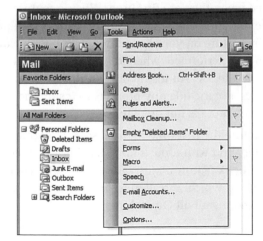

To customize Outlook menus to show full menus, follow these steps:

1. Select **Tools**, **Customize**.

2. Select the **Options** tab in the Customize dialog.

3. Check the **Always show full menus** checkbox, as shown in Figure I.3, and select **Close** to save the change.

FIGURE I.3

The Options tab of the Customize menu enables you to set how menus are displayed.

The setting for full menus affects all Microsoft Office System 2003 applications that support personalized menus. Changing this setting in Outlook also changes the setting in Word, Excel, and the other Office applications.

Outlook Features

In a default Outlook installation, some features are not installed or available, and some features are installed when they are first used. When a feature that is installed on first use is used for the first time, the Office Installer starts and requests access to the Office CD to install the feature on your hard drive. This book assumes a complete Outlook installation was performed, where all features are installed on your hard drive, ready for immediate use. All instructions in this book assume that all features are installed and do not include any prompts to install the feature or error messages displayed when a feature is not available.

The prompt to install a feature the first time it's used seems to occur most often when the CD isn't available, and with today's large hard drives, there really is no reason not to install all Outlook features. Most Office installations performed by computer manufacturers use a typical installation that doesn't install all features, but you can change that and install all Outlook features.

To learn how to install all Outlook features see the "Installing Outlook 2003" and "Adding and Removing Features" sections in Appendix A, "Microsoft Office Outlook 2003 Installation."

Microsoft Office 2003

The default e-mail editor for Outlook 2003 is Microsoft Word 2003. If you purchased Outlook 2003 as a separate application or as an update to a previous version of Microsoft Outlook, Word 2003 will not be available. In those cases, you cannot use Word as the Outlook e-mail editor, nor can you use earlier versions of Word as the e-mail editor for Outlook 2003.

This book assumes Microsoft Office 2003 is installed, and Word 2003 is available for use as Outlook's e-mail editor.

Final Thoughts

I've been using Outlook almost every day since shortly after the first version came out in 1997, and as an Outlook MVP (Microsoft Outlook Most Valuable Professional) I've been providing support for Outlook in the Microsoft Outlook communities since 1998. Over the years, I've learned a lot of time-saving ways of using Outlook to manage my information. In this book, I'll teach you how to use and understand Outlook, and I'll also provide tips about how to use Outlook like a power user. After you read this book, I think you'll find Outlook to be as invaluable to you as it is to me every day.

PART I

OUTLOOK BASICS

IN THIS CHAPTER

- Organizing your information with Outlook.
- Sending and receiving e-mails with Outlook.
- Using Outlook to collaborate with other people.

1

INTRODUCING OUTLOOK

Welcome to Microsoft Office Outlook 2003, Microsoft's premier e-mail client and Personal Information Manager. Outlook is more than just an application for sending, receiving, and filing e-mail. Outlook maintains your address book, stores information about your contacts, manages to-do lists, keeps track of your appointments and meetings, and much more. In this chapter, you will learn how to get organized using Outlook and about the different types of tasks you can perform with Outlook.

Personal Information Management

Personal information management is more than just storing and filing electronic information such as e-mails. *Personal Information Managers (PIMs)* are used to find and group related pieces of information and organize information according to your needs; they serve as the electronic equivalents of paper organizers such as Rolodexes and date books. Outlook not only provides traditional PIM functions, but if you own the Microsoft Office 2003 system, it is designed to integrate and share information with other Office 2003 applications.

Some of the types of information Outlook manages are

- E-mails
- Address books used for addressing e-mails and faxes
- Contact information such as mailing addresses, birthdays, and anniversaries
- To-do lists of tasks
- Appointments, meetings, events, and other information about your schedules
- Diaries and journals
- Notes similar to the sticky notes found on many computer monitors and refrigerators

Outlook provides powerful and flexible tools for managing information, such as

- Storage of collections of information in folders such as E-mail, Contacts, and Calendar folders
- Views of items in folders shown in formats that provide different ways of viewing, sorting, filtering, and grouping information
- Searches for related items of information across different folders
- Reminders for things in your schedule and to-do lists, and for e-mails and contacts
- Contact links with activities such as appointments and e-mails to easily find all activities related to a contact
- Methods for marking and grouping items such as flagging items with colored flags, assigning items levels of importance and privacy, and categorizing items using categories such as Business and Personal
- Rules for performing actions such as moving, copying, and forwarding e-mails as they are received or sent based on conditions you specify
- Virtual folders called Search Folders that show e-mail items from different folders in one place based on criteria that you set

A Day in the Life of Outlook

I use Outlook to manage information for my consulting business. Outlook starts as soon as I start my computer in the morning, and it's the last program I close before I shut down my computer at the end of the day. In this section, I'll briefly describe how I use Outlook during my day. Some of the terms mentioned in this section will be new to you at this time, but the information management concepts should be familiar ones.

The first thing I do in the morning is look at my e-mail. I answer some messages immediately, but others are left for later action. Messages that require some type of follow-up action are flagged with a colored flag so they can be viewed in the For Follow Up Search Folder. Other messages require me to create a new to-do list entry or appointment, and I drag them to a Tasks or Calendar folder where Outlook autocreates a new task or appointment item for me to fill out.

Next, I switch to my Calendar folder, where I look over the day's scheduled events. Reminders give me time to prepare for or travel to the events. My calendar is also configured to show any entries in my to-do list that are due in the next seven days or are overdue. Reminders are set for tasks that absolutely have to be performed that day.

After I've dealt with my e-mail and know what the day's schedule looks like, I glance through the Junk E-mail folder. I do that to make sure nothing I actually want to keep was placed there by Outlook's Junk E-mail filter. I then delete everything in the Junk E-mail folder.

In my experience with the Junk E-mail filter so far, I haven't found any legitimate e-mail that was classified as a spam message. Spam e-mails are messages that are often sent in mass batches by persons or companies (legitimate or not) who've somehow obtained your e-mail address and are "spamming" you with messages. They might be advertisements or other unwanted material. Either way, the Junk E-mail filter in Outlook helps you remove this clutter from your Inbox.

As I work on projects during the day, I make notes that are posted in the Notes folder for the project. These notes remind me of project features, research items, and anything else for which I would use paper "sticky notes." I create journal entries as I work, for example, to time project work, record phone calls and faxes, and work with other Office applications such as Word documents. I create tasks for my project and personal to-do lists and check off the tasks as I complete them. As my schedule changes, I create and change appointments and other scheduled events.

During the course of the day, I periodically look at the Inbox and the For Follow Up and Unread Mail Search Folders to read new e-mails and to follow up on e-mails that were marked for later attention. When I make phone calls or send faxes, I use the Outlook address books to look up the phone or fax numbers. I also use Outlook to manage such personal chores as reminding myself of upcoming birthdays, anniversaries, and appointments.

Outlook has replaced my paper calendars, journals, day planners, and address books and makes it possible for me to track, organize, and analyze the information that I accumulate in the course of the year.

Now that you are familiar with some of the things that Outlook can do, let's look at how Outlook organizes the information it manages.

How Outlook Works

Outlook data is stored in a database called a *data file*. You can have many data files open at the same time in Outlook, but you always have one default data file. Each Outlook data file contains folders that hold Outlook items, such as e-mails and contacts. Outlook creates default folders for you, and you can also create your own folders to organize data in the way that you want. In the following sections, you will learn about Outlook items, folders, and data files.

Outlook Items and Folders

As you use Outlook, you work with a number of different types of items, such as e-mail and contacts. Each type of Outlook item is different and provides fields for entry of data related to that item, such as destination addresses for e-mails and phone numbers and addresses for contacts.

Outlook Items

When you work in Outlook, you will be working with some type of item and that item will be saved to its respective folder. The six main types of items you will work with in Outlook are shown in Table 1.1.

Table 1.1 Outlook Default Items

Item	Description
E-mail	Electronic mail you send or receive
Calendar	Appointments, meetings, and events that you would track in a date book
Contact	Names, addresses, phone numbers, and other information you keep about someone or something
Journal	Diary-like information you keep about someone or some event
Task	To-do list items
Note	Electronic "sticky notes"

You will work with two other types of Outlook items: post items and distribution lists. These items are used less frequently than the six main item types. You will learn about post items in Chapter 4, "Advanced E-mail Techniques," and you will learn about distribution lists in Chapter 6, "Contacts and Address Books."

E-mail items are used to store the e-mails you send and receive. A standard e-mail form (using Microsoft Office Word as the e-mail editor) is shown in Figure 1.1. You will learn more about working with e-mail in Chapter 3, "Sending and Receiving E-mail," and about advanced e-mail issues in Chapter 4.

FIGURE 1.1

E-mails are used not only for communication, but also for sending files and documents to other people.

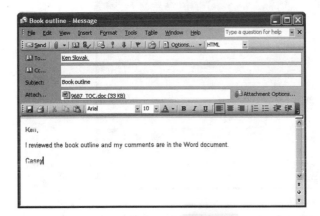

Contact items are used to store contact information and populate your address books. An Outlook contact form is shown in Figure 1.2. You will learn how to create and use contacts in Chapter 6.

FIGURE 1.2

Contacts are your electronic Rolodexes and populate Outlook's address books.

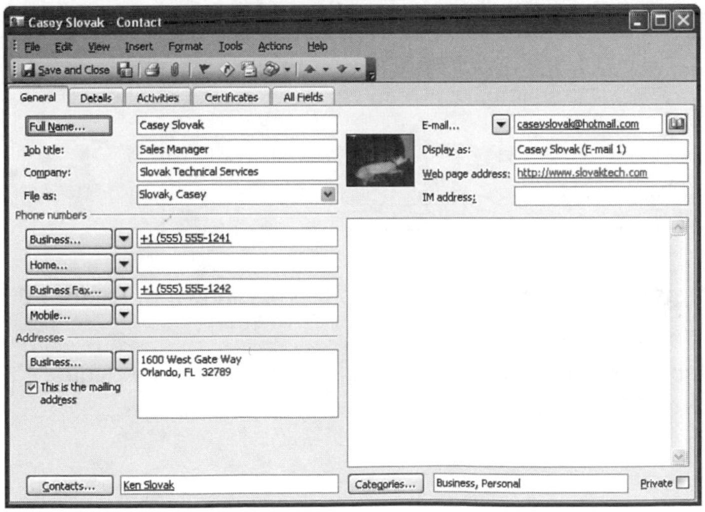

Calendar items store appointments, meetings, and events. An appointment form is shown in Figure 1.3. You will learn about staying organized using the calendar in Chapter 7, "The Calendar."

Journal items are like diary entries, and are also used to track time spent on various activities. A journal form is shown in Figure 1.4. You will learn how using the journal can help you keep track of important information in Chapter 9, "The Journal and Notes."

FIGURE 1.3

Appointments, meetings, and events are used to create your schedule and can be set up to occur at regular intervals.

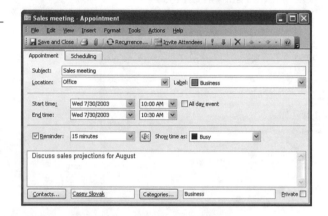

FIGURE 1.4

Journal items are used to replace paper day books and diaries.

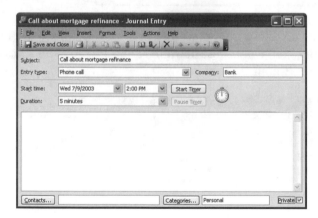

Task items are used for entries in to-do lists, as shown in Figure 1.5. You will learn about Tasks in Chapter 8, "Tasks."

Note items are like paper sticky notes. A Note is shown in Figure 1.6. You will learn about Notes in Chapter 9.

FIGURE 1.5

Tasks are used to create to-do lists and can be assigned to other people in workgroup settings.

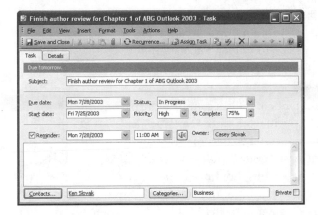

FIGURE 1.6

Outlook Notes are used to provide convenient locations to jot down information.

Outlook Folders

Every Outlook item is stored in a folder, which can be one of the Outlook default folders or one that you create yourself. Outlook folders are specialized folders, unlike the Windows file system folders you see in Windows Explorer. Most Outlook folders can contain only certain types of items. Table 1.2 shows the Outlook default folders and the types of items they can contain.

Table 1.2 Outlook Default Folders

Folder	Folder Holds
Inbox	Any item that has been received via e-mail
Drafts	E-mail and Post items
Junk E-mail	E-mail and Post items
Sent Items	E-mail and Post items
Calendar	Appointments, meetings, and events
Contacts	Contact and distribution list items
Journal	Journal items for diary entries
Notes	Note items
Tasks	Task entries in to-do lists
Outbox	Any item that is being sent out
Deleted Items	Items and folders that have been deleted

The Inbox, Outbox, and Deleted Items folders are the only folders that can hold many different types of Outlook items. All other Outlook folders—Mail and Post, Calendar, Contact, Journal, Note, and Task—can hold only certain types of Outlook items.

Two other special types of folders complete the list of Outlook folders you will work with: Search Folders and Outlook Today. Search Folders are used to group items that meet certain criteria into one easy-to-find place, such as items that haven't been read yet or items that are very large. You will learn about Search Folders in Chapter 5, "Search Folders."

Outlook Today is a special folder that displays selected information about calendar, e-mail, and Task items all in one place. You will learn more about Outlook Today in Chapter 2, "Outlook from the Beginning."

Figure 1.7 shows the list of default Outlook folders in Outlook's Folder List. The folder listed as Personal Folders is the Outlook Today folder.

note

The top folder in your Outlook data file is either called Personal Folders or Mailbox. If you aren't using Exchange server in a business setting, the file is called Personal Folders. This top folder is always used as the Outlook Today folder, which you will learn more about in Chapter 2.

FIGURE 1.7

Outlook default folders are arranged alphabetically in the Folder List.

Outlook Today

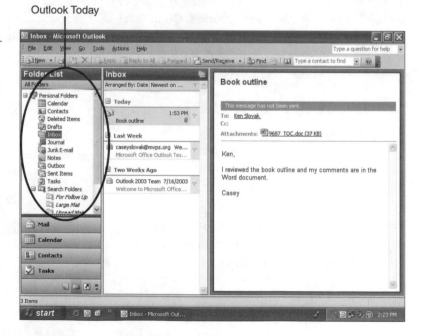

How Outlook Stores Data

If you are a home Outlook user, your default data file is a Personal Folders File (PST file). If you are using Outlook in a business setting, your default data file may be an Exchange mailbox located on a Microsoft's Exchange server computer. All Outlook data is stored in one of these types of data files; there are no separate files for e-mails, calendars, address books, or other Outlook data.

PST Files	Exchange Mailbox
Stored on your hard drive.	Stored on an Exchange server (typically only found in a corporate setting).
Can be opened by only one person at a time, and cannot be shared simultaneously with different people.	Can be shared and opened by more than one person at a time, if the other people have permission to open that mailbox.
Can use only PST files.	Can work with PST files for archiving in addition to the Exchange mailbox.

If you are a home user, the default name for your PST file is Outlook.pst, and its default location is in the C:\Documents and Settings\ <your Windows login>\Local Settings\Application Data\Microsoft\Outlook folder, where <your Windows login> is the name that you use when logging in to Windows.

If you are using an Exchange server mailbox, your mailbox data file is part of a much larger Exchange database stored on a server. An Exchange server mailbox cannot be viewed in Windows Explorer.

Outlook data files can grow to be very large; in Outlook 2003 the standard size limit for a PST file is 20 gigabytes (a gigabyte, or GB, is equal to 1,024 megabytes, or MB), although the theoretical maximum size is about 20 terabytes (a terabyte, or TB, is equal to 1,024 gigabytes). PST files for Outlook 2003 are Unicode compatible, which means they support the use of characters that are 2 bytes in size, thus making them compatible with non-Western languages such as Chinese. Non-Unicode PST files are also supported, for compatibility with older versions of Outlook.

tip

The Local Settings folder is hidden and, by default, cannot be seen in Windows Explorer. To see the Local Settings folder, open Windows Explorer, select **Tools, Folder Options,** and then select the **View** tab. On the View tab, select the **Show Hidden Files and Folders** option and click **OK**.

You can use and work with more than one PST file for your data; for example, you can archive older e-mails to an archive PST file and then open that PST file when you need to work with those e-mails. You will learn about archiving in Chapter 13, "Archiving Data." Exchange users can also work with PST files for uses such as archived data, in addition to the default Exchange mailbox.

Outlook as an E-mail Client

Outlook 2003 is a Personal Information Manager, but it also is a leading e-mail client for Windows platforms. Outlook supports the primary protocols for sending and receiving e-mail:

- POP3, the Internet standard Post Office Protocol version 3 used for downloading e-mail

- IMAP, the Internet standard Internet Message Access Protocol, which is a newer standard than POP3 that is also used for downloading e-mail

- SMTP, the Internet standard Simple Mail Transfer Protocol used for sending e-mail over the Internet

- HTTP mail, used for services such as Hotmail and Yahoo mail

- Exchange server, used for sending and receiving e-mail within organizations using Microsoft Exchange server

- Additional e-mail protocols and servers such as Lotus Notes and cc:Mail using connectors designed to talk to those servers

You will learn about setting up e-mail accounts using these protocols in the "Setting Up E-mail Accounts" section in Chapter 2.

Outlook supports three formats for e-mail, which provide for unformatted and formatted e-mail and enable Outlook to be a universal e-mail client:

- **Plain Text**—Unformatted e-mail that can be understood by any e-mail client

- **HTML**—Formatted e-mail using the same text formatting as used on Web pages and understood by most modern e-mail clients

- **Outlook Rich Text format**—Formatted e-mail using a proprietary Microsoft format that is understood only by Outlook and a few other e-mail clients such as Eudora

In addition to supporting the standard e-mail transfer protocols and e-mail formats, Outlook also supports connecting to e-mail servers using secure methods such as *Secure Password Authentication (SPA)* and *Secure Sockets Layer (SSL)*, used for encrypted communications.

One e-mail feature worthy of mention here is the Outlook 2003 junk e-mail filters. With some estimates saying that more than 60% of all e-mails are unwanted junk e-mails, the new junk e-mail filters are very useful in helping keep the clutter and annoyance of junk e-mail away from your Inbox. You will learn about secure e-mail and the Outlook junk e-mail filters in Chapter 18, "Secure E-mail."

Collaboration Using Outlook

Outlook is more than just a Personal Information Manager and e-mail client; it also is used to work collaboratively with other people. Although many of Outlook's collaborative features such as shared folders and Exchange public folders are available only when you use Exchange server, some collaborative features of Outlook can be used even by individuals; for example, you can publish calendar free/busy information to the Internet and plan meetings. You will learn about using Outlook collaboratively with other people in Chapter 21, "Collaborating with Outlook and Exchange."

Some of the collaborative features of Outlook when using Exchange server are

- Shared folders that people with permission can use to view other people's data
- Private items that can be viewed only by the owner of a folder
- Public folders that can be used for shared information such as address books and calendars and for discussions and bulletin boards
- The capability to delegate access to folders so secretaries and assistants can send e-mails on behalf of other people

You also can do the following:

- Publish calendar scheduling information in the form of lists of free and busy times to aid in planning meetings and events
- Assign tasks to other people and receive status reports on assigned tasks

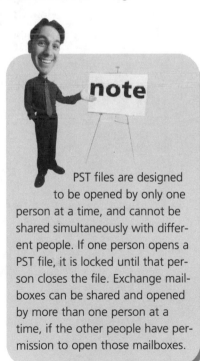

note

PST files are designed to be opened by only one person at a time, and cannot be shared simultaneously with different people. If one person opens a PST file, it is locked until that person closes the file. Exchange mailboxes can be shared and opened by more than one person at a time, if the other people have permission to open those mailboxes.

More Things to Do with Outlook

In addition to the Outlook features mentioned earlier in this chapter, Outlook is also a development platform that can be programmed to create custom applications for collaboration and productivity and to provide additional features for Outlook. Although Outlook development is an advanced topic not covered in this book, you will learn the beginnings of Outlook form development in Chapter 20, "Customizing Outlook Forms."

Many Outlook add-ins and add-ons are available in all price ranges to extend its functionality. You will learn about some of these add-ins and add-ons in Appendix D, "Outlook Tools." Outlook can also be used in conjunction with Personal Digital Assistants (PDAs) and can synchronize data to and from PDAs, making your Outlook data available even when you are away from your computer.

THE ABSOLUTE MINIMUM

In this chapter, you learned what a Personal Information Manager is and how Outlook organizes information. To review, you now know

How Outlook organizes its data.

How Outlook works with different types of data.

That Outlook is used to work collaboratively with other people.

In this chapter, you learned about Outlook's organizational structure. In the next chapter, you will learn about running Outlook for the first time and how to configure it.

2

OUTLOOK FROM THE BEGINNING

In Chapter 1, "Introducing Outlook," you learned how Outlook is organized into a data file, folders, and items. In this chapter, you will learn what happens the first time you run Outlook and how to set up Outlook and your e-mail accounts. You will begin working with Outlook, configure a send/receive group, and learn about Outlook profiles. You will also learn about the Outlook user interface and how to set Outlook user interface preferences.

Before You Begin

When you run Outlook for the first time, you encounter the Startup Wizard, which asks whether you want to set up an e-mail account. You don't have to set up an e-mail account now; you can do that later, but doing it now is easier if you already know your e-mail account information. E-mail account information is supplied by your Internet service provider (ISP) or your Exchange administrator if you are using Microsoft Exchange server for e-mail.

Making Sure You Have an Internet Connection

If you are a home user, you need an ISP to be able to connect to the Internet and to send and receive e-mail. Microsoft Exchange server is used in companies and organizations such as universities. Home users need one of the following types of connections to the Internet:

- A dial-up modem attached to a telephone line. This type of connection is slower than the other Internet connection types mentioned here and ties up a telephone line when you are connecting to the Internet. Setup for a telephone modem is performed using the instructions supplied with the modem.

- A Digital Subscriber Line (DSL) modem supplied by a telephone company. This type of connection is much faster than a telephone line modem. The telephone company either installs the DSL modem and sets up the Windows network connection for it or supplies an installation kit with instructions on configuring and connecting it to the telephone network.

- A cable modem supplied by the local cable TV company. The cable company installs and configures the Windows and cable network connections, which supply a high-speed Internet connection.

- Another type of connection to the Internet, such as a satellite TV Internet connection, which is usually a hybrid connection using a telephone modem to upload information to the Internet and a high-speed satellite feed to download information to the Internet.

America Online (AOL) uses a proprietary e-mail system and is not compatible with Outlook. If you are using AOL as your ISP, you cannot use Outlook unless you also have an additional e-mail account with another provider that is compatible with Outlook.

This book doesn't help you select an ISP if you don't already have one, but finding one isn't hard. Find out from friends which ISPs they use and how happy they are with their service, talk to your telephone company or cable provider about high-speed connections, and decide which ISP to use and start an account.

Running the Network Connection Wizard for the First Time

If you have never connected to the Internet, make sure to run the Network Connection Wizard to set up a networking connection before you start configuring Outlook. To run the Network Connection Wizard for Windows XP, do the following:

1. Select **Start**, **Control Panel**. When the Control Panel opens, select the **Network and Internet Connections** category.

2. Select **Set Up or Change Your Internet Connection** to begin setting up your connection to the Internet.

3. Follow the instructions in the Internet Properties dialog to set up your Internet connection.

If you are running Windows 2000, do the following:

1. Select **Start**, **Settings**, **Control Panel** to open the Control Panel.

2. Select **Network and Dial-up Connections** and then **Make New Connection** to start the Network Connections Wizard.

For help in setting up your Internet connection and using the Network Connection Wizard, select **Start**, **Help and Support** and then select the **Networking and the Web** Help topic. Open the **E-mail and the Web** topic and select the **Make an Internet Connection** task.

If you want to set up an e-mail account, you need the following information, all provided by your ISP or your Exchange administrator if you are using Microsoft Exchange Server for e-mail:

- The e-mail account type. Some types of e-mail accounts are POP3, HTTP, IMAP, and Microsoft Exchange Server.

tip

Outlook 2003 can run on Windows XP and Windows 2000. The illustrations in this book and the instructions for using Windows features assume you are using Windows XP. If you are using Windows 2000 or have changed Windows XP to use the Classic Start menu, some of the instructions and illustrations in this book will not exactly match what you see on your computer. Adjust the instructions to account for the way Windows 2000 works or Windows XP works using the Classic Start menu.

■ The username and password used to log on to the e-mail servers.

■ The names of the incoming and outgoing mail servers. The incoming and outgoing mail servers can have the same or different names. The incoming mail server is the one you receive your e-mail from, and the outgoing mail server is the one you send your e-mail through.

■ Details explaining whether security-related settings are required, such as Secure Password Authentication (SPA); use of Secure Sockets Layer (SSL); and logging on to the incoming e-mail server before logging on to the outgoing e-mail server.

Running Outlook for the First Time

When you start Outlook for the first time, the Windows Installer pops up and completes Outlook's installation phase, which isn't performed during the initial Office installation (see Figure 2.1).

FIGURE 2.1

The Windows Installer finishes Outlook's installation phase the first time you run Outlook.

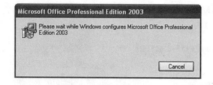

Next, you see the Outlook Startup Wizard screen, as shown in Figure 2.2.

FIGURE 2.2

The Startup Wizard finishes configuring Outlook settings and enables you to set up an e-mail account.

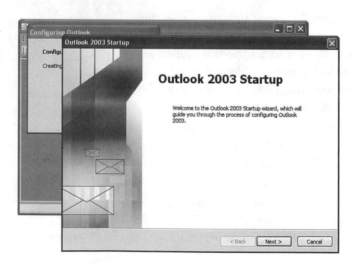

You can select Cancel to close the Outlook Startup
Wizard and open Outlook, or you can proceed
with the wizard and configure Outlook with an
e-mail account. If you've already run Outlook and
canceled the wizard, don't worry; you can configure Outlook with an e-mail account at any time.

Using the Startup Wizard

To configure Outlook using the Startup Wizard,
follow these steps:

1. Click **Next** in the Welcome screen to open
   the first configuration screen.

2. Select **Yes** if you want to configure an e-mail
   account now and **Next** to proceed to the next
   screen. If you don't want to configure an e-
   mail account now, select **No** and then
   Finish to end the Startup Wizard.

3. Select the type of e-mail account you are setting up in the E-mail Accounts screen, as
   shown in Figure 2.3. This figure shows a
   POP3 account already selected. Your ISP or
   Exchange administrator will tell you which
   type of e-mail account you should use.
   Select **Next** to proceed to the main e-mail
   account configuration screen.

tip

To configure an e-mail
account if the Startup
Wizard isn't running, see
the Note below step 2 in
"Using the Startup Wizard."

note

To configure an e-mail
account if the Startup
Wizard isn't running, select **Tool**s,
E-mail Accounts to open the E-
mail Accounts dialog. Select the
Add a new e-mail account
option and click **Next**. Proceed
with the step 3 in "Using the
Startup Wizard."

FIGURE 2.3

Select the e-mail
account type,
which you
find out from
your ISP.

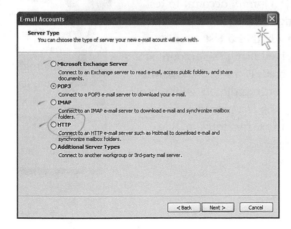

4. On the screen shown in Figure 2.4, you configure the POP3 e-mail account. Fill out the account information using the information provided by your ISP. For HTTP e-mail accounts, select the HTTP Mail Service Provider, and if your selection is Other, enter the Server URL.

FIGURE 2.4

Enter the name, e-mail address, user logon name, password, and incoming and outgoing e-mail server names for your e-mail account.

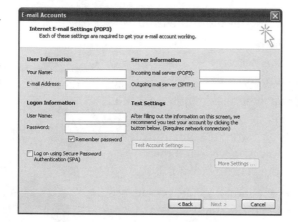

The screens for HTTP and IMAP e-mail accounts are similar to the POP3 configuration screen. Follow the steps in these instructions to configure HTTP and IMAP e-mail accounts.

If you are setting up an Exchange e-mail account, see the section "Setting Up an Exchange E-mail Account Using the Startup Wizard" in this chapter.

5. Check the **Log on using Secure Password Authentication (SPA)** checkbox only if your ISP says it is required.

6. Select **Test Account Settings** if you selected a POP3 e-mail account to test the information you entered. This button checks to see whether a test e-mail can be sent and received using the account settings you entered. Figure 2.5 shows the Test Account Settings dialog, which indicates whether the test passed or failed. If the test fails, the Errors tab shows the errors that occurred.

tip

Check the **Remember password** checkbox to let Outlook remember your password so it can log in automatically when sending and receiving e-mail. If this checkbox isn't checked, you have to enter your password each time you log in to your e-mail server to send or receive e-mails.

FIGURE 2.5

The Test Account
Settings dialog
for POP3 e-mail
accounts shows
the progress of
sending and
receiving a test
e-mail on the
Tasks tab and
shows errors on
the Errors tab.

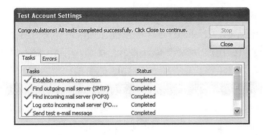

7. Select **Close** to close the Test Account Settings dialog.

If you are using a dial-up modem and aren't connected to a network, this completes
the settings you need for your e-mail account. Select **Next** and then **Finish** to complete the Startup Wizard or E-mail Accounts dialog.

If you use one of the following configurations, you need to make sure your e-mail
connection is set correctly:

- Dial-up modem with a network card installed for a home or work network
- Cable modem
- DSL modem

Select **More Settings** to open the Internet E-mail Settings dialog and then click on
the **Connection** tab, which is shown in Figure 2.6.

FIGURE 2.6

The Connection
tab enables you
to select your
type of Internet
connection, such
as the LAN con-
nection shown.

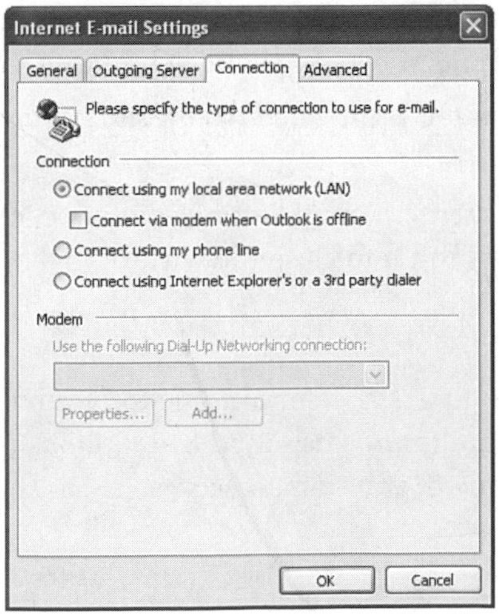

Here, you can make the following selections:

■ If you are connecting Outlook for e-mail using a business network, cable modem, or DSL connection, select **Connect using my local area network (LAN)**.

■ If you want to use a dial-up modem connection when Outlook isn't connected to a LAN, check the **Connect via modem when Outlook is offline** checkbox and select your dial-up modem connection from the **Dial-Up Networking Connection** drop-down in the Modem section at the bottom of the tab. (The Modem area is not active until the Connect via modem when Outlook is offline checkbox is checked.)

■ If you use a dial-up modem to connect to the Internet, select **Connect using my phone line** and select the **Dial-Up Networking Connection** you created using the Network Connection Wizard if you want Outlook to connect to the Internet when it checks for e-mail. This connection will be terminated when you close Outlook, even if you set Outlook so that it does not hang up when it is finished sending and receiving e-mail.

■ If you connect to the Internet before you start Outlook, select **Connect using Internet Explorer's or a 3rd party dialer**. This connection will remain active when Outlook is closed.

Click **OK** to close the Internet E-mail Settings dialog. Then select **Next** and then **Finish** to complete the Startup Wizard or E-mail Accounts dialog.

Advanced E-mail Account Settings

The **More Settings** button opens the Internet E-mail Settings dialog, which has four tabs for POP3 and IMAP e-mail accounts: General, Outgoing Server, Connection, and Advanced. HTTP e-mail accounts show only the General and Connection tabs.

Information about the Connection tab is provided at the end of the previous section and will not be repeated here.

When you are finished with the Internet E-mail Settings dialog, click **OK** to close the dialog. Then click **Next** and then **Finish** to close the wizard.

General Tab

On the **General** tab, Ishown in Figure 2.7, enter a name for your e-mail account if you do not want to accept the default name assigned by Outlook. The default name for your e-mail account is the name of your e-mail server.

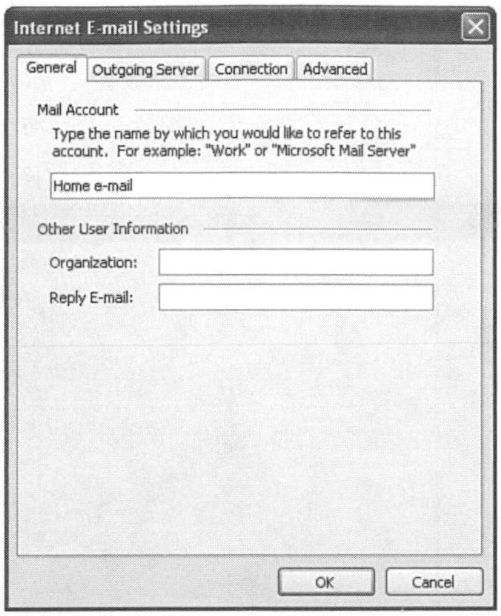

FIGURE 2.7

The General tab enables you to enter a name, organization and reply e-mail address for your e-mail account.

You can leave the **Organization** and **Reply E-mail** settings blank if you do not want to fill them in. If you leave **Reply E-mail** blank, the same e-mail address used to send e-mails will be used as the reply address.

Outgoing Server Tab

On the **Outgoing Server** tab, available for POP3 and IMAP e-mail accounts, you can create settings for your outgoing e-mail server if required.

Figure 2.8 shows the Outgoing Server tab with the My outgoing server (SMTP) requires authentication checkbox checked, which is required before other settings on this tab are enabled.

Use the information provided by your ISP to configure the other settings in the Outgoing Server tab.

note

If settings on the Outgoing Server tab are required, your ISP should have told you to use authentication for your outgoing e-mail server, or Secure Password Authentication for the outgoing e-mail server, or to log in to the incoming e-mail server before sending e-mail from Outlook.

Advanced Tab

On the **Advanced** tab, shown in Figure 2.9, available for POP3 and IMAP e-mail accounts, you can change the ports used for sending and receiving e-mail, enable the use of Secure Sockets Layer (SSL) for encrypted e-mail, change server timeouts, and change how e-mail is delivered.

FIGURE 2.8

The Outgoing Server tab enables you to set special settings your ISP might require for sending e-mails.

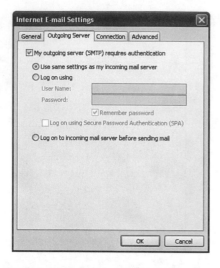

FIGURE 2.9

The Advanced tab enables you to set advanced settings if your ISP requires them for sending and receiving e-mails.

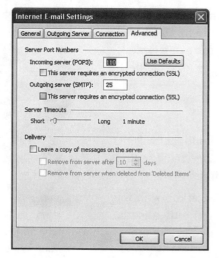

You should use the default settings unless your ISP has told you to use different settings, your e-mail connections time out regularly, or you want to leave e-mail on the e-mail server when you download messages. If your e-mail connections time out regularly, and you get timeout errors when you send or receive e-mail, increase the server timeouts by moving the slider control to the right.

The next section shows how to set up an Exchange e-mail account using the Startup Wizard. Skip this section if you aren't using Microsoft Exchange server.

Setting Up an Exchange E-mail Account Using the Startup Wizard

If you are using Outlook in a business or organizational setting where Microsoft Exchange server is used, your Exchange administrator will either have set up your e-mail account on the Exchange Server for you or have given you the information you need to set up your Exchange e-mail account.

If you are using the Outlook Startup Wizard to configure an e-mail account, select **Microsoft Exchange Server** in the list of e-mail server types; then click **Next** to go to the Exchange Server Settings page where you set up your Exchange e-mail account. To set up your Exchange e-mail account, do the following:

1. Enter the name of your Exchange server and your Exchange username exactly as provided by your Exchange administrator in the Exchange Server Settings dialog, as shown in Figure 2.10. Leave the **Use Cached Exchange Mode** checkbox checked unless your Exchange administrator has instructed you to uncheck this setting.

2. After entering the server and usernames, select **Check Name** to verify the settings you entered and to verify connectivity with your Exchange server. If you have any problems verifying settings or connectivity with

caution

You should leave e-mail on the server only if you also download it from the server into an additional e-mail account that removes the e-mail from the server, or you don't get very much e-mail. The problem with leaving e-mail on the server is that you can fill your mailbox size quota, and new e-mails are then refused until you make room in your mailbox on the e-mail server.

note

You usually don't need to change the settings in the More Settings tab for Exchange e-mail accounts, so this chapter doesn't show these settings or how to change them.

your Exchange server, ask your Exchange administrator or Help desk to help you set up your e-mail account.

3. Unless your Exchange administrator has instructed you to use any other settings or to change the default settings, select **Next** and then **Finish** to create your Exchange e-mail account and open Outlook.

FIGURE 2.10

Use the settings provided by your Exchange administrator to configure an Exchange e-mail account.

Using Outlook for the First Time

Outlook uses activation to verify that you are a legitimate Outlook user and aren't using a stolen or pirated copy of Outlook. *Activation* is a process that can be performed by telephone or on the Internet. If your copy of Outlook wasn't activated previously, perhaps by the store or company from which you purchased your computer, you will be asked to activate Outlook the first time it is run.

If you choose not to activate Outlook, you can start it 10 times before it enters into a reduced functionality mode. If you proceed with activation, the process is automatic if you are connected to the Internet. Phone activation is performed manually.

If you didn't activate Outlook initially, you can activate it at any time by selecting **Help**, **Activate Product**. Once Outlook is activated, you don't have to activate it again unless you make major changes to your computer hardware.

Activation applies to all the Office applications, so if an application such as Word was already activated, you won't be asked again in Outlook.

The first time you open Outlook, the User Name dialog opens. Change the username and initials if you want and click **OK** to open Outlook. Figure 2.11 shows Outlook open for the first time, with the welcome message from the Outlook 2003 team selected in the Inbox folder. If Outlook opens to the Outlook Today window, select the **Inbox** in the All Mail Folders list, as shown in Figure 2.11, to go to the Inbox folder.

Outlook Menus

If you are familiar with Windows, you are already aware of the custom menu feature, which gives you only a partial listing of commands when you open a menu. In Outlook, menus are personalized to show only basic commands when you first start working with it. As you use Outlook more, the commands you use most frequently are shown in menus.

In this book, all the illustrations show full Outlook menus and assume that all Outlook features are installed on your hard drive. Outlook is also shown in full-screen mode to show the maximum amount of detail for illustrations. This book also assumes that Outlook is installed as part of Microsoft Office 2003 and was not purchased as a separate application.

FIGURE 2.11

Outlook opens for the first time showing your mail folders with the welcome message from the Outlook 2003 team selected.

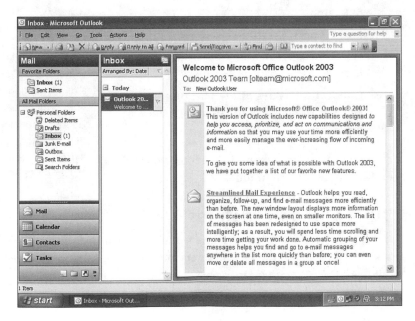

Figure 2.12 shows the Outlook Tools menu using personalized menus. If you leave the menu open for a while, the complete menu is displayed, or you can display more of the menu by moving your mouse cursor over the double down arrow at the bottom of the menu.

FIGURE 2.12

Customized menus show the commands you use most often and hide less often used commands.

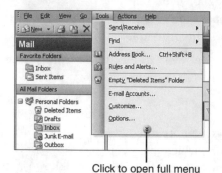

Click to open full menu

As you use Outlook, menu commands you use most often are shown, and commands you use less often are hidden. To show all available menu commands for illustrations in this book, the Outlook menus were customized to show the full menus.

To customize Outlook to always show full menus, do the following:

1. Select **Tools**, **Customize**.

2. Select the **Options** tab in the Customize dialog.

3. Check the **Always show full menus** checkbox and select **Close** to save the change.

Now when you open a menu in Outlook, you will see all the available commands.

> **note**
>
> Changes you make to the personalized menu settings for Outlook affect every other Office application, and changes you make to the personalized menu settings in other Office applications such as Word also affect Outlook.

Installing Other Outlook Features

In a typical Office installation, some features are not installed until they are first used, such as some of the file importers and stationeries, and some features are not available at all. When you try to use a particular feature of Outlook, the Windows

Installer suddenly starts and requests the Office CD to install the requested feature on your hard drive. This book assumes that a complete Outlook installation was used, where all features are installed on your hard drive. The instructions in this book do not include any prompts to install the features. If you choose not to do the full installation, you need to follow any prompts for installing a required feature before you can complete the steps you are working on in this book.

With today's large hard drives, there really is no reason not to install all Outlook features directly on your hard drive. To learn how to install all Outlook features, see the "Installing Outlook 2003" and "Adding and Removing Features" sections in Appendix A, "Outlook Installation."

OUTLOOK AND MICROSOFT OFFICE WORD 2003

The default e-mail editor for Outlook 2003 is Microsoft Word 2003. If you purchased Outlook 2003 as a separate application or as an update to a previous version of Microsoft Outlook, and Word 2003 is not available on your system, you cannot use Word as the Outlook e-mail editor. Nor can you use earlier versions of Word as the e-mail editor for Outlook 2003.

This book assumes Microsoft Office 2003 is installed, and Word 2003 is available for use as Outlook's e-mail editor.

Working in Outlook's User Interface

Outlook's user interface shows folders and items in panes. Other panes are used to navigate from folder to folder and to display information such as Help. In addition to panes, Outlook's user interface uses menus, toolbars, and a status bar. Figure 2.13 shows Outlook displaying four panes, a menu bar, a toolbar, and the status bar.

By default, Outlook shows the Standard toolbar, Navigation Pane, and status bar. The menu bar and Folder Display Pane are always displayed and cannot be turned off. The Reading Pane is displayed in all e-mail folders and can be turned on if desired in other folders. Task panes aren't displayed unless you turn them on or use a function such as Help that shows the Help task pane.

To change which user interface elements are displayed, use the **View** menu. The View menu commands shown in Table 2.1 are used to turn on or turn off user interface elements.

FIGURE 2.13

Most Outlook user interface elements can be turned off or on except for the Folder Display Pane and the menu bar.

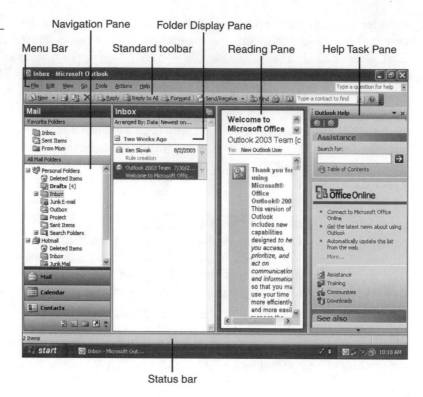

Status bar

Table 2.1   View Menu Commands

Command	Used to Control
Navigation Pane	Toggles the Navigation Pane on and off everywhere in Outlook.
Reading Pane	Opens a submenu that controls the Reading Pane display. Settings are **Right**, **Bottom**, and **Off** on a folder group–by–folder group basis.
Toolbars	Opens a submenu that turns on and off the **Standard**, **Advanced**, **Task Pane**, and **Web** toolbars. **Task Pane** is listed in this submenu after a task pane is first displayed in Outlook, such as the Help task pane.
Status Bar	Toggles the status bar on and off everywhere in Outlook.

The following sections describe working with the user interface elements.

Menus and Toolbars

Most of the menus and toolbars in Outlook are context sensitive. Context-sensitive menus and toolbars change the commands they display based on the current context—typically based on which folder is being displayed. The exceptions are the File, Go, and Help menus and the Web toolbar, which always display the same commands in every context.

The mouse or keyboard can be used to access menu or toolbar commands. To access a menu command using the mouse, click the command. To access a menu command using the keyboard, hold down the **Alt** key and press the underlined hotkey for that menu or toolbar command. For example, to access the File menu, hold down the **Alt** key and press the **F** key .

The Navigation Pane

The Navigation Pane is used as the primary way to navigate from one folder to another and also to display groups of related folders in one place. An alternative to using the Navigation Pane to move from one folder to another is using the Go menu, which lists the default Outlook folders and a **Folder** command that opens a dialog where you can select any Outlook folder. Figure 2.14 shows the Navigation Pane and the buttons for moving between different folder groups.

FIGURE 2.14

The Navigation Pane displays all folder groups by default except for the Journal folders group.

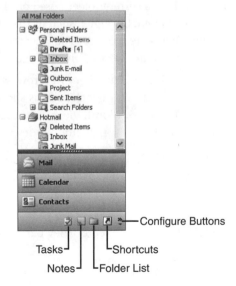

The Navigation Pane contains buttons to display different folder groups: Mail, Calendar, Contacts, Tasks, Notes, and the Journal. The Journal button isn't displayed by default. To display the Journal button in the Navigation Pane, do the following:

1. Select **Configure Buttons** (shown in Figure 2.15) to open the Configure Buttons menu.

2. Select **Add or Remove Buttons**.

3. Select **Journal** to show the Journal folder group.

The Navigation Pane also has buttons to display the Folder List and shortcuts. The Folder List displays all the folders of every type in the Outlook data file. Shortcuts are used to display links to folders or groups of folders that you create. You will learn more about creating Navigation Pane shortcuts as well as customizing the way the Navigation Pane displays items in Chapter 11, "Customizing the Navigation Pane."

To display a related group of folders such as the Mail group, select the button for that group of folders. Each group of folders displays different elements such as lists of folders, available folder views, and favorite folders. Select each Navigation Pane button to see which elements are displayed for that group of folders. To move from one folder to another folder within a group, select the folder in the list of folders.

The Folder Display Pane

The Folder Display Pane shows the items in the current folder based on the current folder view. A folder view may group related items together, such as the default view of the Inbox that groups items by the date they were received. The view may also filter items, such as a view that displays only items that were received in the past seven days.

Folder views can be table-type views that display each item in a row, with information from fields in each item displayed in columns in each row, as shown in Figure 2.15. Other examples of views include Day/Week/Month views for Calendar folders. You will learn more about folder views in Chapter 14, "Outlook Views."

Folders can be one of the following three types:

- **Default folders** are created by Outlook. You can't rename or delete them, and you can't add any default folders to the set that Outlook creates in your data file.

- **User-created folders** are folders that you create. They can be renamed, moved, or deleted.

- **Search Folders** are special folders that display items from one or more e-mail folders that meet the conditions set for the Search Folder. You will learn more about folders in Chapter 10, "Using Folders," and more about Search Folders in Chapter 5, "Search Folders."

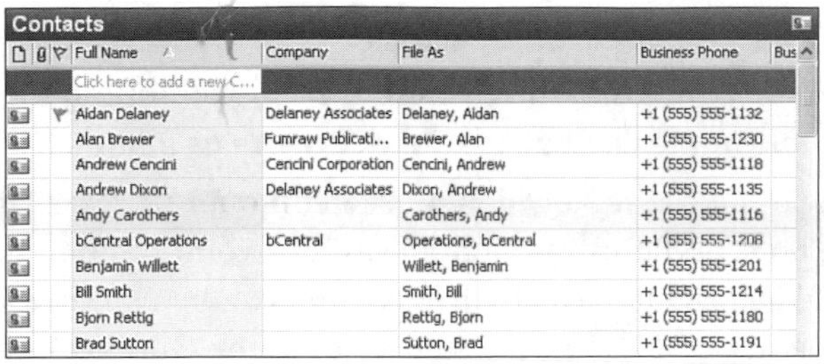

FIGURE 2.15

The Phone List view of a Contacts folder is a table view that shows information for contacts in columns and rows.

The Reading Pane

The Reading Pane is the cleverly titled part of the interface that enables you to read and preview the item selected in the current folder without having to open that item. If you are familiar with an older version of Outlook, this feature is very different from the Preview Pane. You will probably find in time, however, that it is very much an improvement because it enables you to view a great deal more of your item at once without actually having to open it.

The Reading Pane can be displayed either to the right of the folder display (see Figure 2.14) or below the folder display. The Reading Pane is turned on and off on a folder group–by–folder group basis. By default, the Reading Pane is turned on only for e-mail folders.

The default position for the Reading Pane is to the right of the folder display. This position displays approximately twice as much text in the selected item as when the Reading Pane is below the folder display. The disadvantage of the Reading Pane on the right is that it shows fewer fields for each item than when the Reading Pane is below the folder display.

If you display the Reading Pane on the right for one e-mail folder, all e-mail folders display the Reading Pane on the right. The same applies for other groups of folders such as Calendar or Contacts folders. Turning off the Reading Pane in one folder of a group turns the Reading Pane off for that entire group of folders.

To change how, or if, the Reading Pane is displayed, select **View**, **Reading Pane**. Choose **Right**, **Bottom**, or **Off** to configure the Reading Pane for the current folder group.

The Status Bar

The status bar (see Figure 2.14) displays the number of items in the current folder on its left side and other status messages on its right side. Status messages can include online/offline status, update status when using Exchange cached mode, send/receive status, and errors.

The Task Pane

Task panes display special tasks and the results from performing those tasks. The task panes available in the Outlook user interface are as follows:

- **Help** provides a central location for searching for Outlook Help topics, locating downloads and updates, finding Outlook communities, and seeking other help-related assistance. The Help task pane can be used to search for help locally or online, where the latest updates to the Outlook Help files are available.

- **Search Results** displays the results of a search in the Help or Research task panes.

- **Research** provides a way to do online research from reference sources integrated into the Research task pane. Links to updated or additional research sources can be downloaded from the Microsoft Office Online Web site as they become available.

- **Clipboard** displays the contents of the Office Clipboard.

Figure 2.16 shows the selection of task panes available in the main user interface. Additional task panes such as Getting Started, New Document, and Attachment Options are available when you are using Word as the e-mail editor and an e-mail message is open.

FIGURE 2.16

Click the arrow in the task pane's title bar to open the list of other available task panes.

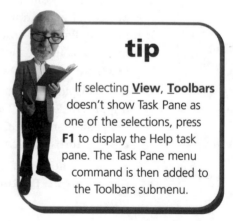

tip

If selecting **View**, **Toolbars** doesn't show Task Pane as one of the selections, press **F1** to display the Help task pane. The Task Pane menu command is then added to the Toolbars submenu.

Outlook Today

Outlook Today is a special Web page that displays unread messages, tasks, and calendar items all in one place, as shown in Figure 2.17.

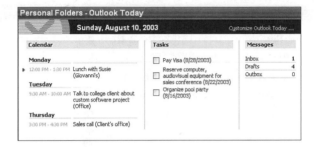

The Outlook Today view can be customized in the following ways:

- The folders it shows unread messages from
- The way tasks are displayed
- The number of days it shows from your Calendar folder
- The Outlook Today display style to use
- The choice whether to open Outlook in the Outlook Today view

To display Outlook Today, select **Personal Folders** in the Mail folders group or the Folder List in the Navigation Pane. If you are using Exchange, display Outlook Today by selecting **Mailbox** in the Mail Folders group or the Folder List.

To customize Outlook Today, select **Customize Outlook Today** at the top of the window. The Outlook Today display changes to the Customize Outlook Today screen, as shown in Figure 2.18.

To customize Outlook Today, do the following:

- Check the **When starting, go directly to Outlook Today** checkbox to open Outlook Today automatically when Outlook starts.
- Select **Choose Folders** to select which folders are shown in Outlook Today. Check the folders to display and click **OK** to save the selections.
- Select the number of days to display from the Calendar folder in the **Calendar** drop-down.
- Select from the **All tasks** or **Today's tasks** options. If you select **Today's tasks**, you can check the **Include tasks with no due date** checkbox if desired. Tasks can be sorted by up to two fields you select from the task sort drop-downs.
- Select the Outlook Today style to use in the **Styles** drop-down. Choosing a style customizes the appearance of the Outlook Today page with various colors, fonts, and layouts.

If you select the **Winter** style, **Customize Outlook Today** is shown at the bottom right of the Outlook Today screen instead of the top right.

To save changes to Outlook Today, select **Save Changes** at the upper right of the screen. To cancel changes, select **Cancel**.

Now that you are familiar with the basics of working with the Outlook interface, you will learn about working online and offline, and using send/receive groups to control how e-mail is sent and received.

Working in Online and Offline Mode

Outlook can be used in both online and offline modes. Outlook is online when it is connected to a mail server for sending and receiving e-mail. If you are using a cable modem, DSL modem, or network connection to send and receive e-mail, you are always connected to the Internet and can choose to always use online mode. If you use a dial-up modem, you are connected while your modem is online using a telephone connection.

The default setting for Outlook is to send e-mail immediately when connected. Outlook can also be configured to send and receive e-mails automatically, at scheduled intervals. If you are using a dial-up modem, you can configure Outlook to dial your ISP and connect to your mail server automatically. If you are using an always-on connection such as cable modem or DSL, no dial-up is needed for Outlook to send and receive e-mail at the scheduled interval or to send e-mail immediately.

So, why would you want to work in offline mode? A major reason you might want to work offline is if you are using a laptop computer and are traveling and aren't online. Some ISP accounts are billed by the number of minutes you are online in a month, so you might want to minimize the amount of time you are online. Even if you are using an always-on connection such as a cable modem or DSL, sometimes you might prefer to work offline, perhaps to work on e-mails without sending them out automatically when you click the Send button.

To control working in online or offline mode, select **File**, **Work Offline**. This menu command is a toggle; each time it's selected, the setting toggles from online mode to offline mode or back to online mode.

The Automatically dial during a background Send/Receive checkbox determines whether Outlook automatically connects when a scheduled send/receive is due.

Working with Send/Receive Groups and E-mail Accounts

A *send/receive group* consists of one or more e-mail accounts and all the settings for sending and receiving e-mail for the group. The default send/receive group is named All Accounts. You can create other send/receive groups, and an e-mail account can belong to one or more send/receive groups.

Send/receive groups are useful in a number of ways, giving you complete control over your e-mail accounts:

- You can enable or disable an individual account in a group without having to remove the account completely.
- You control whether the e-mail accounts in a group send and receive e-mail at scheduled intervals, when Outlook exits, or on demand.
- If you are using a dial-up modem and want to go online only when you send and receive e-mail, you can work offline and have Outlook automatically connect and send and receive e-mail at scheduled intervals or on demand.
- Advanced users can configure settings to work with e-mail headers with e-mails stored on a server and decide whether to download specific e-mails.

To open the Send/Receive Groups dialog, shown in Figure 2.19, select **Tools**, **Send/Receive**, **Send/Receive Settings**, **Define Send/Receive Groups**. An alternative way of opening the Send/Receive Groups dialog is to press the keyboard shortcut **Ctrl+Alt+S**.

FIGURE 2.19

Send/receive groups are used to control sending and receiving settings for one or more e-mail accounts.

Configuring Send/Receive Groups

The default setting for the All Accounts send/receive group, which is automatically created when you create your first e-mail account, is to send and receive e-mail manually only. This means you will receive new e-mails and deliver e-mails you are sending only when you manually send/receive. Automatic send/receives use scheduled intervals to send and receive e-mail, which is usually a more convenient setting. If you want to send/receive e-mail automatically on a schedule, you must configure the group to do that.

- Check or uncheck **Include this group in send/receive (F9)** to include or exclude the group from the F9 send/receive all action. If the group is excluded from send/receive all, you will have to send/receive for that group manually by selecting **Tools**, **Send/Receive** if the automatic sending and receiving setting isn't enabled. This setting is available separately for online and offline mode.

- Check the **Schedule an automatic send/receive every** checkbox and select

To send/receive e-mail manually, press **F9**. You can also send/receive by clicking **Send/Receive** in the Standard toolbar or by selecting **Tools**, **Send/Receive**, **Send/Receive All**.

To control whether Outlook sends e-mail immediately when it's connected, select **Tools**, **Options**, **Mail Setup** tab. Check or uncheck the **Send immediately when connected** checkbox to set the option.

how often to send/receive in the time spin box to have e-mail sent and received automatically at specified intervals. This setting is available separately for online and offline mode.

■ Check the **Perform an automatic send/receive when exiting** checkbox to perform a send/receive when exiting Outlook. Using this setting means you never will exit Outlook with outgoing e-mails sitting in your Outbox, but it will take a little longer to exit when you close Outlook.

■ Select **New** to open the Send/Receive Group Name dialog, where you can name a new group. Click **OK** to create the new group and open the Send/Receive Settings dialog.

■ Select **Copy** to open the Send/Receive Group Name dialog, where you can name the copy of the selected group. Click **OK** to save the copied group and open the Send/Receive Settings dialog.

■ Select **Remove** to delete the selected group.

■ Select **Rename** to open the Send/Receive Group Name dialog, where you can rename the selected group. Click **OK** to save the renamed group.

■ Select **Edit** to open the Send/Receive Settings dialog for the selected group, as shown in Figure 2.20.

When you are finished setting the options on this dialog, select **Close** to save the selected actions for the send/receive groups and exit the dialog.

FIGURE 2.20

The Send/ Receive Settings dialog controls how e-mail is sent and received and if selected e-mail accounts are included in the send/receive group.

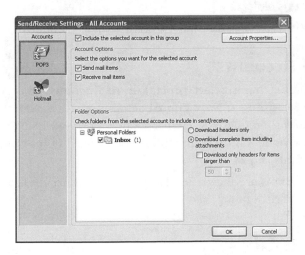

Viewing a Send/Receive Group's Settings

Each type of e-mail account provides somewhat different settings based on the account type. The settings shown in Figure 2.20 are for a POP3 e-mail account—the most common type for home Outlook users.

- Check or uncheck **Include the selected account in this group** to enable or disable the e-mail account in that send/receive group.
- Check or uncheck **Send mail items** to enable or disable sending e-mails from this account.
- Check or uncheck **Receive mail items** to enable or disable receiving e-mails for this account.

The options for downloading e-mail headers or complete items, which is an advanced topic, are not covered in this book.

Selected folders can be included or excluded from a send/receive, but if the Inbox is excluded, no e-mail will be delivered.

To view or change the properties of a selected e-mail account, click the **Account Properties** button in the upper-right corner of the dialog. The Account Properties dialog contains the same information as the dialog for setting up a new e-mail account shown in Figure 2.4 in "Using the Startup Wizard" section in this chapter. Other tabs in this dialog are identical to the tabs in the Internet E-mail Settings dialog, shown in Figures 2.6 to 2.9. See "Using the Startup Wizard" to review the settings available in this dialog.

Click **OK** to save the settings in the Send/Receive Settings dialog.

Creating New E-mail Accounts

To create new e-mail accounts, select **Tools**, **E-mail Accounts** to open the E-mail Accounts Wizard. Select **Add a New E-Mail** account and then **Next** to open the screen for selecting the e-mail account type, as shown previously in Figure 2.4. To set up a new e-mail account, follow the procedure you learned in the "Using the Startup Wizard" section of this chapter.

The new e-mail accounts are shown in all send/receive groups and can be enabled or disabled for use in each group.

Using Outlook Profiles

Outlook keeps all your settings in one or more *profiles*. The default profile, named Outlook, is the only profile you will have unless you create additional profiles. If you create additional profiles, you can maintain different settings and e-mail accounts for each profile. For example, if you sometimes work from home, you can keep your work and personal e-mail accounts, settings, and data file separate. Microsoft Exchange server allows you to log in to only one Exchange server in each profile. If you work with more than one Exchange server, you will need separate profiles.

Another reason more than one profile can be useful is if more than one person shares the same computer and you don't use separate Windows users and logins. In that case, you can create an Outlook profile for each person sharing the computer, which enables the users to have completely different Outlook setups and data files. If you have separate Windows users and logins, each user will have his or her own Outlook setup, independent of every other Windows user.

tip

By creating separate Outlook profiles for each Outlook user, you can maintain separate Outlook data and settings in a multi-user environment.

To create a new profile or view existing profiles, use the Mail icon in the Control Panel. To open the Mail icon, follow these steps:

1. Select **Start**, **Control Panel**.

2. When the Control Panel opens, select the **User Accounts** category.

3. Select **Mail.**

4. Select **Show Profiles** to display the existing Outlook profiles.

   ■ Select **Add** to add a new profile. Enter a name for the profile and click **OK** to open the E-mail Accounts dialog to add an e-mail account to the profile.

   ■ Select **Remove** to delete an existing profile.

   ■ Select **Copy** to open the Copy Profile dialog, where you can enter a name for the copy of the selected profile. Click **OK** to create the copied profile. You can then select **Properties** to make any changes you want to the copied profile.

   ■ If you are using more than one profile and want to select the profile to use when Outlook starts, select the **Prompt for a profile to be used** option for starting Outlook. This setting is also useful if you want to maintain separate Outlook profiles for more than one user.

   ■ Select **Properties** to open the Mail Setup dialog, shown in Figure 2.21. The E-mail Accounts and Data Files options in this dialog are the same as the options in the initial dialog opened from the Control Panel Mail icon, except the Show Profiles option isn't on this dialog.

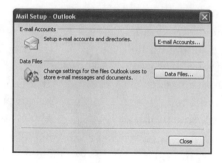

5. In the Mail Setup dialog, select **E-mail Accounts** to view or add e-mail accounts, or select **Data Files** to view or change the Outlook data file used for the profile. Select **Close** to return to the Profiles dialog.

6. Click **OK** to save all profile changes.

User Interface Shortcuts

Two of the best pieces of advice for using Outlook are to right-click everywhere and to drag and drop items.

Many places in the Outlook user interface support right-click menus, also known as *context menus* because their menu commands change based on the current context. A context menu displayed when right-clicking an e-mail item is different from a context menu displayed when right-clicking a task item.

Experiment by right-clicking everywhere in the Outlook user interface and see what commands are available in the context menus that are displayed. In many cases, using the context menus is the easiest way to perform the most common actions within the current context.

The drag-and-drop feature is used not only to move items from one folder to another, but also can be used for what Outlook calls AutoCreate. AutoCreate creates the appropriate item for the destination folder from the source item. For example, if you drag and drop an e-mail into a Contacts folder, a new contact is created with the display name and e-mail address from the e-mail already filled in. All Outlook folders support AutoCreate.

Right-clicking and dragging can be combined to show a menu offering a choice of Move, Copy, or Cancel for a dragged item.

The easiest way to drag and drop items from one folder to another is to drag the item from the current folder to another folder shown in the Navigation Pane. If you are dragging and dropping to AutoCreate items, display the Folder List in the Navigation Pane because it shows all folders of all types.

User Interface Preferences

This section contains an overview of how to configure Outlook settings. Then you will learn how to set the settings that apply to the Outlook user interface and how Outlook works in general. Other settings that apply to items such as e-mails, contacts, and tasks or to topics such as secure e-mail are covered in the chapters where they apply.

Most Outlook user interface settings are located in the Tools, Options dialog. This dialog is organized into tabs that logically group the settings. Tabs in the Options dialog are also called *property pages*. Figure 2.22 shows the Options dialog opened to the first tab shown.

FIGURE 2.22

The Options dialog is the place where you configure the Outlook user interface; it also has settings for different types of items such as e-mails and contacts.

Working with the Options dialog is like working with any other dialog. You can change some settings directly on a tab, and you can select buttons to open additional dialogs for other settings. Any setting changed directly on a tab enables the Apply button. Select **Apply** to save your changes and leave the Options dialog open. Click **OK** to save your changes and close the Options dialog. Or select **Cancel** to close the Options dialog without saving changes.

Additional dialogs opened from buttons have OK buttons to save changes made in those dialogs. If you click **OK** to approve the changes in one of these dialogs, the changes are saved immediately. Returning to the main Options dialog and selecting **Cancel** does not cancel changes already saved in another dialog.

The Other tab of the Options dialog contains user interface options as well as options to control the way Outlook works. Figure 2.23 shows the settings available on the Other tab.

The General section of the Other tab has checkboxes for emptying the Deleted Items folder when you exit Outlook and to make Outlook the default program for your e-mail, contacts, and calendar. If you are using Outlook as your primary e-mail and calendaring application, make sure the default program checkbox is checked. Emptying your Deleted Items folder removes clutter from that folder automatically, but when an item is removed from the Deleted Items folder, it usually is gone forever. The exception is if you are using Exchange server and the Exchange administrator has enabled recovery of deleted items.

FIGURE 2.23

The Other tab has settings to control how Outlook works and appears.

Select the **Navigation Pane Options** button to open the Navigation Pane Options dialog, shown in Figure 2.24. In this dialog, you can select which buttons are displayed in the Navigation Pane and the order in which they are shown. Click **OK** to save the Navigation Pane settings. You will learn more about the Navigation Pane and how to customize it in Chapter 11, "Customizing the Navigation Pane."

FIGURE 2.24

Select the buttons to display in the Navigation Pane and their order.

Selecting the AutoArchive button in the middle of the Other tab opens a dialog in which you can change your automatic archiving settings. You will learn about archive settings in Chapter 13, "Archiving Data."

Select the **Reading Pane** button to open the Reading Pane dialog shown in Figure 2.25, where you can set how the Reading Pane works.

FIGURE 2.25

The Reading Pane can automatically mark messages as having been read.

When an e-mail is selected in the Reading Pane, it can be marked as having been read after a certain amount of time has passed and/or when you select a different item in the Reading Pane. To mark items as read after a time interval, check the first checkbox in the Reading Pane dialog and enter a time to wait before marking the message as read. Check the second checkbox to mark items as having been read when you select a different item in the reading Pane. If neither of these checkboxes is checked, an item will not be marked as read even if you do read it in the Reading Pane. Opening an item always marks it as having been read.

If you check the Single key reading using the space bar checkbox, you can move from one message in the Reading Pane to another message by pressing the spacebar. The setting for moving or deleting an open item in the E-mail Options dialog controls whether the next or previous message is selected after you press the spacebar.

Click **OK** to save your Reading Pane settings and return to the Options dialog.

The Person Names section at the bottom of the Other tab controls whether a Person Names Smart Tag is enabled when you use Word as your Outlook editor. The Person Names Smart Tag recognizes a name in an address field of an e-mail and provides a context menu for that person. Figure 2.26 shows a Person Names Smart Tag context menu.

FIGURE 2.26

The Person Names context menu enables you to schedule a meeting, call, set e-mail sending options, and perform other actions for a contact in an e-mail address.

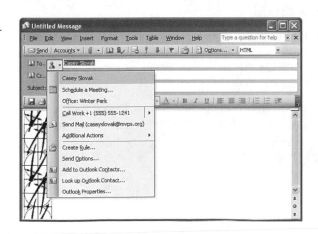

Select the **Display Messenger Status in the From field** checkbox to control whether a sender's Instant Messaging status is displayed in the From field of an open e-mail. If you see significant delays in opening e-mails, try unchecking this check-box to speed up the process of opening e-mails. Messenger status can be displayed only for Windows Messenger.

Select the **Advanced Options** button at the upper right of the Other tab to open the Advanced Options dialog, as shown in Figure 2.27.

FIGURE 2.27

The Advanced Options dialog enables you to select the folder in which Outlook starts up.

To change which folder is displayed when Outlook starts, select **Browse**, select a folder in the Select Folder dialog, and click **OK** to accept your selection. The next time you start Outlook, that folder will be displayed. Outlook's default is to start up in the Outlook Today screen. If that isn't what you want, you might want to change the startup folder to the Inbox to view your e-mail or to the Calendar to view your schedule when Outlook starts.

The Warn before permanently deleting items checkbox near the top of the Advanced Options dialog also controls whether you get a warning when you exit Outlook and the option for clearing the Deleted Items folder when you exit is selected in the Other tab.

The Provide feedback with sound option requires installation of the Office Sounds add-in, which you can download from the Microsoft Office Online Web site. There is a link in the Help menu to the Microsoft Office Online Web site to make it easy for you to find the Web site.

The Show Paste Options buttons option applies only when you are using Word as the Outlook editor. Paste Options buttons are Smart Tags that are similar to the Paste Special button in Word; they enable easy text layout and formatting options.

The Use Unicode Message Format when saving messages option saves messages using the Unicode message format, which uses 2 bytes for each letter in the message. Normally, messages are saved using a format that uses 1 byte for each letter in the message. Messages saved in Unicode format are much larger than messages saved in the standard format. The Unicode message format for saving messages is most useful for messages that use character sets that require Unicode, such as Chinese and Japanese. European languages such as English, French, German, and Spanish do not require Unicode format.

The Enable mail logging (troubleshooting) option is a troubleshooting technique that creates a log entry for every attempt to connect to a mail server and send or receive messages. These logs become very large very quickly, so you should leave this checkbox unchecked unless a support person asks you to turn on diagnostic logging because you are having e-mail problems.

The Reminder Options button at the bottom of the Advanced Options dialog enables you to set whether to display reminders and whether to play a sound when the reminders come due. The sound must be a .WAV file. Click **OK** to save the reminder settings.

The Add-In Manager and COM Add-Ins buttons are used to open dialogs showing which Exchange extensions and Outlook COM add-ins are installed. This advanced topic is not covered in this book.

The Custom Forms button is used to manage custom forms. You will learn about custom forms in Chapter 20, "Customizing Outlook Forms."

The Service Options button opens a dialog containing options for online content searching and updating from the Web, which you will learn about in Appendix B, "Outlook Support and Resources," and customer feedback options. The customer feedback option in this dialog enables participation in the customer experience improvement program, which anonymously collects information about your hardware configuration and software usage; Microsoft uses this information to improve future versions of Outlook and Office. You do not have to participate in this program. If you do decide to participate in the program, rest assured that no personal information is transmitted to Microsoft.

The two checkboxes for allowing scripting in shared and Public Folders near the middle of the Advanced Options dialog apply to Exchange server users and are normally set by the Exchange administrator.

THE ABSOLUTE MINIMUM

In this chapter, you learned about the basics of working in Outlook and how to set up Outlook the first time you run it. To review, you now know how to

- Set up Outlook when running it for the first time using the Startup Wizard.

- Work with Outlook's user interface.

- Use Outlook send/receive groups and profiles.

- Create new e-mail accounts.

- Set Outlook user interface preferences.

With the skills you acquired in this chapter, you can set up additional profiles, send/receive groups, and e-mail accounts, and work with Outlook's interface elements. In the next chapter, you will learn how to work with e-mail.

PART

WORKING WITH
E-MAIL

IN THIS CHAPTER

- Learning about what is shown in the Inbox and how to work in the Inbox.

- Learning about sending and receiving e-mail.

- Knowing about reading e-mail.

- Understanding how to answer and forward e-mail.

- Knowing how to create a new e-mail message.

- Knowing how to set e-mail preferences.

SENDING AND RECEIVING E-MAIL

E-mail has become a major communications medium, and much of the time you spend in Outlook will be e-mail–related time. Of course, the first thing you need to know about e-mail is how to send and receive it; otherwise, you have no e-mail. You also need to know how to read, create, reply to, and forward e-mails. The Inbox is the place where you receive e-mails, so you also need to understand about working in the Inbox. In this chapter, you will learn the ways to work in the Inbox and the basics of working with e-mail.

Working with the Inbox

Before we start working with e-mail, let's take a look at the Inbox folder, shown in Figure 3.1. The Inbox is the folder where your e-mails are delivered, and you will be spending a lot of time working in the Inbox folder, so it's good to know what you will be seeing.

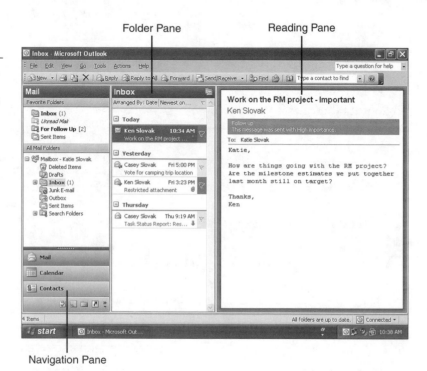

Folder Pane   Reading Pane

FIGURE 3.1

The Inbox view is laid out in three panes; the Navigation Pane, Folder Pane, and Reading Pane.

Navigation Pane

The normal view of the Inbox shows the width of the Outlook window divided into three panes below a menu bar and a toolbar. The toolbar is the Standard toolbar, which contains frequently used commands from the different Outlook menus. The three panes, from left to right, are the Navigation Pane, the Folder Pane, and the Reading Pane.

The Navigation Pane

The Navigation Pane is used to navigate from one folder to another in Outlook. It has buttons for different groups of folders, such as Mail and Calendar. Clicking one of these buttons displays a list of folders related to that button. The Inbox is an e-mail folder, so it is displayed in the Mail group. All folders of every type are displayed if the Folder List button is clicked. Above the All Mail Folders group of folders is the Favorite Folders area, which provides shortcut links to various e-mail folders.

To select a folder to view, click on the desired folder in the list of folders. To view the Inbox, click on the **Inbox** in the All Mail Folders group or in the Favorite Folders area. You will learn more about working with the Navigation Pane throughout this book, and you will learn about customizing it in Chapter 11, "Customizing the Navigation Pane."

The Folder Pane

The Folder Pane displays all the items in the current folder, based on the folder view being used. The default view of the Inbox shows all items in the folder, grouped by the date the items were received. You can learn more about folder views in Chapter 14, "Outlook Views."

The Folder Pane shows quite a bit of additional information about the items in the folder, such as the date/time the items were received, the person who sent the items, and the status of the items. Figure 3.1 shows four e-mails in the Inbox; each item shown illustrates one or more pieces of status information.

The items are grouped by when they were received; the groupings shown are Today, Yesterday, and Thursday. Other groupings you might see in the Inbox include Last Week, Two Weeks Ago, Three Weeks Ago, Last Month; and Older. Groupings are set up to show more detail for newer items and less for older items. You might care when an item was received this week but probably wouldn't care which day three months ago an item was received.

The first item in the Inbox shows the icon for an e-mail that hasn't been marked as read at the left. This icon, called the Unread icon, is a closed envelope symbol. The sender of the e-mail and the time it was received appear next in the first line. At the right of the e-mail is a flag, known as a Quick Flag, that is colored red. Quick Flags are used to mark e-mails so they stand out, and also can provide reminders with alarms and pop-up dialogs to remind you to take some action related to the e-mail. You will find more details on Quick Flags and reminders in Chapter 4, "Advanced E-mail Techniques." The second line of the first e-mail shows part of its subject, and a High importance icon, which is a red-colored exclamation mark.

The second item in the Inbox, in the Yesterday grouping, shows the icon for an e-mail that has been replied to. This icon is an open envelope symbol with a maroon-colored arrow pointing toward the envelope.

The third item in the Inbox, in the Yesterday grouping, shows the icon for an e-mail that has been forwarded to someone. This icon is an open envelope symbol with a blue-colored arrow pointing away from the envelope. This e-mail shows a paper clip icon to the right of the e-mail subject, which indicates that the e-mail has an attachment. An attachment can be a file, document, picture, or other object that is attached to an e-mail. This e-mail shows a green-colored Quick Flag.

The final item shown in the Inbox, in the Thursday grouping, shows the icon for an e-mail that has been marked as read. This icon is an open envelope. This item also shows the icon for an item with Low importance at the right of the second line, a blue-colored down-pointing arrow symbol.

To review, here is a list of the most common pieces of information displayed about items in the Folder Pane:

- Date groupings, which organize e-mails based on the dates they were received. The date groupings become less specific as the dates get further and further in the past.

- E-mail status, which can be read or unread, replied to, and forwarded.

- Flag status, which can be unflagged or show a colored Quick Flag.

- Importance, which can be High, Normal, or Low. E-mails with Normal importance don't show any importance icon.

- Attachment status. E-mails with attachments display a paper clip icon.

- Subject and date/time received. In date groupings that use a day, such as Yesterday, the day of the week and time received are shown. In less specific groupings, such as Last Month, the date the item was received is shown, but not the time. It's more important to show what time an item was received today than it is for an item received months ago.

The Reading Pane

The Reading Pane, the rightmost pane shown in the Inbox, enables you to preview e-mails so you can read them without having to open them. Just below the subject of the e-mail and the sender is the InfoBar, a gray-colored bar that shows additional information about an item in the Reading Pane. In the item shown in the Reading Pane in Figure 3.1, the InfoBar indicates that a follow-up flag is set on the e-mail, and the e-mail was sent with High importance.

Below the InfoBar, you can see the person the e-mail was addressed to, followed by the message in the e-mail.

Now that you are familiar with the layout of the Inbox and what information is displayed for e-mails in the Inbox, you will learn about sending and receiving e-mails.

Sending and Receiving E-mail

In Chapter 2, "Outlook from the Beginning," you learned how to configure e-mail accounts, send/ receive groups, and Outlook profiles. Now you are ready to send and receive e-mail.

If you set up your send/receive group to automatically poll for new e-mails, your e-mail will arrive at regular intervals. If you didn't configure automatic polling for e-mail, you will have to check for e-mail manually. You also can check for new e-mails manually whenever you choose, whether or not an automatic polling interval was set. To manually check for new e-mail messages, do the following:

- ■ To send and receive e-mail manually, press the keyboard shortcut **F9**, which performs the same function as selecting **Tools**, **Send/Receive**, **Send/Receive All**.

- ■ To send only (and not receive) e-mail from all your e-mail accounts, select **Tools**, **Send/Receive**, **Send All.**

In addition to the commands for sending or sending/ receiving for all accounts, you can send/receive for specific e-mail accounts in a send/receive group or for specific send/receive groups. Figure 3.2 shows the Send/ Receive menu for an Outlook setup that has one send/receive group with two e-mail accounts defined in that group.

FIGURE 3.2

The Send/ Receive menu shows your send/receive groups as well as individual e-mail accounts.

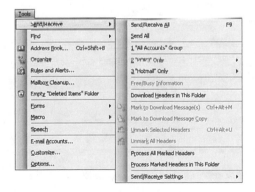

On this menu, you can see that the default All Accounts Group is listed, followed by a menu commands for each e-mail account in the All Accounts Group. If you have more than one send/receive group defined, that group is listed next, followed by the accounts in that group and so on.

Now that you know how to send and receive e-mail, you will learn how to read e-mail in the next section.

Reading E-mail

The most important thing about receiving e-mails is reading them, of course. Outlook provides two methods of reading e-mails. You can read them in the Reading Pane, or you can open individual e-mails.

Working with the Reading Pane

By default, the Reading Pane is shown at the right of mail folder views but optionally can be displayed below the folder view or can be turned off entirely. You saw how the Reading Pane looks on the right of the folder view in Figure 3.1; the Reading Pane displayed at the bottom of the folder view is shown in Figure 3.3. This arrangement displays more information for each e-mail in the folder but shows less of the message text in the e-mail selected in the Reading Pane.

FIGURE 3.3

Displaying the Reading Pane at the bottom of the folder view shows less text than displaying the Reading Pane on the right of the folder view.

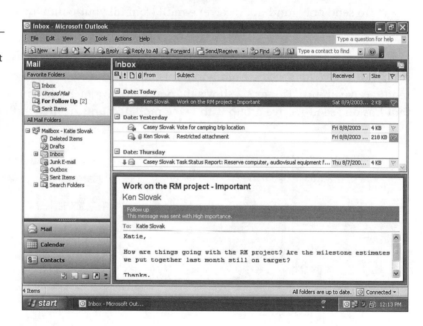

Figure 3.4 shows the Inbox with the Reading Pane turned off.

To change the position of the Reading Pane or to turn it off, do the following:

1. Select **View**, **Reading Pane**.

2. Click **Right** to display the Reading Pane on the right, **Bottom** to display it on the bottom, or **Off** to turn it off.

FIGURE 3.4

When the Reading Pane is turned off, you must open an e-mail to be able to read it.

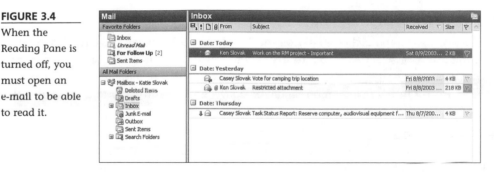

Using the Reading Pane makes it easy to read e-mails without having to open them. If there is more message text than will fit in the Reading Pane screen, you can use the scrollbars to scroll down the message text so that you can read it all. I use the Reading Pane to work with e-mails the vast majority of the time and rarely open an e-mail to read it.

Opening an E-mail

To open an e-mail, either double-click on the e-mail, or right-click on it and select **Open** from the context menu. Opening an e-mail automatically marks it as having been read.

The advantage to reading an e-mail by opening it is that you can view more text at one time in a long e-mail without having to scroll, especially if the e-mail window is maximized. If you prefer to keep the Reading Pane closed, you will have to open your e-mails from the Inbox to be able to read them.

Answering and Forwarding E-mail

You answer e-mails by replying to them, and you can also forward them to other people. Replying to an e-mail automatically addresses the reply to the e-mail's sender. If the original e-mail was sent to more than one person, you can choose to reply to only the sender or to all the original recipients of the e-mail in addition to the sender. You can also add or remove recipients from the e-mail after you begin the reply or forward.

When you are finished entering any text or changing settings for the e-mail, send the replied to or forwarded e-mail by clicking **Send** on the toolbar of the open e-mail or press the key combination **Ctrl+Enter**.

Using Reply and Reply to All

To reply to an e-mail, click **Reply** on the Standard toolbar when the e-mail is selected in the Inbox or select **Actions**, **Reply**. Another way to reply to an e-mail is to right-click a selected e-mail in the Inbox and then select **Reply**. To reply to an open e-mail, select **Reply** in the open e-mail's toolbar. Figure 3.5 shows a reply to an e-mail with the subject *Work on the RM project - Important*.

RE: is always added in front of the original subject of an e-mail when you reply. If the e-mail you reply to is part of a conversation (where related messages are passed back and forth between sender and receiver multiple times), still only one *RE:* appears in the subject line no matter how many times the e-mail is replied to.

To reply to all the recipients of an e-mail, click **Reply to All** on the Standard toolbar when the e-mail is selected in the Inbox or select **Actions**, **Reply to All**. Another way to reply to all recipients of an e-mail is to right-click a selected e-mail in the Inbox and then select **Reply to All**. To reply to all recipients of an open e-mail, select **Reply to All** in the open e-mail's toolbar. Figure 3.6 shows an e-mail being answered using the Reply to All feature. The original e-mail was addressed to two recipients, and the reply is addressed to the other original recipient as well as to the sender of the original e-mail. The subject of the reply shows the addition of the *RE:* modifier.

When you have a reply message open, you can add or remove addressees, change the format of the message, select which e-mail account is used to send the reply if you have more than one e-mail account, and change the message options just as you can with a new e-mail message. You will learn about these topics in later sections of this chapter, as well as in Chapter 4. You will learn to work with e-mail formats in "Working with E-mail Formats" later in this chapter.

FIGURE 3.5

The reply to the original e-mail is already addressed to its sender, and the subject has been modified by the addition of *RE:* in front of the original subject.

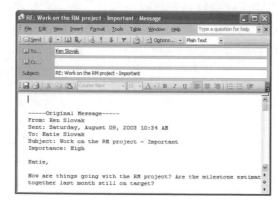

FIGURE 3.6

Reply to All opens a reply e-mail addressed to all the recipients of the original e-mail.

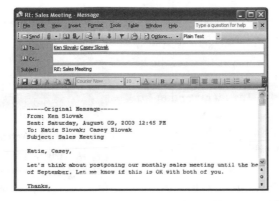

E-mails that are replies don't include any attachments that were included in the original e-mail. This makes sense because all the original recipients of the e-mail received the attachments when they received the original e-mail. The same rule applies to reply to all e-mails.

Forwarding

To forward an e-mail to someone else, select the e-mail in the Inbox and click **Forward** on the Standard toolbar. You also can select **Actions**, **Forward,** or right-click on an item selected in the Inbox and select **Forward**. In an open e-mail, select **Forward** on the toolbar in the open e-mail.

When a message is forwarded to other people, the text *FW:* is added to the message's subject to indicate the message was forwarded. Figure 3.7 shows an e-mail message opened for forwarding.

In most other respects, a forwarded e-mail message is the same as a reply, except that forwarded messages include any attachments that came in the original e-mail. You can add addressees to forwarded messages and change their format and message options just as you can with replies. You will learn about working with e-mail formats later in this chapter, and about setting and changing message options in Chapter 4.

FIGURE 3.6

Forwarded e-mails include any attachments that were included in the original e-mail.

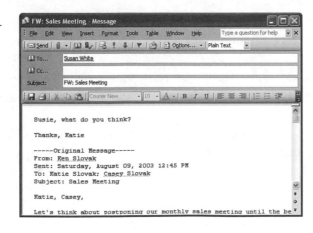

Creating a New E-mail Message

You can create a new e-mail message in a number of ways. The simplest way is to press the key combination **Ctrl+N** when the current Outlook folder is an e-mail folder. The menu option for creating a new message is **Actions**, **New Mail Message**. Selecting this option opens a new e-mail message using the default e-mail editor and e-mail format. You will learn how to set your default e-mail editor and e-mail format in "Setting E-mail Preferences" later in this chapter.

> **tip**
>
> If you are currently in a Contacts folder and have a contact selected, you can select **Actions**, **New Message to Contact** to open a new e-mail message already addressed to that contact. You will learn more about addressing e-mails later in this chapter.

Working with E-mail Formats

Outlook provides three formats in which you can send e-mails:

- **HTML (Hypertext Markup Language)**—An Internet standard for formatted messages and the default format for Outlook 2003 e-mails.
- **Plain Text**—Unformatted e-mails that can be read by any e-mail client.
- **Rich Text Format (RTF)**—A proprietary Microsoft format for formatted messages that can be understood only by Outlook, and another e-mail client named Eudora.

Outlook can use one of two editors for working with e-mail: Microsoft Word and the Outlook editor. Word provides more text formatting options and has the full power of a word processor. The Outlook editor is certainly adequate but doesn't offer the full set of features provided by Word. Both Word and the Outlook editor support all three e-mail formats.

So, which format should you use, and when should you select other formats for specific e-mail messages? Each format has advantages and disadvantages, as shown in Table 3.1.

You can open a new e-mail message using a specific e-mail format by selecting **Actions**, **New Mail Message Using**, and clicking on **Plain Text**, **Rich Text**, or **HTML**.

Some Outlook features that you will learn about later in this book, such as sending an e-mail with voting buttons used to return the recipient's vote to approve or reject a proposal, work only when using Rich Text format. Rich Text format is also required for sending Outlook items such as contacts and tasks correctly to other people. Some people use e-mail clients that don't understand HTML messages; you will want to send e-mail to those people using Plain Text format. You can change the format of an open e-mail message, to send the message to people who use different e-mail clients or to remove or add formatting for messages. If you change the format from HTML or Rich Text to Plain Text, you will be warned that all message formatting will be lost. Select **Yes** to continue with the format change or **No** to cancel changing the message format.

Table 3.1 E-mail Format Advantages and Disadvantages

E-mail Format	Advantages	Disadvantages
HTML	Formatted text. Internet standard. Can show pictures in the body of an e-mail. Can use stationery to provide background images or patterns for formatted e-mails.	Larger size e-mails produced using HTML than the other formats. Older style e-mail readers such as Pine can't understand HTML. Possible to exploit HTML formatting tags to send viruses for spam techniques.
Plain Text	Smallest message size. Cannot be used for inline viruses or spam techniques.	Unformatted text layout.
Rich Text (RTF)	Formatted text. Used for sending custom Outlook forms and Outlook items such as contacts and tasks. Small size for formatted text messages. Can show pictures in the body of an e-mail.	Understood only by Outlook and Eudora.

You change an existing e-mail format differently depending on which e-mail editor you are using:

- **Word editor**—Select the **format** drop-down in the E-mail toolbar and choose the desired format for this message.
- **Outlook editor**—Select the format from the **Format** menu.

Figure 3.8 shows the format drop-down in the E-mail toolbar in an e-mail using Word as the editor.

FIGURE 3.8

The Format drop-down in an e-mail using Word as the editor enables you to change message format.

Table 3.2 shows the alternate formats available in the F̲ormat
menu in the Outlook editor for each e-mail format.

Table 3.2 Alternate Formats with the
Outlook Editor

Current Format	Available Alternate Formats
HTML	Plain Text
Plain Text	HTML, Rich Text
Rich Text	Plain Text

Addressing and Sending an E-mail

Each e-mail has three address fields that you can
use to address the e-mail to other people. An e-
mail can be addressed directly to one or more
people, it can be carbon copied (Cc), or it can be
blind carbon copied (Bcc). You will learn about
carbon copying and blind carbon copying in a
later section of this chapter.

caution

When you send e-mails
to people who do not
use Outlook, never use
Rich Text Format (RTF).
Use only HTML or Plain
Text formats. If the recipient of a
Rich Text e-mail is using an e-mail
client that doesn't understand Rich
Text, he or she will receive a Plain
Text message with an attached
`Winmail.dat` file. This attachment
contains the Rich Text formatting
and cannot be deciphered unless the
recipient is using Outlook or Eudora.

To address an e-mail to one or more people, either type the e-mail address in the To
field or select the **To** button. Selecting the To button opens the Select Names dialog,
shown in Figure 3.9.

FIGURE 3.9

The Select
Names dialog
enables you to
address e-mails
using existing
contact e-mail
addresses.

Highlight the desired recipient or recipients from the address book shown in the Select
Names dialog and click on the **To** button to add the selected e-mail addresses to the

To field of the e-mail. You can also double-click one or more highlighted recipients to add them to the To field. When you are finished adding e-mail addresses to the To field, click **OK** to close the Select Names dialog and return to the e-mail.

When you are finished composing and addressing the e-mail, you can set options for the e-mail, which you will learn about in Chapter 4, before you send it. You can also attach files or Outlook items to the e-mail, which you will learn how to do later in this chapter.

To send the finished e-mail, click **Send** on the toolbar or press the key combination **Ctrl+Enter**.

Sending Rich Text Messages Over the Internet

Sending a Rich Text Formatted (RTF) message over the Internet, required when sending Outlook items such as contacts and tasks, can be difficult to do successfully, especially when you are using Exchange server. Outlook has a tendency to convert Rich Text messages sent over the Internet into HTML messages, which prevents an Outlook item from being received correctly. Some of the settings necessary for correct transmission of Rich Text can be set only by the Exchange administrator.

One setting that is under your control is the format setting for the contact in the contact record. To see this setting in an e-mail message, right-click a recipient in To field and select **Outlook Properties** to open the recipient's contact record. Right-click the e-mail address in the contact record and select **Outlook Properties** again to open the dialog shown in Figure 3.10. If you entered an e-mail address instead of selecting a contact, you have to select **Outlook Properties** only once to display the E-mail Properties dialog.

> ## tip
>
> You can resend an e-mail—for example, if the recipient doesn't originally receive it. To resend an e-mail, open the e-mail and select **Actions**, **Resend This Message**. A new copy of the original message is opened in which you can add or remove recipients, change the subject or message text, add or remove attachments, and change any other message settings or options just as you can with a new e-mail.

FIGURE 3.10

The E-mail Properties dialog enables you to change how e-mails are sent to the contact over the Internet.

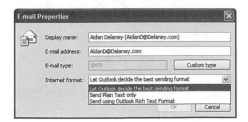

The default setting for Internet format is Let Outlook decide the best sending format. Often, using this setting can lead to the e-mail being converted to HTML. To ensure that Rich Text Format is used for the selected contact, select the **Send using Outlook Rich Text Format** option. Click **OK** to close the E-mail Properties dialog, and if a contact record was opened, select **Save and Close** to save the change and ensure the e-mail is sent in Rich Text Format.

There is a similar setting in the dialog opened by selecting **Tools**, **Options**, **Mail Format**, **Internet Options**. The drop-down for the format used when sending Rich Text messages is a global setting for all messages sent over the Internet by Outlook. The setting you just learned to set is a per e-mail account setting, which gives you much greater control over the way messages are sent.

note

If you don't want to always use Rich Text Format for that contact, change the setting back to Let Outlook decide the best sending format after the e-mail is sent.

If the global setting is changed from Convert to HTML format to Send using Outlook Rich Text format, all Rich Text messages are sent to everyone as Rich Text. The global setting overrides the default Let Outlook decide the best sending format setting in the contact's e-mail address properties. This can result in accidentally sending Rich Text messages to people whose e-mail clients can't understand Rich Text, with possible loss of information or formatting. The best way to control who gets Rich Text formatted messages is on a per e-mail account basis, as you learned how to do in this section.

Carbon Copying and Blind Carbon Copying

In addition to sending e-mails directly to people on the To address line, you also can carbon copy and blind carbon copy an e-mail to people.

Carbon copying people in an e-mail is similar to sending interoffice memos in business, with the memo sent directly to some people and with other people in the Cc (carbon copy) address field. The distinction between sending directly to someone and sending a Cc of a message is that people in the To field are expected to take some action as a result of the message, such as replying to it. People who are carbon copied with the message aren't expected to take any action; they are copied so they are aware of the message.

Blind carbon copying (Bcc for blind carbon copy) is a method of copying someone with a message without enabling any of the other recipients of the message to know the person was copied. The only person who can see the Bcc address field in a message is the person who sent the message. Although Bcc has many legitimate uses, you should be aware that it is also a technique used by spammers. Many of the spam e-mails you receive won't show that the message was addressed to you, an indication the message was Bcc'd to your e-mail address.

The Cc address field is always shown in an e-mail message. The Bcc address field is not shown by default. The method for showing the Bcc address field in an e-mail message depends on which e-mail editor you're using—Word or the Outlook editor:

■ For e-mails using Word as the e-mail editor, show the Bcc address field by clicking the down arrow to the right of the Options button on the E-mail toolbar in an open e-mail and selecting **Bcc**, as shown in Figure 3.11.

■ For e-mails using the Outlook editor, show the Bcc address field by selecting **View**, **Bcc Field** in an open e-mail.

FIGURE 3.11

To show the Bcc Address field in an e-mail using Word as the e-mail editor, you use the Options drop-down.

Showing the Bcc address field is a toggle setting. After you show the Bcc address field, it will continue to be displayed in all e-mail messages until you toggle the setting again.

Adding a recipient to the Cc or Bcc address fields follows the same procedure as adding a recipient to the To field, which you learned how to do earlier in this chapter. You either type a valid e-mail address in the Cc or Bcc address field or select **Cc** or **Bcc** to open the Select Names dialog. In the Select Names dialog, highlight the Cc or Bcc recipient and click on either the **Cc** or **Bcc** button.

caution

If you blind carbon copy someone in an e-mail, and the Bcc'd recipient doesn't realize he or she was Bcc'd on a message and then uses Reply to All, the rest of the original recipients will also receive a copy of the reply. They will then know that person was copied without the other recipients' knowledge. If an e-mail contains extremely sensitive content, you might consider sending a separate e-mail to the person instead of blind carbon copying him or her.

Sending Attachments

E-mail messages can have attachments, which can be either files or Outlook items. Some examples of Outlook items are tasks, contacts, and other e-mails. You should attach Outlook items only when you are sending to people who also use Outlook. Other e-mail software applications don't know how to handle Outlook items, so it is useless to send Outlook items to people who do not use Outlook. If you attach Outlook items, you also must send the e-mail in Outlook Rich Text Format, which you learned about earlier in this chapter.

You can't add an attachment to a received e-mail message; you can only add an attachment to new e-mails or to open e-mails that are being replied to or forwarded.

The Paperclip icon in the toolbar enables you to attach files (not Outlook items) to an open e-mail. Selecting the **Paperclip** icon in an open e-mail opens the Insert File dialog, shown in Figure 3.12.

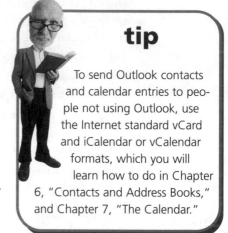

tip

To send Outlook contacts and calendar entries to people not using Outlook, use the Internet standard vCard and iCalendar or vCalendar formats, which you will learn how to do in Chapter 6, "Contacts and Address Books," and Chapter 7, "The Calendar."

FIGURE 3.12

The Insert File dialog enables you to attach files to e-mails.

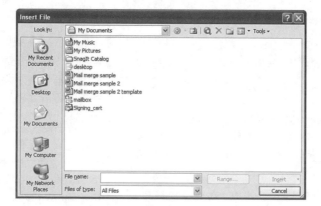

Select the file to attach to the e-mail in this dialog and then select **Insert** to insert the file as an attachment.

To attach an Outlook item to an e-mail, click the down arrow next to the Paperclip icon and select **Insert Item** to open the Insert Item dialog, shown in Figure 3.13. If you are using the Outlook editor, select **Insert**, **Item** to open the Insert Item dialog.

In the Look In section at the top of the dialog, select the folder where the item you want to insert is located. Scroll through the Items section at the bottom of the dialog and select the item to insert; then click **OK** to attach the Outlook item to the e-mail.

If you are using the Outlook editor, you can choose to insert the item as an attachment, as text only, or as a shortcut. Selecting **Attachment** attaches the Outlook item to the e-mail message just as it does when you attach a file. Selecting **Text Only** inserts information from the Outlook item as text in the e-mail. Selecting **Shortcut** inserts a shortcut link to the item and is not useful unless you are using

Exchange server and the Outlook item is in a folder accessible to the recipient of the e-mail message.

FIGURE 3.13

The Insert Item dialog enables you to attach Outlook objects to e-mails.

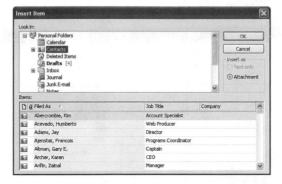

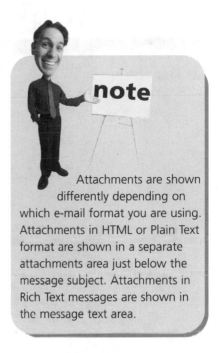

Attachments are shown differently depending on which e-mail format you are using. Attachments in HTML or Plain Text format are shown in a separate attachments area just below the message subject. Attachments in Rich Text messages are shown in the message text area.

Setting E-mail Preferences

Outlook provides many settings for configuring e-mail, your default e-mail format and editor, and your e-mail options. Most of these settings are available when you select **Tools**, **Options**, click on the **Preferences** tab, and then select **E-mail Options**. Some other e-mail–related settings are located on the Mail Setup, Mail Format, Spelling, and Other tabs. You learned about the settings in the Mail Setup tab in Chapter 2.

The E-mail Options Dialog

In the top section of the E-mail Options dialog, shown in Figure 3.14, you set message handling options. In the bottom section, you set the appearance of e-mails you reply to or forward. Two buttons in this dialog, Advanced E-mail Options and Tracking Options, open additional dialogs.

Message Handling Options

The top section of the E-mail Options dialog is the Message handling options section. These options control how messages are handled when you move or delete, read, send, reply, or forward e-mails.

For the After moving or deleting an open item setting, you can choose the following:

- Open the previous item in the folder. This is the default setting.
- Open the next item in the folder.
- Return to the Inbox.

FIGURE 3.14

In the E-mail Options dialog, you set most of the e-mail handling and sending appearance options.

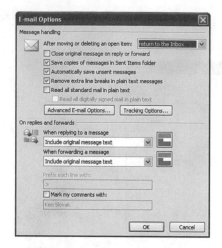

The Close original message on reply or forward setting selects whether to close an open e-mail after you reply to it or forward it.

If Save copies of messages in Sent Items folder is checked, copies of all messages you send are saved in the Sent Items folder. This setting interacts with the In folders other than the Inbox, save replies with original message setting in the Advanced E-mail Options dialog. Table 3.3 shows how these two settings interact.

Table 3.3 Interaction of Save Copies Setting with Save Replies Setting

Settings	Result
Save copies checked, save replies checked	Original messages, replies to items in Inbox saved to Sent Items. Replies to items in other folders saved in the original folder.
Save copies checked, save replies not checked	Original messages, replies from any folder saved in Sent Items.
Save copies not checked	Original messages, replies from any folder not saved at all.

If Automatically save unsent messages is checked, messages that haven't been saved or sent are automatically saved to the Drafts folder or another folder selected in the Advanced E-mail Options dialog. The autosave frequency is set in the Advanced E-mail Options dialog.

The Remove extra line breaks in plain text messages setting is used to condense Plain Text messages by removing extra blank spaces between lines of the messages. Extra line breaks are not shown but are not actually removed from the message. If extra line breaks are removed from an e-mail, the InfoBar for the e-mail notes the removal. To show the e-mail with the extra line breaks, click on the InfoBar and select **Restore line breaks**.

The Read all standard mail in plain text setting displays e-mails in Plain Text format. This option removes formatting and inline pictures from the display of HTML and Rich Text messages. The formatting is still there in the messages; it just isn't shown. If you remove this setting, the messages will be displayed with their original formatting. This option is used mostly to prevent active content such as links to Web sites in messages that might carry viruses from executing the active content.

The Read all digitally signed mail in plain text setting is enabled only if the setting to read all standard e-mail in plain text is checked. This setting is similar to the one for standard e-mails but applies to secure digitally signed e-mails only. The reason for a separate setting is that, because signed e-mails carry traceability to the originator and can be checked for forgery and tampering, they are less likely to be carrying a virus than unsigned e-mails. You will learn more details about digitally signed and secure e-mails in Chapter 18, "Secure E-mail."

On Replies and Forwards Options

When you reply to or forward a message, you can select whether to include the original message text in your reply or forward, and you can choose how the original text is inserted in the reply or forward. The following settings can be used for replies and/or forwards:

- **Attach original message**—This setting includes the original message as an attachment to the reply or forward. This is similar to the way forwards received from AOL (America Online) users appear.

- **Include original message text**—This setting places the original message below the text for the reply or forward. **Include and indent original message text** is similar, but the original text is indented from the left margin of the reply or forward. Both settings place a separator line between the original text and the reply or forward text, and also list the sender, the date/time the original message was sent, and the person to whom it was sent below the separator line.

- **Prefix each line of original message**—This setting includes the original message below a separator line with the sending information the same as in the previous settings, but it also places a prefix character at the beginning of each line of the original message.

You use the Mark my comments with setting when you use Word as the e-mail editor, and you enter comments mixed into the original text of a message that is replied to or forwarded. The text entered is placed between brackets and serves to identify comments that are interspersed with the original text.

Click **OK** to save the E-mail Options settings.

Advanced E-mail Options

Select **Advanced E-mail Options** to open the Advanced E-mail Options dialog, as shown in Figure 3.15.

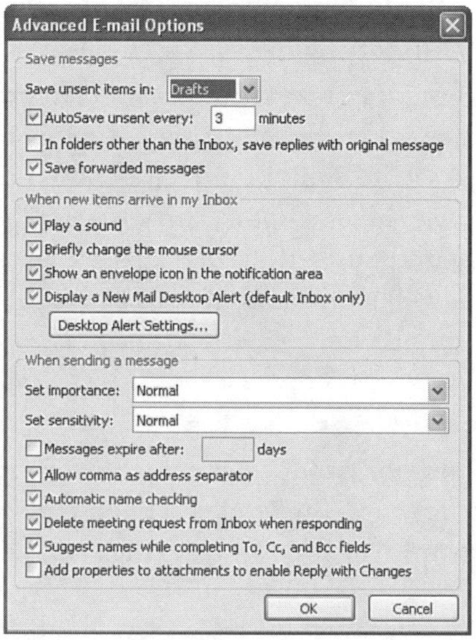

FIGURE 3.15

The Advanced E-mail Options dialog has additional, advanced e-mail settings.

The settings in the Advanced E-mail Options dialog are broken into groups for message-saving settings, actions to take when new e-mail messages are delivered to the Inbox, and settings used when sending messages. The first group of settings is for saving messages.

Save Message Settings

The Save unsent messages in setting enables you to choose to save unsent messages in the Drafts, Inbox, Outbox, or Sent Items folder. The default is to save unsent messages in the Drafts folder.

The AutoSave unsent every setting enables you to set how often to save unsent messages. The default setting is to save unsent messages every 3 minutes.

The effects of the In folders other than the Inbox, save replies with original message setting, combined with the Save copies of messages in Sent Items folder setting on the E-mail Options tab, are shown in Table 3.3.

The Save forwarded messages setting also works with the Save copies of messages in Sent Items folder setting on the E-mail Options tab. If both settings are checked, forwarded messages are saved in the Sent Items folder.

The next group of settings is for actions to take when new e-mail messages are delivered to your Inbox.

Actions Taken on Arrival of New Messages

The Play a sound setting in the Advanced E-mail Options dialog plays the Windows New Mail Notification sound when new e-mails arrive in the Inbox. The new mail sound doesn't play every time a new e-mail arrives; it plays at intervals of approximately 5 minutes. If new mail arrives more often than at 5-minute intervals, the new mail sound may not play for each new mail arrival.

To change the sound used for the New Mail Notification sound, follow these steps:

1. Select **Start, Control Panel** and then **Sounds, Speech, and Audio Devices**. If Control Panel is not shown in the Start menu, open the Control Panel by selecting **Start**, **My Computer,** and from the Address drop-down, select **Control Panel**.

2. Select **Sounds and Audio Devices**; then in the Sounds and Audio Devices Properties dialog, select the **Sounds** tab.

3. Scroll the sounds listed under Program events until **New Mail Notification** is selected, as shown in Figure 3.16.

4. Select the sound you want played in the Sounds drop-down, or if the desired sound isn't shown in the Sounds drop-down, select **Browse** and navigate to the sound you want to use and click **OK**. The sound must be in a .WAV file. Click **OK** to save the selection for the new mail sound.

The Briefly change the mouse cursor setting in the Advanced E-mail Options dialog displays a visual signal that a new e-mail has arrived in the Inbox. If you have a relatively fast computer, you may not see the cursor change; it happens too fast to notice.

The Show an envelope icon in the notification area setting shows an envelope signaling a new e-mail has arrived in the Inbox. The envelope icon is displayed until an e-mail is marked as read, is replied to, forwarded, or deleted. Figure 3.17 shows the envelope icon signaling new mail has arrived.

FIGURE 3.16

The default sound played when new e-mails arrive is Windows XP Notify.wav.

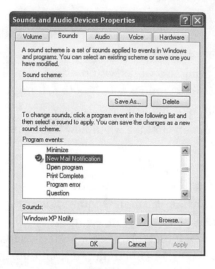

FIGURE 3.17

The envelope icon is shown in the notification area when new e-mails arrive in the Inbox, as is a Desktop Alert.

The Display a New Mail Desktop Alert setting shows an alert message when a new e-mail arrives; this alert shows the subject of the message and part of its text. Desktop Alerts are shown only when e-mail arrives as a result of a scheduled e-mail send/receive. E-mails that arrive after you manually send/receive do not trigger a Desktop Alert. Select the **X** in the alert to close it. Select the down arrow in the alert to open the incoming e-mail. A Desktop Alert for an incoming e-mail message is shown in Figure 3.17.

Select **Desktop Alert Settings** to open the Desktop Alert Settings dialog, shown in Figure 3.18, to change the configuration of Desktop Alerts.

You can set the length of time a Desktop Alert is displayed, its degree of transparency, and whether it should be hidden behind applications running in full-screen mode in the Desktop Alert Settings dialog. Experiment with the settings and select **Preview** to see how your settings appear. When you are satisfied with the Desktop Alert settings, click **OK** to save them.

The final group of settings in the Advanced E-mail Options dialog control settings used when sending e-mails. These settings are the defaults used for all e-mails, although you can change many of these settings in an e-mail before you send it.

FIGURE 3.18

The Desktop
Alert Settings
dialog enables
you to configure
how the alert
appears and
how long it is
displayed.

Send Message Settings

The Set importance setting in the bottom section of the Advanced E-mail dialog enables you to set the default importance of e-mails to Low, Normal, or High. The Set sensitivity setting enables you to set the default sensitivity of e-mails to Normal, Personal, Private, or Confidential. You will learn about e-mail importance and sensitivity in Chapter 4.

The Messages expire after setting enables you to set how long sent messages exist before they expire. Expired messages are shown as crossed out but otherwise remain available.

The Allow comma as address separator setting enables you to use a comma as well as a semicolon as a separator when you enter e-mail addresses in the To, Cc, or Bcc fields of an e-mail. The default is that only semicolons are acceptable as separators for e-mail addresses.

The Automatic name checking setting enables you to make sure an e-mail address is entered in an acceptable format. Automatic name checking is performed after you tab out of the e-mail address fields. This feature also checks names entered in e-mail address fields to verify they match a name that has an e-mail address in your contacts. Automatic name checking doesn't check for the validity of an e-mail address, only that it is formatted correctly. If you enter an e-mail address that does not exist but is in the correct format, it will pass automatic name checking. Names and e-mail addresses that pass automatic name checking are underlined.

The Delete meeting requests from Inbox when responding setting determines whether meeting requests you respond to are deleted or remain in the Inbox. You will learn more about meetings and meeting requests in Chapter 7.

The Suggest names when completing To, Cc, and Bcc fields setting presents suggestions for completing names after you start typing in the e-mail address fields. This Outlook feature is called *autocompletion*. You can do the following:

- To accept a suggestion, press **Tab** or **Enter** when the highlighted suggestion is correct.

■ To accept alternate suggestions, use the arrow keys to highlight the suggestion you want to use.

■ To use none of the suggestions, continue typing to complete the name you want to enter.

The Add properties to attachments to enable Reply with Changes setting enables you to add tracking information to Office documents sent as attachments to e-mails. When the attachments are edited by the e-mail recipient and sent back using Reply with Changes, the changes are tracked in the attached document.

Click **OK** to save your advanced e-mail settings.

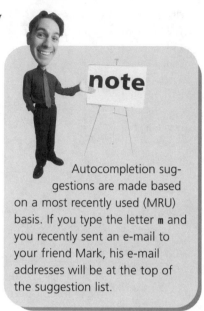

note

Autocompletion suggestions are made based on a most recently used (MRU) basis. If you type the letter **m** and you recently sent an e-mail to your friend Mark, his e-mail addresses will be at the top of the suggestion list.

Tracking Options

Select **Tracking Options** to open the Tracking Options dialog, as shown in Figure 3.19.

FIGURE 3.19

The Tracking Options dialog enables you to configure options for read and delivery receipts and for meeting requests.

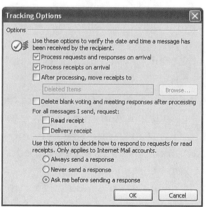

When Outlook receives meeting and other requests, the requests can be processed automatically during free time when Outlook isn't doing anything else, or they can be processed only when you open the items. The same is true for requests for read and delivery receipts. Delivery receipts are similar to certified mail that you must sign for when it is delivered by the postman, and read receipts are similar but are generated when you read an e-mail.

After a receipt is processed, you can have it automatically deleted or moved to a folder. Check **After processing, move receipts to** and then select **Browse** to open the Select Folder dialog. Select a folder to move receipts to and then click **OK**.

The next setting, Delete blank voting and meeting responses after processing, determines whether voting and meeting responses are deleted if you don't enter a reply message in the response.

The For all messages I send, request setting enables you to request read and/or delivery receipts for all e-mails you send. The use of receipt requests is generally encouraged only for important items, and some e-mail clients don't support sending delivery or read receipts. Consequently, even if you request receipts, they may not be returned to you. Some e-mail clients also enable you to prevent receipts from being sent. If a recipient using one of those e-mail clients doesn't want a receipt to be sent out, it won't be.

The first two settings in the Tracking Options dialog control whether requests and receipts are processed automatically or only when the items are opened.

The final setting in the Tracking Options dialog controls whether you return receipts requested over Internet e-mail. You can select to always send back a receipt, never send one, or decide each time a receipt is requested whether you want to send it back.

Click **OK** to save the tracking settings.

Junk E-mail Options

Select **Tools**, **Options**, click on the **Preferences** tab, and then select **Junk E-mail** to open the Junk E-mail Options dialog, shown in Figure 3.20. The Junk E-mail Options dialog has four tabs: Options, Safe Senders, Safe Recipients, and Blocked Senders. You will learn about using the Safe Senders, Safe Recipients, and Blocked Senders tabs in Chapter 4.

FIGURE 3.20

The Junk E-mail Options dialog enables you to configure how the junk e-mail filter works.

The Options tab enables you to select the degree of Junk E-mail filtering you want Outlook to use. You can choose from the following settings:

- **No automatic filtering**—This setting completely turns off the junk e-mail filtering.

- **Low**—This setting moves obvious junk e-mail into the Junk E-mail folder. Microsoft estimates that this setting catches between 50% and 70% of all junk e-mails.

- **High**—This setting is a more restrictive filter. Microsoft estimates that it catches 90% or more of all junk e-mail and moves it to the Junk E-mail folder.

> **caution**
>
> Even if you haven't had false positives filtered into the Junk E-mail folder in a long time, the last setting on the Options tab can cause deletion of e-mails you wanted to keep, so be very careful before you enable it.

- **Safe lists only**—This setting moves all e-mails except those from people or domains listed in your safe senders list to the Junk E-mail folder. You can select to trust anyone in your contacts in the safe senders list, but this setting is the most restrictive and will probably filter a significant number of non-junk e-mails into the Junk E-mail folder.

The checkbox for deleting suspected junk e-mail doesn't permit you a second chance to decide that an e-mail isn't junk, so check this setting only if you haven't had e-mail you want to keep filtered into the Junk E-mail folder for a while.

Click **OK** or **Apply** to save the junk e-mail settings.

Mail Format Tab Settings

Select **Tools**, **Options** and then click on the **Mail Format** tab to display the tab shown in Figure 3.21; it contains options for setting your default e-mail format, e-mail editor, Internet format, and international options. You will learn about the remaining tab settings for stationery, fonts, and signatures in Chapter 4.

FIGURE 3.21

The Mail Format tab enables you to set your default e-mail format and editor.

On this tab, you can do the following:

■ Select your default e-mail message format from the message format drop-down. Your choices are HTML, Rich Text, or Plain Text.

■ Check the **Use Microsoft Office Word 2003 to edit e-mail messages** checkbox to enable Word as your editor for all new e-mail messages. This setting also applies to messages you reply to or forward.

■ Check the **Use Microsoft Office Word 2003 to read Rich Text e-mail messages** checkbox to enable Word as your editor when you open Rich Text format messages.

■ Select **Internet Format** to open the Internet Format dialog, as shown in Figure 3.22. This dialog has settings for sending copies of pictures over the Internet instead of sending links to the pictures, converting Outlook Rich Text messages to HTML format when sending the messages over the Internet, and using line wrapping for Plain Text messages and encoding attachments in Plain Text messages. Generally, you should leave these settings at their defaults. You can restore the defaults by clicking **Restore Defaults**. To save any changes in this dialog, click **OK**.

■ Select **International Options** to open the International Options dialog, shown in Figure 3.23. You should generally leave these settings at their defaults.

FIGURE 3.22

The Internet Format dialog enables you to control how messages sent over the Internet are sent out.

caution

Usually, you should not change the settings for international e-mail options. Changes in these settings can make your e-mails unreadable in English.

FIGURE 3.23

The International Options dialog controls how messages are encoded when using languages other than English.

Spelling Options

Select **Tools**, **Options** and then click on the **Spelling** tab to display the tab shown in Figure 3.24; this tab contains options for spell checking in e-mails. The settings are similar to those used for setting spell checking options in Microsoft Word and won't be covered in any detail in this book. The spelling options are somewhat misleading because, except for the Always check spelling before sending and Ignore original message text in reply or forward settings, these settings apply only when the Outlook editor is used for e-mail, not when Word is used as the e-mail editor.

The custom dictionary supplements the standard dictionary and enables you to add words that otherwise would be flagged as misspelled. Select **Edit** to open the Custom.dic file in Notepad to add, remove, or edit words in your custom dictionary. This custom dictionary is shared with Word. When you select **Edit**, you see a dialog saying that changes may not be reflected in open messages. Click **OK** to close this dialog and check **Please do not show me this dialog again** to never display the dialog when you edit your custom dictionary. When you are finished editing the custom dictionary, select **File**, **Save** to save your changes and **File**, **Exit** to close the editor and return to Outlook.

FIGURE 3.24

Spelling settings control spell checking when you send e-mail.

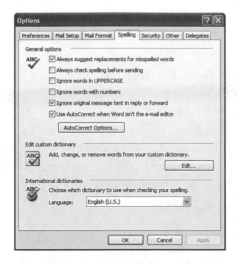

You can select the primary dictionary used for spell checking by selecting your preferred language from the Language drop-down in the Spelling tab.

Click **OK** or **Apply** to save the spelling settings.

E-mail Options on the Other Tab

Some additional e-mail or e-mail related settings are located in the Other tab of the Tools, Options dialog.

Reading Pane Options

Select **Tools**, **Options**, click on the **Other** tab, and select **Reading Pane** to open the dialog shown in Figure 3.25. In this dialog, you can set how the Reading Pane works.

FIGURE 3.25

The Reading Pane enables you to read messages without opening them and can automatically mark messages as read.

When an e-mail is selected in the Reading Pane, it can be marked as having been read after a certain amount of time has passed and/or when you select a different item in the Reading Pane. To mark items as read after a time interval, check the first checkbox in the Reading Pane dialog and enter a time to wait before marking the message as read.

If you select a different item before the time interval has expired, and you haven't checked the second checkbox for marking items as read when the selection changes, the e-mail will not be marked as having been read.

If the Single key reading using space bar checkbox is checked, you can move from one message in the Reading Pane to another message by pressing the spacebar. The setting for moving or deleting an open item in the E-mail Options dialog controls whether the next or previous message becomes selected after you press the spacebar.

Click **OK** to save your Reading Pane settings.

Person Names Options

Select **Tools**, **Options**, click on the **Other** tab, and use the Person Names settings at the bottom of the tab to control whether a Person Names Smart Tag is enabled when you use Word as the Outlook editor. The Person Names Smart Tag recognizes a name in an address field of an e-mail and provides a context menu for that person.

The Display Messenger Status in the From field checkbox controls whether a sender's Instant Messaging status is displayed in the From field of an open e-mail. Messenger status can be displayed for Windows Messenger.

Click **OK** or **Apply** to save the Person Names settings.

E-mail Options in the Advanced Options Dialog

Select **Tools**, **Options**, click on the **Other** tab, and then select **Advanced Options** to display the remaining e-mail settings.

Check **When selecting text, automatically select entire word** to enable this option. This setting is enabled only when you are using Word as the e-mail editor.

Paste Options buttons are Smart Tags that are similar to the Paste Special button in Word; they enable easy text layout and formatting options. This option applies only when you are using Word as the Outlook editor.

Click **OK** to save these settings.

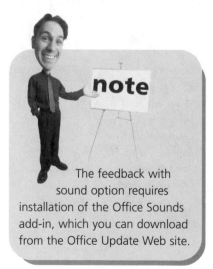

note

The feedback with sound option requires installation of the Office Sounds add-in, which you can download from the Office Update Web site.

Posting Items to Folders

Outlook includes a feature called a *Post item*. Post items can't be sent by e-mail but are "posted" in e-mail folders. Post items typically are used for discussions in Exchange public folders and for other collaborative work, as you will learn in Chapter 21, "Collaborating with Outlook and Exchange." However, you can use Post items to place notes and reminders to yourself in e-mail folders and to serve as containers for such files as Word documents or Excel worksheets.

To add a Post item to a folder, select **File**, **New**, **Post in This Folder** to open a new Post item, as shown in Figure 3.26.

FIGURE 3.26

Post items can be used for discussions, notes in folders, and containers for attachments.

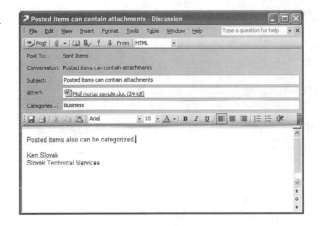

Enter a subject and select **Categories** to open the Categories dialog if you want to add a category to the Post. If you add a category, click **OK** to close the Categories dialog. Enter any text you want in the message area and add any attachments, as you learned in "Sending Attachments" earlier in this chapter. Select **Post** in the toolbar of the open Post item to add it to the current e-mail folder.

You will learn about posting replies to Post items and replying directly to the original poster in Chapter 21.

THE ABSOLUTE MINIMUM

In this chapter, you learned about the basics of working with e-mails in Outlook 2003. To review, you now know how to

Send and receive e-mails.

Read e-mails.

Reply to e-mails and forward them to other people.

Create a new e-mail message and select its format.

Carbon copy and blind carbon copy people in outgoing e-mails.

Attach files and Outlook items to e-mails.

Set e-mail preferences.

Work with Post items.

With the skills you acquired in this chapter, you now know how to work with Outlook e-mails. In the next chapter, you will learn advanced e-mail techniques such as using signatures and stationery and flagging e-mails with Quick Flags and reminders.

IN THIS CHAPTER

- Learning how to create e-mail signatures.
- Understanding how to use stationery with e-mail.
- Knowing how to add attachments to e-mails.
- Learning how to send e-mail links to the Web.
- Knowing how to deal with junk e-mail.
- Understanding how to flag e-mails and set e-mail reminders.
- Understanding how to set e-mail message options.

4

ADVANCED E-MAIL TECHNIQUES

In this chapter, you will learn advanced techniques for working with your e-mail. These e-mail techniques include creating and using signatures for your messages, such as your name and address; using stationery in HTML e-mails to provide patterned backgrounds for your messages; adding attachments and links to Web sites to your e-mails; and setting Quick Flags and reminders for e-mails. You will also learn how to set message options such as message importance and sensitivity and how to deal with junk e-mails. These topics will provide you with the knowledge you need to become an advanced Outlook e-mail user.

Creating and Using Signatures

Most e-mail you send will contain a *signature* at the end of the message text. It might consist of only a salutation and your name, or it could include a title, company name, address, phone number, secondary e-mail address(es), and so on.

Instead of typing a signature in every e-mail you send, you can create a signature that is automatically inserted in your e-mails. You can use different signatures for new e-mail messages or replies and forwards, and if you use Word as your e-mail editor and have more than one e-mail account, you can even have different signatures for each e-mail account. If you are using the Outlook editor instead of Word as your e-mail editor, you won't get individual signatures for each e-mail account; however, you can insert a specific signature whenever you want.

In addition to a default signature that is inserted in every e-mail you send or to which you reply, you also can insert a signature in an e-mail on a custom basis for that particular e-mail. This type of signature is often referred to as a *one-off signature*. For example, my default signature includes my name and company, but I use a different signature if I want to provide complete contact information and another one for e-mails to friends and family.

You create and select signatures in the Mail Format tab of the Outlook Options settings, as shown in Figure 4.1. To display the Mail Format tab, select **Tools**, **Options** and click on the **Mail Format** tab. In the Signature section of the Mail Format tab, you can choose from settings for signatures to use for each account for new e-mails and for replies and forwards.

FIGURE 4.1

The Mail Format tab enables you to create signatures and assign which signatures are used for specific e-mail accounts.

Creating a New Signature

To create a new signature, follow these steps:

1. Select **Signatures** at the bottom right of the Mail Format tab to open the Create Signature dialog, as shown in Figure 4.2.

FIGURE 4.2

The Create Signature dialog enables you to create new signatures and edit or remove existing signatures.

2. Select **New** to open the Create New Signature dialog, as shown in Figure 4.3.

FIGURE 4.3

The Create New Signature dialog enables you to create a new signature starting from a blank signature, an existing signature, or a file.

3. Enter a name for your new signature. The name should be easy to recognize so that when you choose a signature for an e-mail you can easily pick out the correct signature for that particular e-mail. (I use **Default Signature** as the name for my default signature.) You can then choose from one of the two options described here:

- **Start with a blank signature**—Selecting this option opens the Edit Signature dialog, where you type your desired signature.

- **Use this file as a template**—Selecting this option enables you to use an existing text file as the starting point for your new signature. Click on **Browse** to locate the text file in the file system. All the text lines in the file are used for the new signature.

4. Select **Next** to proceed to the Edit Signature dialog, as shown in Figure 4.4.

FIGURE 4.4

The Edit Signature dialog enables you to enter text, set fonts and formatting, and include vCards in your signature.

5. Enter the text for your signature in the **Signature text** area. If you selected a text file as the starting point for your signature, the contents of the text file are already in the Signature text area.

6. If you are using HTML or Rich Text as your e-mail format, you can use the **Font** and **Paragraph** buttons to select a font for the signature, select paragraph alignment, and decide whether to use bullets in the signature.

7. To remove all the text in the Signature text area and start over, click on the **Clear** button.

8. Select the **Advanced Edit** button to open Word so that you can edit the signature, or open Notepad if you are using the Outlook editor for e-mail. You can edit the signature in this editor, and you will return to the signature when you close the editor.

tip

You can attach a vCard to your signature if you want. A *vCard* is an Internet standard for transmitting contact information. If you have a contact record for yourself, you can use this information to create or select a vCard that contains your contact information. You will learn more details about vCards in Chapter 6, "Contacts and Address Books."

9. Select **Finish** when you are finished editing the signature to return to the Create Signature dialog. You can edit the new signature by highlighting it and selecting **Edit,** and you can delete it by highlighting it and selecting **Remove**. You can also create additional signatures by selecting **New** again and repeating steps 3–5.

10. Click on **OK** to close the Create Signature dialog.

Adding a Signature to an E-mail

After you create a signature, it is available in the Signature for new messages and Signature for replies and forwards drop-downs on the Mail Format tab. The default is to use the new signature for new messages and no signature for replies and forwards.

Select which signatures to use for new messages and for replies and forwards in the drop-downs. If you have more than one e-mail account set up, you can make individual signature selections for new messages and for replies and forwards for each e-mail account. Select the e-mail account in the Select signature for account drop-down and the signatures for each message type.

Click on **OK** to save your selections and close the Options dialog, or select **Apply** to save your selections and leave the Options dialog open.

After you set your signature options, your new signature will be inserted automatically in each e-mail you create, reply to, or forward based on your settings.

Inserting a Signature Manually Using the Outlook Editor

The methods for inserting a nondefault signature in an e-mail depends on which e-mail editor you are using. Inserting a signature in an e-mail item when you use the Outlook editor is simple: Just select **Insert**, **Signature** and select the signature

note

A signature you create is available no matter whether you are using HTML, Plain Text, or Rich Text Format.

caution

If you have a signature that is inserted automatically, the Outlook editor doesn't replace the default signature with one you insert manually. You must delete the automatically inserted signature to avoid having two signatures in the e-mail.

you want to use in the signature list. Select **More** to open the Select a Signature dialog, which has a complete list of signatures you've created.

Inserting a Signature Manually Using the Word Editor

Inserting a signature when you use Word as the e-mail editor is somewhat more complicated; you can use two methods. The first method requires you to create signatures as Word AutoText entries; the second method requires you to have a default signature set up. When you use the second method, the default signature is replaced by the signature you insert.

The AutoText method of creating a signature is limited to a one-line signature, but you can create new signatures as you need them:

1. Open an e-mail message, place the cursor in the message area of the e-mail, and select **Insert**, **AutoText**, **AutoText** to open Word's AutoText tab, shown in Figure 4.5.

FIGURE 4.5

One-line signatures can be created using Word AutoText entries, which can be inserted into your e-mails.

2. In the **Enter AutoText entries here** text box, type the text you want to use as a signature. Select **Add** and then click on **OK** to save your new AutoText entry.

You can add as many one-line signatures as you want as AutoText entries. To add more signatures, repeatedly select the **Insert**, **AutoText**, **AutoText** menu commands in an open e-mail.

You can now insert this signature anywhere you want in an e-mail message by selecting **Insert**, **AutoText**, **Normal**. Select the signature from the list for Normal.

To use the default signature method, make sure you have a default signature created and set for use in new messages and replies and forwards. If you don't want to always use a signature, you can create a blank signature that has no text. A blank signature will be enough to enable you to insert signatures as described in the following steps. This method will not work if you have no signature created.

1. Open a new e-mail by pressing the keyboard shortcut **Ctrl+N** when you are in an e-mail folder.

2. Right-click on the signature that appears on the blank e-mail and select the signature you want to use in this e-mail from the signature list. The signature you select will replace the existing signature. If you are using a blank signature, count down three lines from the top of a new e-mail message and right-click; this is the same as right-clicking a visible signature.

3. If you select **E-mail Signature**, the E-mail Options dialog opens, as shown in Figure 4.6. Here, you can select an existing signature or create a new signature. If you create a new signature in this dialog, you can right-click it again to see the new signature in the list of signatures in the context menu.

caution

When you close Outlook, Word may prompt you to save the global template, `Normal.dot`. Select **Yes** to save the signatures you created in the AutoText entries. If you select **No**, any signatures you created will be lost.

tip

One often-asked question is how to add a disclaimer or some standard text to outgoing e-mails. You might want to add a confidentiality notice, a privacy statement, a humorous quote, or any other standard text. You can use a signature to perform this function. If you add the text you want in lines below your name in the signature, this standard text, also known as *boilerplate text*, will be inserted when your signature is inserted.

FIGURE 4.6

The E-mail Options dialog enables you to add an existing signature to an e-mail or to create a new signature.

Using Stationery

Microsoft supplies an assortment of different stationery you can use, and additional stationery is available for you to download from the Office Update Web site. You can also create your own stationery from any .HTM file, but you need to remember that the graphics you use should not prevent the e-mail text from being easily readable. Figure 4.7 shows an e-mail message using the Tech Tools stationery as a background graphic.

FIGURE 4.7

The Tech Tools stationery is one of many available stationeries for Outlook.

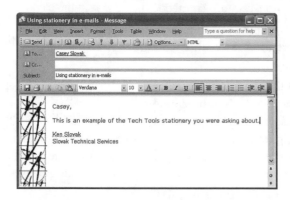

To select stationery, do the following:

1. Select **Tools**, **Options** and click on the **Mail Format** tab.

2. Select the **Use this stationery by default** drop-down to display a list of all installed stationery. Stationery installed in the C:\Program Files\Common Files\Microsoft Shared\Stationery\ folder is automatically displayed in the stationery list.

You can also select stationery by using the Stationery Picker dialog, which enables you to preview existing stationery, download additional stationery, or create your own stationery:

1. Select **Tools**, **Options** and click on the **Mail Format** tab.

2. In the **Stationery and Fonts** section, select **Stationery Picker** to open the Stationery Picker dialog, as shown in Figure 4.8.

3. Highlight a stationery in the **Stationery** section and view it in the Preview area to see how it looks.

4. To download additional stationery from the Office Update Web site, first select **Get More Stationery**. Then select the additional stationery to download from the Web site. Follow the directions on the Web site to download and install the additional stationery you select.

5. Highlight the stationery you want to use and click on **OK** to use this stationery as your default.

FIGURE 4.8

The Stationery Picker dialog enables you to select from among the available stationeries.

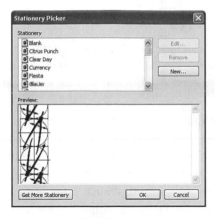

If you select a stationery to use as the default, that stationery is used for all new HTML e-mail messages you create. Stationery is not used when you create a new Plain Text or Rich Text e-mail message. You learned about different e-mail formats in Chapter 3, "Sending and Receiving E-mail." If you use a default stationery for HTML and want to create a new e-mail message that doesn't use stationery or uses a different stationery, select **Actions**, **New Mail Message Using** to do that. This menu is shown in Figure 4.9.

FIGURE 4.9

The New Mail Message Using menu enables you to select a nondefault stationery or to create e-mails that don't use the default stationery.

The entries at the top of this menu are stationeries you've used recently. Selecting the **More Stationery** command opens the Stationery Picker dialog where you can select any stationery to use for the new e-mail message. Selecting stationery in this dialog doesn't change your default stationery. To open an e-mail message using no stationery, select the **HTML (No Stationery)** menu command. This menu is also useful if you don't have a default stationery selected and want to create a new e-mail message that uses stationery. You can use this menu to create a new e-mail message using a different e-mail editor or using nondefault message formats, as you learned in Chapter 3.

Working with Attachments

In Chapter 3, you learned about attaching files to Outlook e-mails. You also learned that some files are restricted as attachments because the attached files can be executed. In this section, you will learn more about sending and receiving restricted file attachments.

Outlook restricts access to certain attachments based on their file extensions. These attachments are restricted because they are file types that can be executed, which means they are like programs that can be run. A few years ago, many Outlook users were besieged with e-mails containing attached viruses, which often masqueraded as legitimate file attachments. Despite warnings that such attachments could contain viruses, the users often opened such attachments without a second thought, leading to their computers becoming infected with viruses.

Microsoft's solution was to restrict access to such attachments in received e-mails and to warn the senders of such attachments that the recipient might not be able to access the attachment. Microsoft implemented two levels of attachment security. Access to Level 1 attachments is completely restricted; these attachments are not available in the received e-mail even though they still exist as attachments in the e-mail. A second level of attachments, known as Level 2 attachments, can be accessed but have to be saved to the file system before they can be opened. By default, there are no Level 2 attachments. You must add attachments to the Level 2 list, or an Exchange administrator can add attachments to the Level 2 list if you are using Exchange server.

Sending and Receiving E-mail with Restricted Attachments

If you attach a file to an e-mail, and the file type is a Level 1 restricted attachment, you will see the warning dialog shown in Figure 4.10 when you send the e-mail.

FIGURE 4.10

When you attempt to send a Level 1 attachment to someone, the restricted attachment dialog is displayed.

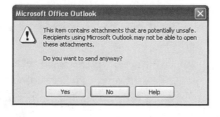

You can choose to send the e-mail with the restricted attachment by clicking **OK** in the restricted attachment dialog, but the e-mail's recipient may not be able to access the attachment. Different versions of Outlook implement different lists of restricted Level 1 attachments, so some attachments that are restricted in Outlook 2003 aren't restricted in Outlook 2002 and vice versa. For a complete list of all Outlook 2003 restricted attachments, press F1 to open the HelpTask Pane and search on the phrase "attachment file type blocked by Outlook".

If you receive an e-mail whose attachments are restricted by Outlook, the e-mail contains an InfoBar that tells you which attachments were restricted. Figure 4.11 shows an e-mail message containing a restricted attachment.

FIGURE 4.11

Restricted attachments are hidden when they are received in e-mails.

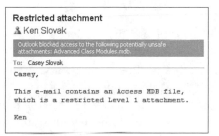

To avoid the problem of restricted attachments, you can compress the file into a ZIP file using one of the many programs that can compress files. However, this solution also has problems because many virus-scanning programs look inside ZIP files and remove or quarantine restricted files within the ZIP files. A better solution is to rename the original file extension and provide instructions in the e-mail for the recipient to rename the file back again after saving the attachment to the file system. For example, if you are sending a file named Restricted.exe to someone as an attachment, you can rename the file Restricted.ex_ and in the e-mail tell the recipient to rename the file back to Restricted.exe.

tip

You can either avoid the problem of restricted attachments or remove selected file types from the restricted list in a number of ways. To remove file types from the restricted list, you can edit the Windows Registry; this process is not covered in this book. You can also use a shareware tool I provide named Attachment Options that you can download from my Web site at http://www.slovaktech.com/attachmentoptions.htm.

Receiving E-mail with Unrestricted Attachments

When you receive an attachment in an e-mail, the e-mail indicates there is an attachment by showing a paperclip icon in the folder view of the e-mails. The attachment is also listed in the Reading Pane. An e-mail with an attachment is shown in Figure 4.12.

To open an e-mail attachment that is completely unrestricted, double-click on the attachment name in the Reading Pane or an open e-mail, or right-click on the attachment name and select **Open** in the Reading Pane or an open e-mail. Some examples of unrestricted file types are Word document files, Excel worksheets, and text files.

FIGURE 4.12

E-mails with unrestricted attachments show the attachment filename and the size of the attachment.

> **Unrestricted attachment**
>
> 👤 Ken Slovak
> To: Casey Slovak
> Attachments: 📄 9096xcc.doc (43 KB)
> ─────────────────────────
> Casey,
>
> This e-mail has a Word doc as an attachment,
> which is an unrestricted attachment.
>
> Ken

When you attempt to open most file attachments, Outlook displays a dialog offering the choice of opening the file or saving it to the file system; the Opening Mail Attachment dialog is shown in Figure 4.13. I recommend saving the file and scanning it with antivirus software with the latest signature files before opening the attachment. Doing this takes more time, but it's better to be safe and make sure that an attachment isn't infected with a virus than to have your system become infected.

FIGURE 4.13

Attempting to open most attachments directly from an e-mail displays the Opening Mail Attachment dialog.

You can uncheck the **Always ask before opening this type of file** checkbox to be able to directly open attachments of that file type. However, assuming that certain file types will never be virus carriers might be dangerous, and that extra step of saving the attachment to the file system and then preferably scanning it with antivirus software can save you a lot of grief and corrupted data if an attachment is infected with a virus.

When you attempt to open a Level 2 attachment, Outlook will only permit you to save it to the file system; you cannot open it directly. By default, there are no Level 2 attachments; all file extensions are either Level 1 or unrestricted. Level 2 attachments are created when you remove a file extension from the Level 1 list, or if you are using Exchange, and an Exchange administrator adds a file extension to Level 2. Figure 4.14 shows the Attachment Security Warning dialog shown for Level 2 attachments.

FIGURE 4.14

The Attachment
Security Warning
dialog is shown
when you
attempt to
open a Level 2
attachment.

note

You cannot change a
Level 2 attachment into an
unrestricted attachment. You can
remove a file type from the Level
2 attachment list only if you are
using Exchange server and the
Exchange administrator removes
the file type from the Level 2 list.

Using the Attachment Options Pane

After you attach a file to an e-mail, an
Attachment Options button appears. Clicking
this button opens the Attachment Options pane,
shown in Figure 4.15.

The Attachment Options pane enables you to share
an attachment on a Microsoft Windows SharePoint
Services shared workspace. This workspace is set up
on a Windows 2003 Server and can be used for
shared documents, contacts, and calendars. Most often, a shared workspace is set up
on a corporate server or a SharePoint Portal Server and used for corporate workgroups. Microsoft Windows SharePoint Services shared workspaces can also be set up
on public servers and accessed over the Internet.

FIGURE 4.15

The Attachment
Options pane
has options for
sending attach-
ments as regular
or shared
attachments.

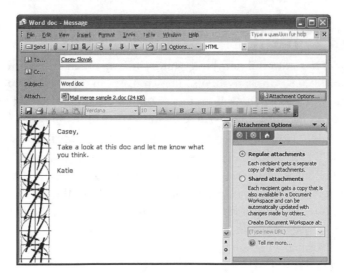

If you are using Outlook as an individual user, you probably won't be interested in the Attachment Options pane. Disable showing the Attachment Options pane in e-mail messages with attachments by unchecking the **Show when attaching files** checkbox. The Attachment Options button is always present in an e-mail with attachments, so if you later need to use the Attachment Options pane to work with a shared workspace, click on the **Attachment Options** button to show the pane. To close the Attachment Options pane, click on the **X** at the top right of the pane.

E-mailing Links to the Web

One common type of blocked attachment is a URL attachment to a Web page. An attachment of this type is created by selecting **File**, **Send**, **Link by E-mail** in Internet Explorer. Unless the URL file extension has been moved to Level 2, the attachment will be blocked completely, and even if the URL file extension has been moved to Level 2, you must save the URL attachment to the file system before you can open it.

Instead of sending a link using Link by E-mail in Internet Explorer, open a new e-mail message in Outlook and copy and paste the Web address you want to send directly in the text of the e-mail message. That link will not be restricted by Outlook, and if the user clicks it in an e-mail, his or her Web browser will open to that URL. Highlight the address of the Web page in the address field in Internet Explorer and right-click on the link. Select **Copy Shortcut**. Move the focus to an e-mail message, right-click, and select **Paste** to paste the link into the e-mail message.

Filtering Junk E-mail

Outlook 2003 has powerful new junk e-mail filtering based on research done at Microsoft for MSN 8. Junk e-mail, also known as spam, has become a huge problem for everyone who receives e-mail. In fact, recent studies indicate that as much as 60% of all e-mail is junk e-mail. These e-mails waste time and e-mail bandwidth, and often contain content that is not suitable for family viewing, so the new e-mail junk filtering in Outlook 2003 is a welcome feature.

You learned about enabling the junk e-mail features in Chapter 3. If you receive a message that is classified as junk e-mail, it is moved from the Inbox to the Junk E-mail folder. You can then examine the items in the Junk E-mail folder occasionally and make sure they are really junk before deleting them.

Adding Senders to the Junk E-mail List

If a junk e-mail that is not caught as spam arrives in the Inbox, you can add the e-mail's sender to a junk senders list so future e-mails from that sender will be tagged as spam when they arrive. To add the sender of an e-mail to the junk senders list, do the following:

1. Right-click on the e-mail and select **Junk E-mail**, **Add Sender to Blocked Senders List**. The dialog shown in Figure 4.16 confirms the addition to the junk senders list.

FIGURE 4.16

The Add to blocked senders list dialog confirms the sender of an e-mail was added to the blocked senders list.

2. If you don't want to see this dialog again, check the **Please do not show me this dialog again** checkbox.

3. Click on **OK** to close this dialog.

You can also add entire e-mail domains to the junk senders list as follows:

1. Select **Actions**, **Junk E-mail**, **Junk E-mail Options** to open the Junk E-mail Options dialog.

2. Click on the **Blocked Senders** tab and select **Add** to open the Add address or domain dialog, shown in Figure 4.17.

FIGURE 4.17

The Add address or domain dialog enables you to add entire domains to the blocked senders list.

3. Either enter a complete e-mail address to add to the junk senders list or enter a domain to assign the entire domain to the junk senders list. A domain entry consists of the domain name and the domain—for example, `junksender.com`. You can enter the @ (at sign) before the domain name, but if you don't enter the @, it will be added automatically.

4. Click on **OK** to complete the addition of the domain or sender to the junk senders list. You then return to the Blocked Senders tab, as shown in Figure 4.18.

FIGURE 4.18

The Blocked
Senders tab
enables you to
add blocked
senders or
domains and to
export and
import blocked
senders lists.

To remove an entry from the junk senders list, highlight the entry and select
Remove. To edit an entry in the junk senders list, highlight the entry and select
Edit to open the Edit Address or Domain dialog. Edit the entry and click on **OK** to
save your changes.

Importing and Exporting the Junk Senders List

The junk senders list can be exported as a text file, so you can use the list on other
computers or share your list with other people. Follow these steps to export your
junk senders list:

1. Select **Actions**, **Junk E-mail**, **Junk E-mail Options** to open the Junk E-
   mail Options dialog; then click on the **Junk Senders** tab.

2. Select **Export to File** to open the Export Junk Senders dialog.

3. Navigate to the place where you want to save the exported junk senders list,
   enter a filename for the exported list, and save it to the file system by selecting
   Save.

To import a junk senders list saved as a text file into your junk senders list, follow
the preceding set of steps, but instead of Export to File, select **Import from File** to
open the Import Junk Senders dialog. Navigate to the place where the text file is
stored in the file system, select the file, and complete the import by selecting **Open**.
Senders and domains that are imported are added to your junk senders list.

Adding Senders to a Trusted Senders List

Legitimate e-mails are sometimes mistakenly tagged as junk e-emails. You can add
the senders of those legitimate messages to a safe senders list so that e-mails sent by

these people aren't tagged as junk again. To add a sender to the safe senders list, highlight an e-mail from the sender, right-click, and select **Junk E-mail**, **Add Sender to Safe Senders List**. You can also open the safe senders list by selecting **Actions**, **Junk E-mail**, **Junk E-mail Options** to open the Junk E-mail Options dialog and then selecting the **Safe Senders** tab, as shown in Figure 4.19.

 In the safe senders list, you'll find a checkbox used for trusting any e-mails sent by someone in your Contacts list. This checkbox is checked by default. If you do not want to automatically trust e-mails sent by people in your Contacts list, uncheck the **Also trust e-mail from my Contacts** checkbox. Then click on **OK** to save the new setting and close the dialog, or click on **Apply** to save the new setting and leave the dialog open.

FIGURE 4.19

The Safe Senders tab enables you to add senders whom you consider safe and to trust everyone in your Contacts list.

The safe recipients list is used for newsletters and mailings that are legitimate but not addressed directly to you. For example, a newsletter might be addressed to mailinglist@slovaktech.com with your e-mail address in the BCC field. If you want to receive this newsletter and not have it tagged as a junk e-mail, highlight the e-mail, right-click, and select **Junk E-mail**, **Add Recipient to Safe Recipients List**. To view the safe recipients list, select **Actions**, **Junk E-mail**, **Junk E-mail Options** to open the Junk E-mail Options dialog and then select the **Safe Recipients** tab.

On the Safe Senders and Safe Recipients tabs, you can directly add, edit, or remove entries the same way you do in the Blocked Senders tab, by selecting **Add**, **Edit**, or **Remove**. You also can export or import text files of these lists in the same way you can with the junk senders list, by selecting **Import from File** or **Export to File.**

One final junk e-mail command is available by right-clicking on an e-mail and selecting **Junk E-mail**. You can even add an entire domain to the safe senders list by selecting **Add Sender's Domain (@example.com) to Safe Senders List**.

Working with Messages in the Junk E-mail Folder

If an e-mail is tagged as junk e-mail and moved to the Junk E-mail folder in error, you can mark the e-mail as not being junk by going to the Junk E-mail folder, highlighting the e-mail, and either selecting the **Not Junk** button on the Standard toolbar, or right-clicking on the e-mail and selecting **Junk E-mail**, **Mark as Not Junk** to open the Mark as Not Junk dialog. In this dialog, you can choose to add the sender to the trusted senders list and to always trust e-mails sent to the address used in that e-mail.

Check the **Always trust e-mail from** checkbox to add the sender to your trusted senders list. If you leave the checkbox unchecked, only the highlighted e-mail is tagged as not junk. Click on **OK** to save the settings in the Mark as Not Junk dialog. E-mails marked as not junk are automatically moved from the Junk E-mail folder to your Inbox.

Flagging E-mails and E-mail Reminders

Individual e-mails can often get lost among all the other e-mails in a folder but may require some further action such as a reply, follow-up, or review. Outlook provides a way of marking such e-mails so they stand out; this process is known as *flagging*.

Flagged e-mails stand out in a folder view of e-mail items so that they can easily be seen and also are shown in the For Follow Up Search Folder. You will learn about Search Folders in Chapter 5, "Search Folders." Flagged e-mails can also have attached reminders that show a reminder dialog when the reminder is due. Flags can also be color-coded and grouped by flag colors when you view them in a folder. These color-coded flags, called Quick Flags, are a new feature in Outlook 2003.

To flag an e-mail with the default Quick Flag color, highlight the e-mail and click in the flag column. Right-click an e-mail and select **Follow Up**, or right-click in the flag column to open the flagging context menu, shown in Figure 4.20.

FIGURE 4.20

The flagging context menu enables you to add a Quick Flag to an e-mail.

In the flagging menu, you can flag an e-mail with a color other than the default flag color, mark the flagged e-mail as complete, add a reminder to the flag, clear the flag, or set the default flag color. When a flag is marked as complete, the flag is cleared, and a check mark appears in the e-mail's flag column.

To add a reminder to an e-mail, select **Add Reminder** in the flagging context menu; select the **flag** icon in the Standard toolbar of an open e-mail; or select **Actions**, **Follow Up**, **Add Reminder** in an open e-mail to open the Flag for Follow Up dialog, as shown in Figure 4.21.

FIGURE 4.21

In the Flag for Follow Up dialog, you can change a flag's color and add a reminder to an e-mail.

Set the text for the flag in the Flag to drop-down. This text field can hold any text, not just the default choices. To enter different text for the flag, type the entry you want into the drop-down's text box. You cannot add to or change any of the default choices, which are:

Call

Do Not Forward

Follow Up

For Your Information

Forward

No Response Necessary

Read

Reply

Reply to All

Review

In the Flag Type drop-down, select the flag color you want to use for the reminder. If you select None, the e-mail will have a reminder but won't be flagged and won't show up in the For Follow Up Search Folder.

In the Due By drop-down, select the down arrow to open a calendar date picker to select when the reminder is due. You can also type a date in the Due By drop-down's text field. In addition to accepting dates entered in standard date format, this intelligent input field accepts shorthand notation for dates. Some of the shorthand formats the field accepts are d, w, m, and y for day, week, month, and year. For example, 4d is interpreted as 4 days from now, 3m is interpreted as 3 months from now, and 1y is interpreted as 1 year from now.

In the Time drop-down, which is next to the Due by drop-down, select a time for the reminder to be shown. You can also type a time in either AM-PM format or in 24-hour format. Both 3:00 PM and 15:00 are interpreted as 3:00 PM.

The Flag for Follow Up dialog also provides a Completed checkbox that enables you to mark the flag as completed and a Clear Flag button that enables you to clear the flag on the e-mail.

When you have the flag and reminder set up as you want, click on **OK** to save the flag and reminder settings. When the reminder is due, a Reminder dialog is displayed, as shown in Figure 4.22. It enables you to dismiss the reminder, dismiss all reminders, open the highlighted item in the Reminder dialog, and *snooze* the reminder. Snoozing a reminder is similar to hitting the snooze button on an alarm clock; the reminder will fire again after the set period of time for the snooze expires.

FIGURE 4.22

The Reminder dialog enables you to dismiss or snooze a reminder alarm.

The Reminder dialog shows all reminders that are due or overdue and all snoozed reminders in one place. To dismiss one or more reminders, highlight the reminders you want to dismiss and click on **Dismiss**. To open one or more items shown in the Reminder dialog, highlight the items and select **Open Item**. Click on **Dismiss All** to dismiss all reminders listed in the Reminder dialog.

To snooze a reminder so that it fires again later, highlight the item you want to snooze, click the down arrow in the Snooze drop-down to select a snooze interval, and then select the **Snooze** button. The Snooze drop-down is also an intelligent input field. You can enter a time as 3 minutes or as 3m; you can also use shorthand such as h for hours, d for days, w for weeks, mo for months, and y for years.

note

Dismissing a reminder for an e-mail doesn't clear a flag on the e-mail. The item remains flagged until you specifically clear the flag.

The Reminder dialog displays reminders for all Outlook items that are due, overdue, or snoozed, not only e-mail items. So if you have reminders set for appointments and tasks as well as for e-mails, they all are displayed in the Reminder dialog.

Additional E-mail Options

In addition to all the e-mail settings you have learned about so far in this chapter, others are available in the InfoBar that is displayed in the Reading Pane, in open items, and in the Message Options dialog. In this section, you will learn about these settings.

Blocked Content

Many e-mails contain links to pictures or other content located on the Internet. When the link is activated, the content is downloaded and displayed in the e-mail. This technique is also used for other less benign purposes, however, such as Web beacons, which are tiny, invisible links that let a spammer know that your e-mail address is a valid one. Other techniques load content that takes you to a Web page that you might or might not want to visit. Microsoft has added content blocking to Outlook 2003 and displays information about blocked content in the InfoBar that is displayed at the top of an e-mail viewed in the Reading Pane or in an open e-mail item.

Click in the InfoBar to open a menu enabling you to view the blocked content and to set content blocking settings. This menu and the selected InfoBar are shown in Figure 4.23.

FIGURE 4.23

In the Blocked content menu, you can select to download pictures or configure your automatic download settings.

Select **Download Pictures** to view the content that was blocked by Outlook. Select **Change Automatic Download Settings** to open the Automatic Picture Download Settings dialog, shown in Figure 4.24.

FIGURE 4.24

In the Automatic Picture Download Settings dialog, you can configure settings for how Outlook downloads external content.

Check the **Don't download pictures or other content automatically in HTML e-mail** checkbox to block Web beacons and other external content. The other checkboxes in this dialog provide for content blocking exceptions for downloads in e-mails from senders and to recipients in your safe senders and safe recipients lists, content linked to locations in the Trusted Zone, and for being warned when external content is downloaded. The Trusted Zone is used only for trusted or internal locations. By default, all the checkboxes in the Automatic Picture Download Settings dialog are checked. Click on **OK** to save any changes you make in this dialog.

Message Options Dialog

Various other advanced settings are grouped in the Message Options dialog, such as message settings, voting and tracking options, delivery options, contact linking, and categories. Some of these settings can be set only in new e-mails before you send them; others can also be set in sent e-mails and e-mails that you have received. To open the Message Options dialog in an open e-mail message, select **Options** in the E-mail toolbar. To open the Message Options dialog in an e-mail in a folder view, right-click on the e-mail and select **Options**. The Message Options dialog for a new e-mail message is shown in Figure 4.25.

Setting Importance Level

The importance of an e-mail can be set to Low, Normal, or High in the Importance drop-down. Importance is an arbitrary setting that can be set for an e-mail you are sending and for e-mails that are already received. You can group by or sort by importance, to arrange e-mails by their importance in a folder view.

- High importance e-mails are indicated by a red exclamation point.
- Low importance e-mails are indicated by a blue down-pointing arrow.
- Normal importance e-mails don't have any Importance symbol.

FIGURE 4.25

Settings such as importance, sensitivity, and message tracking options can be set in the Message Options dialog.

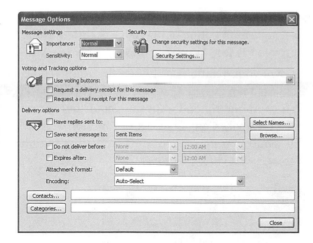

Setting a Sensitivity Status

The sensitivity of an e-mail can be set to Normal, Personal, Private, or Confidential in the Sensitivity drop-down. You can set the sensitivity of an e-mail only before you send it. Sensitivity is mostly used when you are using Exchange server, although it is not limited to use with this server.

■ E-mails with normal or confidential sensitivity can be viewed in another person's mailbox if you have permissions to open that mailbox from the **File**, **Open**, **Other User's Folder** menu command.

■ E-mails with private sensitivity cannot be viewed when opening a mailbox from the **File**, **Open**, **Other User's Folder** menu command.

■ E-mails with personal sensitivity can be viewed when opening a mailbox from the **File**, **Open**, **Other User's Folder** menu command.

For all e-mails with a sensitivity other than normal, the Sensitivity setting is shown in the e-mail's InfoBar.

Security Settings

The Security Settings button at the top of the Message Options dialog is used to send secure e-mail. You will learn about secure e-mails in Chapter 18, "Secure E-mail." A secure e-mail can be sent with a digital signature that verifies the sender and indicates whether the message was tampered with, and it can be sent encrypted so that no one but you can read its contents.

Voting Buttons

Voting options are enabled when you check the **Use voting buttons** checkbox in the Message Options dialog. When you send an e-mail with voting buttons, the e-mail recipients can vote, and their votes are tallied in the original e-mail as the replies are returned to you. The default voting button choices, listed in the Voting Buttons drop-down, are Approve or Reject, Yes or No, and Yes or No or Maybe.

You can create your own voting buttons by typing the voting choices separated by semicolons in the text field next to the **Use voting buttons** checkbox. For example, if you are planning a camping trip and want the people going on the trip to vote for Yellowstone, Yosemite, or Devil's Canyon as the destination, enter those voting choices separated by semicolons to create the custom voting buttons. Figure 4.26 shows an e-mail message with voting buttons.

FIGURE 4.26

Voting buttons are used to poll recipients for their choices and can be tracked for voting results.

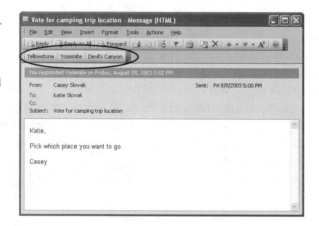

When you receive an e-mail with voting buttons, the InfoBar in the Reading Pane shows that the e-mail has voting buttons, and you can click on the InfoBar to display a menu with the voting choices, enabling you to vote without opening the e-mail. The voting choices are also present in the Actions menu when an e-mail with voting buttons is open. After you vote, the InfoBar changes to show your vote and the date and time your vote was cast. You can change a vote as many times as you want; only the last vote is counted. To change a vote, open the e-mail and select the button for your new choice. The InfoBar will change to show your new vote. Figure 4.27 shows an open e-mail after voting, displaying the voting information in the InfoBar.

Outlook can automatically tabulate votes as they come in, but setting up this feature properly can be tricky. Votes are tabulated only if the original voting message is stored in the Sent Items folder and was sent and replied to in Rich Text Format. Votes are processed when the returned votes are opened, or they can be tabulated automatically, but it can take up to 10 minutes from the time a vote comes in before it is tabulated.

FIGURE 4.27

Information about voting buttons is shown in the InfoBar.

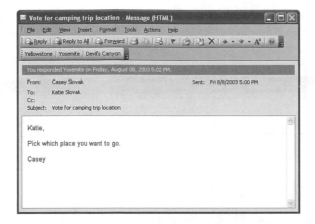

When you reply to an e-mail with voting buttons, you are offered the choice of sending the response now or opening the response to edit the message before sending it. I recommend opening the e-mail and checking to make sure the e-mail will be sent in Rich Text Format. To check the sending format for each recipient of the e-mail, select the entry in the **To** field and right-click on it. In the context menu, select **Outlook Properties.** If the e-mail address is that of a contact, the contact record will open. Select the e-mail address of the contact, right-click, and select **Outlook Properties** again to open the E-mail Properties dialog. If the address is not that of a contact, the E-mail Properties dialog opens directly. In the E-mail Properties dialog, select **Send using Outlook Rich Text Format** in the Internet Format drop-down and click on **OK** to make sure that Rich Text is sent to the recipient.

If everything is set up correctly, the original e-mail sent with the voting buttons and stored in the Sent Items folder displays a Tracking tab when it is opened, as shown in Figure 4.28. This tab shows the vote count in the InfoBar and a list of all the voters and how they voted.

There is no way to close the voting for a voting e-mail, but you can simulate closing a vote by moving the original e-mail into a folder other than Sent Items.

Tracking Options

You can request a delivery receipt for an e-mail by checking the **Request a delivery receipt for this message** checkbox in the Voting and Tracking Options section of the Message Options dialog. You can request a read receipt by checking the **Request a read receipt for this message** checkbox. Delivery receipts are sent when an e-mail is delivered to the recipient of an e-mail. Read receipts are sent when the recipient reads the message. These receipts are most reliable when everyone is using Outlook and Exchange server.

FIGURE 4.28

The Tracking tab shows the vote count in the InfoBar and lists the voters and their choices.

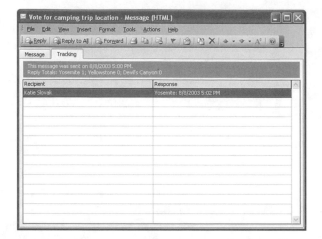

If you decide to request receipts for e-mails, do so sparingly and don't be surprised if you don't receive any. Some e-mail clients don't support delivery or read receipts, so the receipts are never sent. Some Internet providers strip the receipt request from the received e-mail so that it is never requested from the e-mail client. Many e-mail clients, including Outlook, enable you to refuse to send delivery or read receipts, so a receipt is never sent when the user refuses to send one. Many people refuse to send receipts on principle, figuring it's no one's business if they received or read the e-mail.

If delivery or read receipts are requested and received, the date and time a receipt was generated are shown in the e-mail's InfoBar.

Delivery Options

Replies are normally sent to the same e-mail address that sent the original e-mail. If you want replies to an e-mail sent to a different e-mail address, check the **Have replies sent to** checkbox in the Message Options dialog; then either enter a valid e-mail address in the text field, or click on **Select Names** and choose a recipient in the Have Replies Sent To dialog. This dialog is similar to the Address Book dialog shown when you select the To button in an e-mail. Select the name of the recipient and click on **OK** to add the recipient to the text field.

If your default setting is to save sent messages in the Sent Items folder, the **Save sent message to** checkbox is checked and sent items are listed in the text box. If you changed the default setting to save sent messages in a folder other than Sent Items, the checkbox is not checked. Whatever your default for sent messages, you can change the setting for a specific e-mail by checking or unchecking this checkbox. To save the message to a different folder than Sent Items, select **Browse** and pick a destination folder from the Select Folder dialog. After selecting a folder in this dialog, click on **OK** to enter the folder in the text field.

Check the **Do not deliver before** checkbox to prevent an e-mail from being delivered before the time you select. The date is automatically set to today's date, and the time is set to the end of your work day as set in your Calendar options. Select a different date and time from the Date and Time drop-downs to change the defaults. When you set this option on an e-mail, the message is sent to your Outbox when you send the e-mail but remains in the Outbox until the designated date and time; it then is sent out in the next scheduled or manual send/receive.

caution

When using the Do not deliver before option, make sure Outlook is running when the desired date and time arrive; otherwise, the message won't be sent until the next time you open Outlook.

The **Expires after** checkbox sets an expiration date and time for the e-mail. The date is automatically set to today's date, and the time is set to the end of your work day as set in your Calendar options. Select a different date and time from the Date and Time drop-downs to change the defaults. Expired e-mails are indicated by information in the message's InfoBar and are shown as crossed out in a folder view. E-mails that are expired do not disappear from the recipient's mailbox and can still be opened and replied to. This cosmetic setting doesn't really change any functionality of the e-mail. An example of an e-mail you might want to expire is a time-limited offer for free merchandise.

Some e-mail clients do not understand the default attachment format and message encoding of MIME. This is true particularly of some older e-mail clients that some of your e-mail recipients might be using. In those cases, you may want to select one of the alternate attachment formats of uuencode or BINHEX. Many older Unix e-mail clients use uuencode, and some older Macintosh e-mail clients use BINHEX. Most newer e-mail clients do understand MIME formatting, so unless you are instructed to change your format by an e-mail recipient, leave this setting alone. Encoding is always set to Auto-Select, so you also should leave this setting alone.

Contacts

Selecting the **Contacts** button near the bottom of the Message Options dialog opens the Select Contacts dialog. This dialog, which is similar to the Address Book dialogs, enables you to link the e-mail to one or more of the contacts in your Contacts folders. When you open the contact record for a linked contact, you can view all linked items related to that contact in the contact's Activities tab. You will learn more about contact linking and activities in Chapter 6.

Categories

You can assign a category to an e-mail and use the categories assigned to e-mails to group them. This way, you can group all related items together in a view. You also can filter e-mails on their categories; for example, you might assign the category Business to an e-mail and then filter on Categories Contains Business to show only e-mails that have Business as one of their categories. You will learn more about grouping, sorting, and filtering views in Chapter 14, "Outlook Views."

To assign one or more categories to an e-mail, select **Categories** to open the Categories dialog, as shown in Figure 4.29.

Check one or more categories shown in the master category list and click on **OK** to add those categories to the e-mail. You can also type a custom category in the text area at the top of the dialog and click on **OK** to use that custom category and also add it to your master categories list. Select **Add to List** to add the custom category to your master category list without closing the Categories dialog.

FIGURE 4.29

The Categories dialog contains predefined categories, and you can add your own categories either just for an item or to the master categories list.

To edit the master category list, select **Master Category List**. To add a new category to the master list, type it into the **New Category** text field and select **Add**. To remove a category from the master list, highlight it and select **Remove**. To reset the master list to the default categories, select **Reset**. Click on **OK** when you are finished with the master category list.

You can type any text in the Categories text field in the Message Options dialog to use as a category. I recommend not doing this unless you are entering

note

When you remove a category from the master list, it is not removed from any e-mails that already contain that category. The removed category is no longer available for use in new e-mails but remains in existing e-mails.

text for a category that will be used only that one time. If you intend to use that category again another time, use the Categories dialog (shown earlier in Figure 4.29). This way, you can make certain that you don't spell a custom category differently in different items. Any spelling difference or difference in capitalization creates a new category. For example, *Business* and *business* are different categories and will not group or filter e-mails with those categories together.

Internet Headers

Internet headers are a record of the paths an e-mail takes from the sender's computer to yours. In most cases, you won't be concerned about the Internet headers for e-mails, but they can be useful in some cases, such as tracing back to the source of a spam e-mail or a virus-carrying e-mail.

To view the Internet headers for an e-mail item, right-click on that item in a folder and select **Options**. In an open e-mail message, you can view the Internet headers by selecting **View**, **Options**.

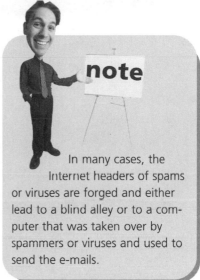

note

In many cases, the Internet headers of spams or viruses are forged and either lead to a blind alley or to a computer that was taken over by spammers or viruses and used to send the e-mails.

THE ABSOLUTE MINIMUM

In this chapter, you learned about advanced e-mail settings in Outlook 2003. To review, you now know how to

- Create and use signatures using both Word and the Outlook default editor.
- Add stationery to an e-mail.
- Work with restricted attachments.
- Send and receive links to Web pages that aren't restricted.
- Work with junk e-mail and use the junk e-mail filter.
- Flag e-mails with a level of importance as well as a reminder.
- Work with advanced e-mail options and settings.

With the skills you acquired in this chapter, you can now be sure you are making the most of Outlook when you send and receive e-mail. In the next chapter, you will learn about Outlook Search Folders.

IN THIS CHAPTER

- Learning what Search Folders are.
- Understanding the predefined Search Folders.
- Learning how to create custom Search Folders.

5

SEARCH FOLDERS

A Search Folder shows e-mails located in different folders all in one place. What makes Search Folders so powerful and useful is you can work with e-mails in a Search Folder one after another without caring where they are actually located. In this chapter, you will learn how to use, create, and customize Search Folders.

What Search Folders Do

Think of a Search Folder as a virtual folder. Even though an e-mail might be in the Sent Items folder, you can perform any action, such as reading it or replying to it, while you are working in a Search Folder in which it appears. The next e-mail in the folder might be located in the Inbox or a custom folder such as Personal E-mail, but you can work with it without leaving the Search Folder and navigating to the Personal E-mail folder.

You can use Outlook's predefined Search Folders, or custom Search Folders you create, to group e-mails based on almost any search criteria. Some examples of Search Folder search criteria are

- Unread items
- Items with High importance
- Items that were received in the past month
- Items that have been assigned the Business category
- Items from or to your boss

Each Search Folder has search criteria, which determine what items it shows, and a list of folders in which it searches. If an item changes so it no longer meets the search criteria, it will no longer be shown in the Search Folder.

Search Folders have two limitations you should be aware of:

- Search Folders work only with e-mail items.
- A Search Folder can search in only one Outlook data file; it can't search across multiple data files.

Changes made to an item in a Search Folder are made to the item in its actual location. If you change an item in a Search Folder so it no longer matches the folder's search criteria, that item will still exist in its original location. An example of this is the Unread Mail folder. If you mark a new e-mail message read in the Search Folder, it won't be shown there, but it will still be in the Inbox.

tip

The Search Folder display doesn't update to show changes until the display is refreshed. To refresh the Search Folder display, press **F5**, or switch to another folder and back using the Navigation Pane.

Predefined Search Folders

Outlook comes with 13 predefined Search Folders, but only 3 of them are enabled when you first start Outlook. You can enable any of the other predefined Search Folders, disable the Search Folders that are enabled by default, and create your own custom Search Folders. The following predefined Search Folders are enabled by default when you open Outlook:

- For Follow Up
- Large Mail
- Unread Mail

Figure 5.1 shows these three Search Folders in the Folder List in the Navigation Pane.

FIGURE 5.1

The For Follow Up, Large Mail, and Unread Mail Search Folders are enabled when you first start Outlook.

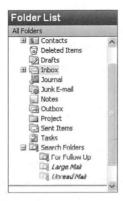

Outlook's Predefined Search Folders

Table 5.1 shows all 13 predefined Search Folders and the search criteria they use.

Table 5.1 Predefined Search Folders

Search Folder	Search Criteria
Unread mail	E-mails that are unread.
Mail flagged for follow up	E-mails with a colored flag.
Mail either unread or flagged for follow up	E-mails that are either unread or that have a colored flag.
Important mail	E-mails with High importance.
Mail from and to specific people	E-mails sent to or received from selected people.
Mail from specific people	E-mails received from selected people.
Mail sent directly to me	E-mails where the To field has your name.
Mail sent to distribution lists	E-mails sent to selected distribution lists.
Large mail	E-mails larger than a limit you specify. The size of an e-mail includes any attachments.
Old mail	Sent or received e-mails that are older than a threshold you set.

Table 5.1 (continued)

Search Folder	Search Criteria
Mail with attachments	E-mails with attachments.
Mail received this week	E-mails received this week.
Mail with specific words	E-mails that have words you specify in their text.

Each predefined Search Folder has a default view, which you can change, arrange on a different field, or customize. Customizing a Search Folder view is the same as customizing the view of any other folder in Outlook and is not described in this chapter. You will learn about changing and customizing views in Chapter 14, "Outlook Views."

In the following sections, you will learn how to enable, disable, and rename Search Folders.

Enabling and Disabling Search Folders

Only 3 of the 13 predefined Search Folders are enabled when you first start Outlook, but you can enable or disable any of the predefined Search Folders. You enable and disable Search Folders using the Search Folder context menu. The Search Folder context menu for the Large Mail folder is shown in Figure 5.2. To open a Search Folder context menu, right-click on Search Folders or one of the enabled Search Folders in the Folder List or the Mail folder group in the Navigation Pane.

FIGURE 5.2

The Search Folder context menu enables you to customize, rename, and delete a Search Folder.

To enable any of the predefined Search Folders, follow these steps:

1. Open the Search Folder context menu and select **New Search Folder** to open the New Search Folder dialog, as shown in Figure 5.3. The New Search Folder dialog shows all 13 predefined Search Folders and the groups in which they are arranged.

2. In the New Search Folder dialog, select the Search Folder you want to enable and click **OK**.

FIGURE 5.3

The New Search Folder dialog shows the predefined Search Folders and enables you to create a custom Search Folder.

The newly enabled Search Folder is added as a subfolder of Search Folders.

To disable any of the predefined Search Folders, do the following:

1. Select the Search Folder you want to disable.

2. Right-click and select **Delete**.

3. Click **Yes** in the dialog asking you to confirm the deletion.

The items in the Search Folder are not deleted when you delete a Search Folder; the items still exist in their original folder location. In the case of a predefined Search Folder, even though the folder is deleted, the folder definition remains, so you can enable the Search Folder again to re-create it.

caution

If you delete a custom Search Folder, the folder and its definition are deleted. If you change your mind after deleting a custom Search Folder, you will have to create it again from the beginning.

Renaming Search Folders

To rename a Search Folder, right-click the folder in the Folder List or the Mail folder group in the Navigation Pane and select **Rename.** The text field for the folder name becomes editable, and you can change the name of the folder. After you name the folder to your satisfaction, press **Enter**.

Search Folders and Favorite Folders

Search Folders can be added to the Favorite Folders group the same way any other e-mail folder can be added to Favorite Folders. Right-click the folder in the Folder List or the Mail folder group in the Navigation Pane and select **Add to Favorite Folders**. You will learn more about Favorite Folders in Chapter 11, "Customizing the Navigation Pane."

Customizing Predefined Search Folders

You can customize all predefined Search Folders by changing the folders they search, and you can even customize the search criteria of some predefined Search Folders. To begin customizing a predefined Search Folder, right-click on the folder in the Navigation Pane and select **Customize this Search Folder** to open the Customize dialog, as shown in Figure 5.4. The dialog shown in this figure is for a Search Folder whose search criteria cannot be customized.

FIGURE 5.4

The Customize dialog enables you to change the folders that are searched and in some cases edit the search criteria for the Search Folder.

The following sections will guide you step by step through customizing the folders and search criteria for an existing Search Folder. After you define custom Search Folders, the procedure for changing them is the same as for customizing a predefined Search Folder.

Changing the Folders a Search Folder Searches

To change the folders searched for a Search Folder, follow these steps:

1. Open the Customize dialog, which you learned to do earlier in this chapter.
2. Select **Browse** to open the Select Folder(s) dialog, as shown in Figure 5.5.
3. If you want to clear the current folder settings, click **Clear All**.
4. To automatically select subfolders of a folder when it is selected, check **Search subfolders**.
5. Check each folder you want to search for this Search Folder.
6. Click **OK** to save the folder settings.

If you don't want to change the Search Folder's search criteria, or if the Criteria button is disabled, click **OK** to save the customizations. If you want to change the folder's search criteria, follow the steps in the next section.

FIGURE 5.5

The Select
Folder(s) dialog
enables you to
clear existing
folder settings
and select the
folders to search
for the Search
Folder.

FIGURE 5.5

The Select
Folder(s) dialog
enables you to
clear existing
folder settings
and select the
folders to search
for the Search
Folder.

Changing a Search Folder's Search Criteria

This example shows how to change the size of e-mails that are shown in the Large
Mail Search Folder. To change the size used for the Large Mail search criteria, do the
following:

1. Select the Large Mail Search Folder in the Navigation Pane.

2. Right-click on **Large Mail** and select **Customize this Search Folder** to
   open the Customize dialog.

3. Click **Criteria**.

4. In the Mail Size dialog, shown in Figure 5.6, select the size and enter a new
   size, or use the up- and down-arrow controls to increase or decrease the size.

FIGURE 5.6

The Mail Size
dialog enables
you to change
the size for the
Large Mail
Search Folder.

5. Click **OK** to save the new search criteria.

6. Click **OK** to save the newly customized Search Folder.

The next example shows how to enable a predefined Search Folder and customize its
search criteria at the same time. Just follow these steps:

1. Right-click on **Search Folders** in the Folder List and select **New Search
   Folder**.

2. In the New Search Folder dialog, scroll down the list of Search Folders and select
   Old mail. (You saw the New Search Folder dialog previously in Figure 5.3.)

3. Click **Choose** to open the Old Mail dialog, as shown in Figure 5.7.

FIGURE 5.7
The Old Mail
dialog enables
you to change
the age items
must exceed for
the Old Mail
Search Folder.

4. Enter a number in the Show mail older than area or use the up- or down-arrow controls to change the age to look for.

5. Use the drop-down to select **day(s)**, **week(s)**, or **month(s)** as the time period to use.

6. Click **OK** to close the Old Mail dialog.

7. Click **OK** to enable the Search Folder and use the customized search criteria.

If you used the default search criteria of older than one week, the Search Folder is now named Older Than One Week. Some Search Folder names can become very long depending on their search criteria. You can rename a Search Folder, as you learned earlier in this chapter, but you should try to use names that will be meaningful to you at a later date if you shorten any Search Folder names.

note

You cannot reset a predefined Search Folder's search criteria after you have customized the search criteria. To remove customized search criteria from a predefined Search Folder, first delete the existing Search Folder and create a new instance of the predefined Search Folder.

Creating Custom Search Folders

Microsoft has defined quite a number of useful Search Folders for you already, but sometimes none of them quite meet your needs. That's when you will want to define your own custom Search Folders. Remember, though, Search Folders can search only in e-mail folders.

The example in this section creates a custom Search Folder that searches for e-mails that have been assigned a category of Business. To define the custom Business Search Folder, follow these steps:

1. Select a Search Folder in the Navigation Pane and right-click it.

2. Select **New Search Folder**.

3. In the New Search Folder dialog, scroll down the list of Search Folders and select **Create a Custom Search Folder** in the Custom group.

4. Click the **Choose** button to open the Custom Search Folder dialog, as shown in Figure 5.8.

FIGURE 5.8

The Custom Search Folder dialog enables you to give your custom Search Folder a name, create the search criteria for the Search Folder, and select which folders to search.

5. Enter **Business** as the name for your new Search Folder.

6. Click **Browse** to set the folders to search in the Select Folder(s) dialog, which you learned to do earlier in this chapter.

7. Click **OK** to close the Select Folder(s) dialog.

8. Click **Criteria** to open the Search Folder Criteria dialog, as shown in Figure 5.9.

9. Select the Advanced tab, shown in Figure 5.10.

note

The Search Folder Criteria dialog is similar to the Advanced Find dialog you will learn how to use in Chapter 12, "Finding Things Anywhere." To learn how to define more complex search criteria than shown in this chapter and how to use the different tabs in the Search Folder Criteria dialog, refer to Chapter 12.

FIGURE 5.9

The Search Folder Criteria dialog enables you to enter custom search criteria for a custom Search Folder.

FIGURE 5.10

The Search
Folder Criteria
Advanced tab
enables you to
create search cri-
teria using any
Outlook e-mail
field.

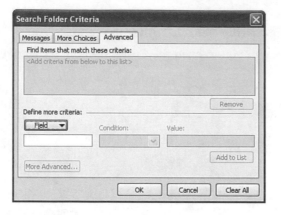

10. Click **Field** to show the available fields and select **All Mail Fields** to display all the Outlook mail fields you can use for search criteria.

11. Select **Categories**.

12. Enter `Business` in the Value field and leave the Condition as `contains`.

13. Click **Add to List** to add the criteria. The Advanced tab should now look like Figure 5.11.

FIGURE 5.11

The search crite-
ria can contain
one or more
conditions to use
for the Search
Folder.

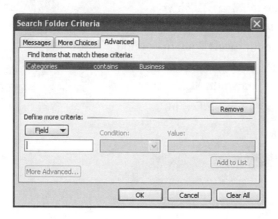

14. Click **OK** three times to create the new Business Search Folder.

You can now assign the Business category to any e-mail, and it will be shown in the Business Search Folder.

THE ABSOLUTE MINIMUM

In this chapter, you learned about Outlook's new Search Folders feature. To review, you now know

What Search Folders are and how to use them.

Which Search Folders are predefined by Outlook.

How to modify existing Search Folders.

How to create custom Search Folders.

With the skills you acquired in this chapter, you can work more efficiently with Outlook Search Folders. In the next chapter, you will learn how to work with Outlook contacts and address books.

PART

MANAGiNG iNFORMATiON iN OUTLOOK

IN THIS CHAPTER

- Learning to create and use Outlook address books.

- Understanding the methods used to create new contacts in Outlook.

- Using distribution lists to send e-mails to groups of people.

- Viewing activities related to a contact and creating new activities views.

- Learning how to set Contacts options.

6

CONTACTS AND ADDRESS BOOKS

Contact items in Outlook are used to store information about your contacts and are also used to provide data for address books. Outlook uses address books to address e-mails and faxes. Address books can also consist of information from sources other than contacts. In this chapter, you will learn about working with Outlook contacts and about using different types of address books.

Working with Outlook Address Books

The distinction between an address book and a Contacts folder can be confusing because they both sound as though they should be the same thing. A Contacts folder can be used to provide entries for an address book, but you don't have to use a particular Contacts folder as an address book; that's your decision. Each Contacts folder has a setting that determines whether it is displayed as an address book. You will learn how to enable and disable showing a Contacts folder as an address book in this chapter.

You can use more than one address book, with each address book consisting of entries that come from a specific source. The most common sources of entries for an address book, which you will learn about in this chapter, are

- **Outlook Contacts folders**—Your default Contacts folder is usually enabled as an address book unless you disable it from being used as an address book.

- **Exchange Global Address List (GAL)**—If you are using Exchange server, the corporate Exchange user list can be displayed as an address book.

- **Lightweight Directory Address Protocol (LDAP) directories**—These directories use an Internet standard protocol and are available for many companies, universities, and other organizations.

When you first set up Outlook, which you learned to do in Chapter 2, "Outlook from the Beginning," the Outlook Address Book service is automatically added to your configuration. Outlook uses the Outlook Address Book service to display Contacts folders as address books. To display an Outlook address book, select **Tools**, **Address Book**. Figure 6.1 shows an address book displaying Outlook contacts.

FIGURE 6.1

The Address Book dialog shows the name, display name, e-mail address, and address type when displaying contacts.

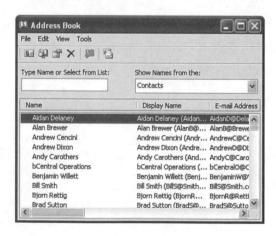

You will learn about using contacts and how to set up other sources for address books in the following sections of this chapter.

Using Contacts Folders as Address Books

Contacts folders are the primary source for your Outlook address books. You always have at least one Contacts folder in your Outlook data file, and by default that folder is used as your Outlook address book. In addition to the default Contacts folder, you also can create other Contacts folders and use them as address books.

To use a Contacts folder as an address book, you must install the Outlook Address Book service and enable the Contacts folder as an address book.

Although the Outlook Address Book service was installed by default when you first started Outlook,

note

Only contacts that have at least one e-mail address or fax number are displayed in a Contacts address book.

you may need to remove the service or reinstall it in some circumstances. Some reasons you might need to remove and reinstall the service are if you get errors when trying to display a Contacts folder as an address book or if the setting to enable a Contacts folder as an address book is disabled.

Removing the Outlook Address Book Service

To remove the Outlook Address Book service, follow these steps:

1. Select **Tools**, **E-mail Accounts** to open the E-mail Accounts Wizard, as shown in Figure 6.2.

FIGURE 6.2

The E-mail Accounts Wizard enables you to add, remove, and change address books as well as to add, remove, and change e-mail account settings.

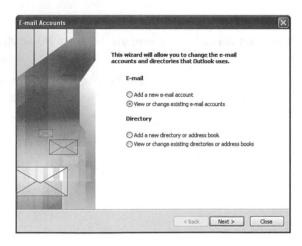

2. Select the **View or change existing directories or address books** option and click **Next** to move to the next wizard screen.

3. Highlight **Outlook Address Book** and click the **Remove** button.

4. Select **Yes** in the dialog asking whether you want to remove the Outlook Address Book.

5. Select **Finish** to complete removal of the Outlook Address Book service.

After the Outlook Address Book service is removed, Contacts folders are no longer shown in the Address Book dialog.

Reinstalling the Outlook Address Book Service

To reinstall the Outlook Address Book service, do the following:

1. Select **Tools**, **E-mail Accounts** to open the E-mail Accounts Wizard.

2. Select the **Add a new directory or address book** option and click **Next** to move to the next wizard screen.

3. Select the **Additional Address Books** option and click **Next** to move to the next wizard screen.

4. Highlight **Outlook Address Book** and click **Next**.

5. Click **OK** in the dialog telling you that the e-mail account you just added will not start until you exit and restart Outlook.

Displaying a Contacts Folder as an Address Book

To display a Contacts folder as an Outlook address book, follow these steps:

1. Right-click on a Contacts folder in the Navigation Pane and select **Properties**.

2. Select the **Outlook Address Book** tab.

3. Check the **Show this folder as an e-mail Address Book** checkbox, as shown in Figure 6.3.

4. If you want the address book to use a different name than the folder name, enter a new name for the address book in the **Name of the address book** entry field.

5. Click **OK** to show the folder as an Outlook address book.

FIGURE 6.3

The Outlook
Address Book
tab of the folder
Properties dialog
enables you to
show the folder
as an address
book and to give
the address book
a different name
than the folder
name.

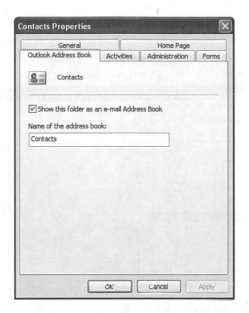

Using Address Books Other than Contacts Folders

Outlook can use other sources for its address books
in addition to Contacts folders. The following sections describe the additional built-in Address Book
services that are available for use in Outlook. Other
applications, such as ACT!, also can add their own
providers for Address Book services. If you are using
such an application, any address books or contact
lists in that application will be available for use in
Outlook as an address book when the service for
that address book is enabled.

Outlook considers
e-mail addresses and fax
numbers to be valid electronic
addresses, and displays both for
contacts in an address book. Each
electronic address is displayed in
a separate entry in the address
book, so if a contact has e-mail
and fax addresses, each is displayed in a separate entry for
that contact.

Global Address Lists (GALs)

The Global Address List (GAL) is an address book that is available if you are using
Microsoft Exchange server. The GAL lists every person with a mailbox account on
the Exchange server and can also be used to list special entries, known as *custom
recipients*, that don't have Exchange mailboxes.

If you have an Exchange e-mail account set up in your Outlook profile, you don't
have to do anything to view the GAL as one of your address books; it automatically
is shown as an Outlook address book. The GAL is stored on the Exchange server and
can be changed only by an Exchange administrator. Users cannot add or remove
entries in the GAL or edit them; all changes are made by administrators.

The address book displaying the GAL shows information available in each Exchange recipient's record and is different than the address book display of a contact. The GAL can also contain *distribution lists*, which are collections of e-mail addresses used to send e-mail to groups of people. Figure 6.4 shows a GAL displayed in an address book.

FIGURE 6.4

The Global Address List displays information from the Exchange server as an address book.

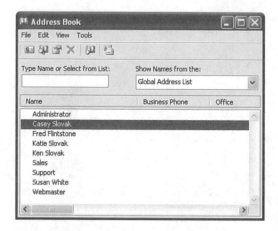

Lightweight Directory Address Protocol (LDAP) Address Books

Lightweight Directory Address Protocol (LDAP) address books use an Internet standard that is supported by many universities and other organizations. Generally, if you are using an LDAP address book, the administrators of the LDAP service will provide the configuration information you need to make Outlook's LDAP Address Book service connect to the LDAP server.

To install the LDAP Address Book service, follow these steps:

1. Select **Tools**, **E-mail Accounts** to open the E-mail Accounts Wizard.
2. Select the **Add a new directory or address book** option and click **Next** to move to the next wizard screen.
3. Select the **Internet Directory Service (LDAP)** option and click **Next** to move to the Directory Service (LDAP) Settings screen, as shown in Figure 6.5.
4. Enter the name of the LDAP server supplied to you, and if you are required to log in to the server, check the **This server requires me to log on** checkbox to enable the Logon Information area. Supply the login information you were given for logging in to the LDAP server in the Logon Information area. You may also be required to enter a search string or other settings in the More Settings dialog, depending on what login information is required for your LDAP server.
5. Select **Next** and click **OK** in the dialog telling you that the e-mail account you just added will not start until you exit and restart Outlook.
6. Select **Finish** to add an LDAP address book.

Personal Address Books (PABs)

Personal Address Books (PABs) are available in Outlook 2003 for compatibility with
earlier versions of Outlook. Microsoft discourages the creation and use of PABs
unless you need to use a PAB that was created in an earlier version of Outlook.

Some earlier versions of Outlook did not support the creation of distribution lists in
Contacts folders. Distribution lists are collections of e-mail addresses used to send e-
mail to groups of people. You needed a PAB to be able to store distribution lists on
your computer for use in Outlook. For users with no access to an Exchange server,
using a PAB was the only way to have distribution lists in earlier versions of
Outlook.

To install a PAB service in Outlook for use with a PAB created in an earlier version,
follow these steps:

1. Select **Tools**, **E-mail Accounts** to open the E-mail Accounts Wizard.

2. Select the **Add a new directory or address book** option and click **Next** to
   move to the next wizard screen.

3. Select the **Additional Address Books** option and click **Next** to move to the
   next wizard screen.

4. Highlight **Personal Address Book** and click **Next**.

5. Click **OK** in the dialog telling you that the e-mail account you just added will
   not start until you exit and restart Outlook.

Instead of using a PAB in Outlook, you can import the contents of a PAB into a
Contacts folder. This approach is recommended by Microsoft when you don't need to
maintain the PAB for compatibility with an older version. A PAB can be imported
only into an existing Contacts folder, so make sure the folder you want to import to
exists before starting the import.

To import a PAB into an existing Contacts folder, do the following:

1. Select **File**, **Import and Export** to open the Import and Export Wizard.

2. Highlight **Import from another program or file** and click **Next**.

3. Highlight **Personal Address Book** and click **Next**. If you have the Personal Address Book service installed, the installed PAB will automatically be used. Installation of the Personal Address Book service isn't required to import the contents of a PAB file into Outlook.

4. If you don't have the Personal Address Book service installed, enter the name and path of the PAB to import in the **File to import** field, or select **Browse** to open the screen shown in Figure 6.6, and navigate to the location of the PAB file. If you browsed to the file, click **OK** to use that file.

FIGURE 6.6

The Browse screen enables you to find the PAB file to import and opens with the file extension .PAB already selected.

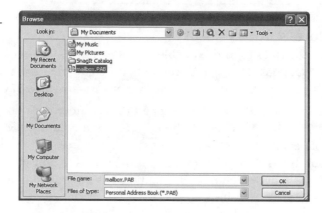

5. Select the destination folder in which to import the PAB and click **Next**.

6. Select **Finish** to complete the PAB import.

After a PAB isimported into a Contacts folder, you can remove the Personal Address Book service as follows if you do not need it to access another PAB that isn't imported into Outlook:

1. Select **Tools**, **E-mail Accounts** to open the E-mail Accounts Wizard.

2. Select the **View or change existing directories or address books** option and click **Next** to move to the next wizard screen.

3. Highlight **Personal Address Book** and click the **Remove** button.

4. Select **Yes** in the dialog asking whether you want to remove the Personal Address Book.

5. Select **Finish** to complete removal of the Personal Address Book service.

Using the Address Book Dialog

Although you can open the Address Book dialog at any time, you will most often work with address books when you are addressing e-mails or other items you are sending, such as task requests.

Let's look more closely at the Address Book dialog, shown in Figure 6.7.

FIGURE 6.7

The Address Book dialog can be used to add new entries, display entries from different address books, and display details about address book entries.

■ Select **New Entry** to add a new entry to the selected address book. You can add new entries to contacts and Personal Address Books. Most LDAP address books allow only entries made by an administrator, and you cannot add new entries to an Exchange GAL.

■ Select **Find Items** to open the Find dialog. Depending on which address book is selected, you may be able to search for names or other information in the address book entry.

■ Select **Properties** to open a dialog showing additional information about the selected address book entry.

■ Select **Delete** to remove an entry from an address book. You cannot delete entries from the GAL or from most LDAP address books.

■ **Add to Contacts** is enabled only when an address book other than Contacts is selected. The selected entry is added to a new contact item, which is opened to enable entry of additional data. Select **Save and Close** on the Standard toolbar to save the new contact item.

■ Select **New Message** to open a new e-mail message already addressed to the selected address book entry.

Changing How the Address Book Looks

To change the width of a column in the Address Book dialog, move the mouse cursor over a column heading divider until the cursor becomes a bar with a double arrow. Drag the column heading to the left or right to expand or contract the size of the column. You cannot add additional columns or change the order in which columns are displayed. Address books are sorted based on how the source for the address book is sorted; the sort order of an address book can't be changed in the Address Book dialog.

Changing Which Address Book Is Used First to Check E-mail Addresses

To change the order in which address books are displayed and used for checking e-mail addresses, do the following:

1. Open the Address Book dialog by selecting **Tools**, **Address Book**.

2. In the Address Book dialog, select **Tools**, **Options** to open the Addressing dialog, as shown in Figure 6.8.

FIGURE 6.8

The Addressing dialog sets the order in which address books are shown, the place where personal addresses are kept, and the order address books are used to check names for address resolution.

3. Select which address book is shown first when opening the Address Book dialog in the **Show this address list first** drop-down.

4. To change where personal addresses are kept, select an address book in the **Keep personal addresses in** drop-down. Only Contacts folders and Personal Address Books can be used in this drop-down, and because Personal Address Books are used only for compatibility with older versions of Outlook, this setting should be left at Contacts.

5. To add an address book to the list of address books checked for names when addressing an e-mail, select **Add** to open the Add Address List dialog. Select the desired address book from the list of available address books and select **Add**. The dialog remains open to permit the addition of address books. Select **Close** to close the Add Address List dialog.

6. Click **Remove** to remove an address book from the list of address books checked for names when addressing an e-mail.

7. To display the properties of a selected address book, select **Properties**. The information displayed in the Properties dialog depends on what type of address book is selected. For Contacts folders, the information is the folder name and Outlook data file in which the folder is located.

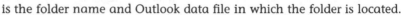

note

If you have more than one Contacts folder enabled as an Outlook Address Book, you can select any of those Contacts folders to use for storing personal addresses.

8. Use the up and down arrows to change the order in which address books are checked for names. When you address an e-mail, the address books are searched in the order shown in this list to find an e-mail address for that name.

9. Click **OK** to save the new address book settings.

Now that you are familiar with the different Outlook address books, you are ready to learn more about contacts—the primary sources for Outlook's address books.

Adding Contacts

As you learned in the previous sections, you can add a new contact from the Address Book dialog, either by importing a contact from a selected address book entry or by using **New Entry**. However, you usually add contacts when working in a Contacts folder, not from the Address Book dialog.

Creating a Contact in Table View

This section could also be called the "easy way" to create a contact. If you are viewing a Contacts folder in a table view, such as Phone List, you can add a new contact by entering a name in the **Click here to add a new contact** field. This field is located just below the column headings in the table view (see Figure 6.9).

Press **Tab** to move to another field to continue entering information for the new
contact. You can enter information in any field that is visible in the current view.
Press **Enter** to complete creation of the new contact.

Creating a Contact Using the New Contact Form

Just as the preceding section outlined the "easy way" to create a contact, this section
covers the more complete way to create a contact—the new contact form. Select
Actions, **New Contact** to open a new contact form, as shown in Figure 6.10.

FIGURE 6.10

Contact forms
provide space
for up to 19
phone/fax num-
bers, 3 e-mail
addresses, and 3
mailing
addresses.

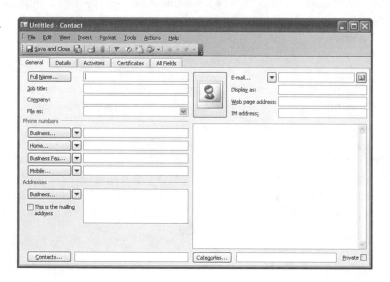

Enter information for the new contact and select **Save and Close** on the Standard
toolbar to save the new contact.

The following list details the various entries you can make for a contact:

- Select **Full <u>N</u>ame** to open the Check Full Name dialog, which enables separate entry of a title, first name, middle name, last name, and suffix. This dialog is opened automatically when a name is incomplete or unclear unless the Show this again when name is incomplete or unclear checkbox is unchecked. Click **OK** to save the entries in this dialog.

- Select one of the buttons next to the phone number fields to open the Check Phone Number dialog, which enables separate entry of a country or region, a city or area code, a local number, and an extension. Click **OK** to save the information in this dialog.

- Select a down arrow next to a button in the phone number fields to display a different type of phone number. Nineteen different types of phone and fax numbers can be entered for each contact.

- Select the down arrow next to the Addresses section to select the Business, Home, or Other address.

- Select the address type button to open the Check Address dialog, which enables separate entry of street, city, state or province, ZIP or postal code, and country or region information. This dialog is opened automatically when an address is incomplete or unclear unless the Show this again when address is incomplete or unclear checkbox is unchecked. Click **OK** to save the entries in this dialog.

- Select the down arrow next to the E-mail field to display and enter one of the three available e-mail addresses.

- Select the **Add a Picture** thumbnail to open the Add Contact Picture dialog, where you can browse to an image of the contact in one of the supported graphics formats.

Click **OK** to add the picture to the contact. The picture is added as an attachment to the contact. A contact with a picture is shown in Figure 6.11.

You cannot rename or delete the existing 19 phone/fax fields, 3 mailing address fields, and 3 e-mail fields, nor can you add additional phone/fax, mailing address, or e-mail address fields to a contact.

Adding a picture to a contact is a good way to personalize the contact form and provides identification for the contact if you don't already know what the contact looks like.

The graphic formats supported for use as pictures in a contact include BMP, EMF, ICO, JPG, JPEG, GIF, and TIF.

The General tab of the contact form also has space to enter Web page and Instant Messaging addresses, job title, and company. There is a checkbox for selecting the mailing address for the contact and a Private checkbox to keep the contact from being seen if the Contacts folder is shared with other people. Buttons and fields are available to enter categories and link other contacts to this one. You will learn more about using the Contacts field later in this chapter in the section "Viewing Activities."

FIGURE 6.11

Adding a picture of the contact is a good way to personalize the contact item.

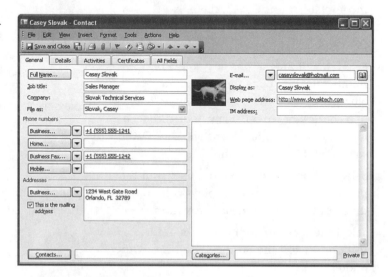

Additional information for the contact can be entered in the Details tab, as shown in Figure 6.12. If you enter a birthday or anniversary for a contact in the Details tab, a recurring event with a reminder is created in the calendar for that birthday or anniversary.

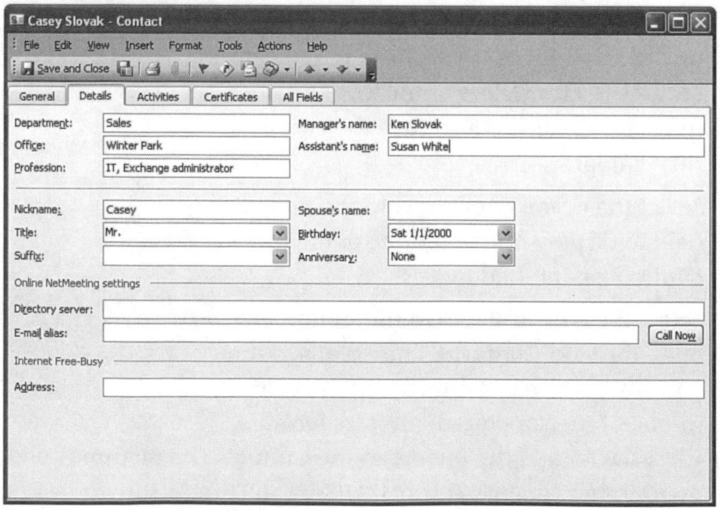

FIGURE 6.12

The Details tab of a contact form enables you to add birthdays and anniversaries for a contact.

The All Fields tab shows all the fields in a contact and the values for those fields. The Certificates tab shows all installed certificates for the contact, which are used for sending and receiving digitally signed and encrypted e-mails. You will learn about digitally signed and encrypted e-mail in Chapter 18, "Secure E-mail."

Adding a Contact from an E-mail

To create a new contact item for the sender of an e-mail, follow these steps:

1. Open the e-mail item by double-clicking it.
2. Right-click the **From** address of the e-mail and select **Add to Outlook Contacts**. A new contact form opens with the name and e-mail address of the new contact already filled in.
3. Add whatever other information you want to the contact and save it by selecting **Save and Close** in the Standard toolbar.

Viewing and Organizing Your Contacts

The default view of a Contacts folder is the Address Cards view, which is similar to a paper address book or Rolodex file. Various table-type views are also available for Contacts folders. You can also customize views of Contacts folders to display additional fields or to group contacts within a view. You will learn about views and customizing views in Chapter 14, "Outlook Views."

To change a view of a Contacts folder, select **View**, **Arrange By**, **Current View** and select a view to display.

To show the available views for a Contacts folder in the Navigation Pane, select **View**, **Arrange By**, **Show Views in Navigation Pane**.

Address Card views of contacts display the contacts similar to the way entries are displayed in a paper address book, in last name order. Table views of contacts can be sorted by most fields visible in the view. If you try to sort contacts on a field that doesn't allow sorting, such as Categories, you will receive an error message. Click **OK** to close the error message.

Contacts can be grouped by Category, Company, Location, or Follow-up Flag. Grouped contacts are divided into groups based on the selected view and then are sorted within the groups by the selected sort field or fields.

To sort contacts in a table view, click in the column heading you want to sort by. An up arrow in the selected field indicates the field is sorted in ascending order, where field values starting with the letter A are sorted first, as shown in Figure 6.13. A down arrow in the field indicates the field is sorted in descending order, with the letter Z sorted first. To change the sort order, click again in the same field. The sort order is toggled each time you click in a field heading.

FIGURE 6.13

Contacts can be sorted in ascending order for most fields, as shown in the Full Name column, or in descending order.

Recording Contact Activities

Every Outlook item, such as an e-mail or a task, has a Contacts field that is used to link the item to one or more contacts. The Activities tab in a contact form shows Outlook items linked to the contact. Activities support basic contact management functionality by providing a location where you can view everything stored in Outlook related to the contact.

Creating a Link to a Contact

You create a link to a contact in the item you want to link to that contact. For example, to link an appointment to a contact, do the following:

1. Open an appointment, as shown in Figure 6.14, by selecting **File**, **New**, **Appointment** and click **Contacts**.

FIGURE 6.14

Outlook items are linked to contacts by using the Contacts button.

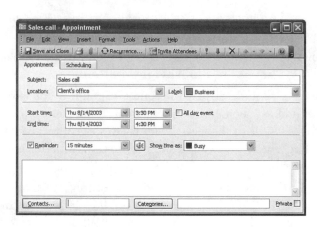

2. Select the contact that you want to link to the appointment from the list of contacts in a selected Contacts folder, as shown in Figure 6.15.

FIGURE 6.15

The Select
Contacts dialog
enables you to
link one or more
contacts to an
Outlook item.

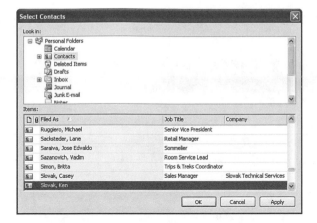

FIGURE 6.15

The Select
Contacts dialog
enables you to
link one or more
contacts to an
Outlook item.

3. Click **Apply** to add the contact link and leave
   the Select Contacts dialog open to add links to
   other contacts, or click **OK** to add the contact link and close the dialog.

Viewing Activities

Activities views are used to show items in selected
folders that are linked to a contact. You can choose
which view to use by clicking the down arrow next
to the Show field at the top of the Activities tab.
Each view shows linked items in one or more folders; for example, the All Items view shows all items
in all folders and subfolders of your default data
file that are linked to the contact.

When you open a contact and display the contact's Activities tab, Outlook searches in all folders defined for an Activities view for items linked
to that contact, as shown in Figure 6.16.

The default view for the Activities tab is the All
Items view, which searches for any item linked to
the contact in the default data file. Activities
views search in one or more folders in an
Outlook data file.

The other default views of Activities that are
available are Contacts, E-mail, Journal, Notes

note

You must save a newly
created item before you
can link it to a contact, and each
Contacts field is limited to about
30 contact links.

tip

You can change the fields
displayed in an Activities
view the same way as in
folder views. See
"Customizing Views" in
Chapter 14, "Outlook
Views," for information
about customizing fields in views.

and Upcoming Tasks/Appointments. You can also define your own custom Activities views, as you will learn in the next section.

FIGURE 6.16

The Activities tab of a contact form in All Items view shows items linked to the contact, such as tasks and appointments.

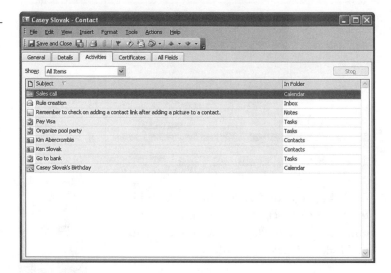

Creating and Modifying Activities Views

The predefined Activities views search in specific folders; for example, the All Items view searches in all Outlook folders, and the Contacts view searches in all Outlook Contacts folders. If you want to be able to use Activities views that search only in folders you specify, you must create a new view or modify an existing view.

To create new Activities views or modify existing Activities views for a Contacts folder, follow these steps:

1. Right-click on the Contacts folder in the Navigation Pane and select **Properties**.

2. Select the **Activities** tab, as shown in Figure 6.17. The Activities tab shows all the Activities views defined for that Contacts folder.

3. Highlight an Activities view that you want to modify or copy and click the **Modify** button or **Copy** button. Select **New** to create a completely new Activities view. The View Title and Folders dialog opens, as shown in Figure 6.18 for a new Activities view.

> **tip**
>
> An Activities view can search in only one Outlook data file and cannot search across multiple data files. If you are searching in an Exchange Public Folders data file, you can search for activities in only one folder in that data file in each Activities view, which is a limitation of Exchange.

FIGURE 6.17

The Activities tab enables you to create and modify Activities views and select the default Activities view for a Contacts folder.

FIGURE 6.18

Select the folders to search for activities by checking the checkboxes next to the folder names.

tip

If you want to search all folders in an Outlook data file, check the **Search Subfolders** checkbox and the folder at the top of the folder list, labeled as **Personal Folders** or **Mailbox**.

4. If you are copying an existing view or creating a new view, enter a name for the view in the **Name** field.

5. In the window in the middle of the dialog, check the checkboxes next to the folders that you want Outlook to search for activities in the new Activities view you are creating.

6. If you want to search subfolders of checked folders, make sure the **Search Subfolders** checkbox is checked.

7. To clear all selected folders, select **Clear All**.

8. To save the new or modified Activities view, click **OK**.

9. To change the default Activities view for the Activities tabs in all contacts in the folder, select your new default Activities view in the **Default activities view** drop-down (refer to Figure 6.17).

10. To reset a view to its original settings, highlight the view and select **Reset**. Click **Yes** in the dialog asking whether you want to reset the folder group.

11. Click **OK** to save the Activities views changes.

The procedures in this section enable you to create a new Activities view or modify an existing view, specifying which folders to search for the view. You also learned how to set the default view used when an Activities tab in a contact is first displayed and how to reset the folders used in a predefined Activities view.

Sharing Contact Information with Others

Outlook provides two ways to send contact information about a contact to another person. You can send the information as a vCard or forward a contact from within one of your Contacts folders. vCards are an Internet standard way of transmitting contact information as a text file and can be understood by most modern e-mail clients, but the vCard specification doesn't support all the possible fields in an Outlook contact item. vCards are also known as electronic business cards. Forwarded Outlook contacts contain all the contact fields but can be used only by people running Outlook.

- To send a contact to another person, highlight the contact and select **Actions**, **For_w_ard**. A new e-mail message is opened with the selected contact attached to the e-mail message.

- To send a vCard to another person, highlight the contact and select **Actions**, **Forward as _v_Card**. A new e-mail message is opened with a vCard file (.VCF) of the selected contact attached to the e-mail message. When a vCard file is opened, Outlook creates a new contact item.

tip

You can include a vCard as part of your signature, and it will be attached to every e-mail in which the signature is used. See the "Creating and Using Signatures" section in Chapter 4, "Advanced E-mail," to learn how to use a vCard in a signature.

■ To save a vCard to the Windows file system, open a contact and select **File**, **Export to vCard file**. Select the filename and location in the VCARD File dialog and select **Save** to save the vCard file.

Using Distribution Lists

Distribution lists are used to send e-mails to groups of people. Distribution lists can be created and used over and over again, eliminating the need to repeatedly select the same group of people when composing or forwarding messages. Distribution lists are stored in Contacts folders and can be selected for use in most places where you can use a contact.

Creating a Distribution List

To create a distribution list, follow these steps:

1. Select **Actions**, **New Distribution List** to open a new distribution list form, as shown in Figure 6.19.

FIGURE 6.19

Distribution lists make it easy to repeatedly send e-mails to the same group of people.

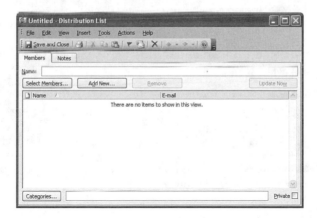

2. Enter a name for the distribution list in the **Name** field.

3. To add contacts or entries from any address book to the distribution list, select **Select Members.** Highlight each member to add in the Select Members dialog and click **Members** to add the highlighted contacts to the distribution list, as shown in Figure 6.20. Click **OK** to close the Select Members dialog and save the selections.

4. To add distribution list members that aren't in one of your address books to the distribution list, select **Add New**. In the Add New Member dialog, enter a

display name and e-mail address for the new member and check the **Add to Contacts** checkbox if you want the new member automatically added to your contacts. Click **OK** to add the new member.

FIGURE 6.20

You can add people from multiple address books to a single distribution list by clicking the Members button when one or more address book entries is selected.

tip

You can add more than one person at a time to a distribution list by clicking on each new member while holding down the **Ctrl** key. After selecting the members to add to the distribution list, click on the **Members** button to add all the selected entries to the distribution list.

5. To remove a member from a distribution list, highlight the member and select **Remove**.

6. If e-mail addresses of distribution list members have changed, select **Update Now** to update the distribution list with the new e-mail addresses.

7. If you want to add notes to the distribution list, enter the note information in the Notes tab. Notes are purely for information, and they aren't used when the distribution list is used.

Distribution lists are shown in table views in bold text and use a different icon than contacts. In an Address Card view, a distribution list shows an icon in the address card, as shown in Figure 6.21.

caution

Some ISPs have limits on the number of recipients to whom you can send a message to prevent sending junk e-mail from their mail servers. If your ISP has such a limit, you will receive an error message if you attempt to send a message to a distribution list that exceeds the limit. Check with your ISP to see whether it has such a limit.

FIGURE 6.21

Distribution lists use different icons than contacts and show an icon in Address Card view.

Working with Distribution Lists

Distribution lists are selected for use in e-mails and for other addressing uses just as contacts are selected—from an Address Book dialog. When you add a distribution list as a recipient for an item, the name of the distribution list is added to the item (see Figure 6.22).

The distribution list is shown with a plus (+) sign to the left of the distribution list name. To expand the distribution list and show all the members of the list, select the +. Click **OK** to expand the list, which replaces the distribution list with the e-mail address display names for the members of the distribution list. An expanded list cannot be converted back to the distribution list again after it is expanded.

Distribution lists are not automatically updated with new information from the contacts that make up the distribution lists.

FIGURE 6.22

Distribution lists are expanded into the list of members when an item is sent.

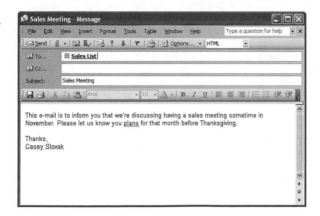

Flagging Contacts

Flagging a contact is useful to remind you to take some action regarding the contact or to make it stand out in a table view of contacts. You learned about flagging items in "Flagging E-mails and E-mail Reminders" in Chapter 4.

To flag a contact in a table view, select the contact and click in the Flag column. Select the desired flag from the drop-down list of flags, as shown in Figure 6.23.

To add a followup flag and a reminder for a contact item, do the following:

1. Right-click the contact and select **Follow Up**.

2. In the Flag for Follow Up dialog, shown in Figure 6.24, select the flag text in the **Flag To** drop-down or enter new text for the flag in the drop-down's text area.

3. If you want a reminder for the flag, select the date and time for the reminder in the date and time **Due by** drop-downs. You can type times in the time field or change a selected time to one that isn't in the list, as you can with other time fields.

4. Click **OK** to save the new flag and reminder.

5. To clear a flag, right-click the contact and select **Clear Flag**.

6. To mark a flag as complete, right-click the contact and select **Flag Complete**.

> **tip**
>
> Sometimes you want to send a message to most of a distribution list but not to all its members. In this case, expand the distribution list; then select and delete members to whom you do not want to send the message. This way, you can retain the distribution list without modification but still send to a subset of its members.

FIGURE 6.23

Flags and reminders for contacts are useful to remind you of such things as calling or e-mailing the contact.

FIGURE 6.24

Flagging a contact draws attention to it and can fire a reminder for the contact.

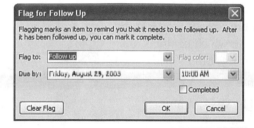

Changing Contact Options

Contact options are used to change the order contacts are listed in a Contacts folder table view, determine how the File As field is generated by Outlook, and check for duplicate contacts when a new contact is created. You can also show an Address Cards Rolodex index in a second, alternative language in addition to your default language.

To change contact options, select **Tools**, **Options**, **Preferences**, **Contact Options** to open the Contact Options dialog, as shown in Figure 6.25.

Select how to show contact names in the **Default "Full Name" order** drop-down. Names can be shown in the following orders:

- First name followed by an optional middle name and then the last name
- Last name followed by the first name
- First name followed by two last names

note

You can flag contacts just as you can flag e-mail items, although contacts flagged for followup don't appear in the For Follow Up Search Folder.

FIGURE 6.25

On the Contact Options dialog, you can control how names are shown and filed.

Select how the File As field is set up for contacts in the **Default "File As" order** drop-down. The File As field is used to set the order in which contacts are displayed. The available settings are

- Last name, first name
- First name followed by the last name
- Company name
- Last name, first name, followed by the company name in parentheses
- Company name followed by last name, first name, with the names in parentheses

Check the **Check for duplicate contacts** checkbox to check for duplicates when you create a new contact.

Alphabetic index tabs like those in a Rolodex are displayed when a Contacts folder is viewed in an Address Card view. The **Show an additional Contacts Index** checkbox controls whether an additional set of index tabs is shown in an alternative language.

Click **OK** to save the Contacts settings.

note

Changing the Full Name and File As orders affects only contacts you create after the orders are changed. To change the orders for existing contacts, you must open each existing contact and change the Full Name and File As orders manually.

THE ABSOLUTE MINIMUM

In this chapter, you learned about Outlook's contacts and address books. To review, you now know

What address books are and how to use them.

How to use Outlook contacts to store information about people and companies.

How to associate activities with a contact and how to set up ways to view them.

How to send electronic business cards to other people.

How to use distribution lists to send e-mail to groups of people.

How to change the default options for contacts.

With the skills you acquired in this chapter, you now know how to work with contacts and address books. In the next chapter, you will learn how to work with Outlook's calendar.

IN THIS CHAPTER

- Learning how to navigate in the calendar and use different calendar views.

- Learning how to create new appointments, meetings, and all day events.

- Understanding how to set up appointments, meetings, and all-day events that occur on a regular schedule.

7

THE CALENDAR

The Outlook calendar enables you to view, create, and arrange the appointments, events, and meetings that make up your schedule. Maintaining your schedule is probably your most important information management task, and Outlook's calendar has features that enable you to plan meetings and all-day events, view multiple calendars individually or side by side, view group schedules, and even view your to-do list alongside your calendar. In this chapter, you will learn about working with all these features of the Outlook calendar.

Navigating in the Calendar

To display Outlook's calendar, select the **Calendar** button in the Navigation Pane or select **Go**, **Calendar**. The default view of the calendar shows one month in the Date Navigator with the current day's schedule displayed in the main folder window, as shown in Figure 7.1. The Date Navigator is the little calendar that is displayed in the Calendar folder to enable you to move from one date to another.

FIGURE 7.1

The Day view of the calendar shows your working hours in a light color and indicates the current time of the day.

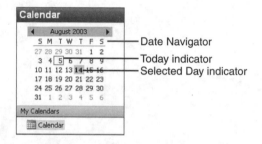

— Date Navigator
— Today indicator
— Selected Day indicator

The currently selected date is shown in the Date Navigator as a colored day, with today's date outlined in red. You can do the following to move around in the calendar:

- To show your schedule for a different day in the current month, select the day in the Date Navigator.

- To show a different month, click the left or right arrows at the top of the Date Navigator to show past or future months. Continue clicking the left or right arrows until the month you want to display is shown.

- To display the current day in the calendar, select **Today** in the toolbar or select **Go**, **Today**.

tip

To customize the font used for the Date Navigator select **Tools**, **Options**, the **Other** tab, and then select **Advanced Options**. In the **Appearance options** section, select the font used for the Date Navigator by selecting the **Font** button. Click **OK** after you set the font, font style, and size you want used in the Date Navigator.

The calendar displays the time in user-selectable increments in Day view, with an indicator line showing the current time. To change the default 30-minute time increments shown in the Day view, do the following:

1. Right-click the day heading shown at the top of the day and select **Customize Current View**.

2. Select **Other Settings** to open the Format Day/Week/Month View dialog.

3. Select the time increments in the **Time Scale** drop-down. The available increments are 5, 6, 10, 15, 30, and 60 minutes.

4. Click **OK** twice to save the new time increment.

Later in this chapter, in the "Switching Calendar Views" section, you will learn about using different calendar views, but now it's time to learn what can be displayed in an Outlook calendar.

note

Another way to change the time increments is to right-click in the time column in a Day view and select the desired increment in the context menu.

Using Calendar Items

Three types of calendar items are used with Outlook calendars:

- **Appointments**—Activities scheduled for a specific time frame. Appointments don't require that other people agree to attend the activity.

- **Events**—All-day appointments. Events are assumed to begin when your work day begins and end at the end of your work day. You will learn how to set your work day hours in the "Setting Calendar Options" section later in this chapter.

- **Meetings**—Appointments that others are scheduled to attend. Meetings are scheduled with other people and can have required and optional attendees.

All three types of calendar items are related; for example, events are appointments for which the All day event checkbox is checked. If you uncheck the All day event checkbox in an event form, the event is converted into an appointment. An appointment form is shown in Figure 7.2. The event form is identical to the appointment form, except no times are shown because an event is an all-day appointment.

Meetings are appointments that other people have been scheduled to attend. If you invite other people to an appointment, the appointment is converted into a meeting. If you invite other people to an all-day event, that event is converted into an all-day meeting. You will learn about scheduling meetings in the "Scheduling Meetings" section of this chapter and the "Scheduling Meetings" section in Chapter 21, "Collaborating with Outlook and Exchange."

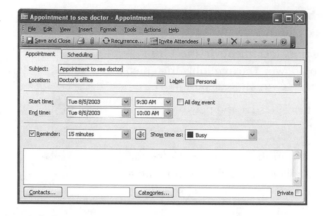

Switching Calendar Views

The default calendar view is the Day view shown in Figure 7.1, but you can use other views to get different pictures of your schedule.

The most commonly used calendar views are Day/Week/Month views, which show the calendar in the same ways as many paper day planners do. Table views of the calendar such as Active Appointments, Events, Annual Events, Recurring Appointments, and By Category are also available but are less commonly used.

To switch views of the calendar, select **View**, **Arrange By**, **Current View** and select the view you want from the list.

Day/Week/Month Calendar Views

The Day/Week/Month views are

- **Day**—Shows the schedule for the selected day
- **Work Week**—Shows the schedule for your workweek days
- **Week**—Shows the schedule for the selected week
- **Month**—Shows the schedule for the selected month

> **tip**
>
> To display a list of the available views for the calendar in the Navigation Pane, select **View**, **Arrange By**, **Show Views in Navigation Pane**. If you show the available views in the Navigation Pane, changing views is quicker than using the menu commands. This way, you also can see the Customize Current View command under the list of available views in the Navigation Pane.

You will learn how to set your workweek days later in this chapter in the section "Setting Calendar Options." Figure 7.3 shows the Work Week view, with the working days highlighted with a colored bar in the Date Navigator.

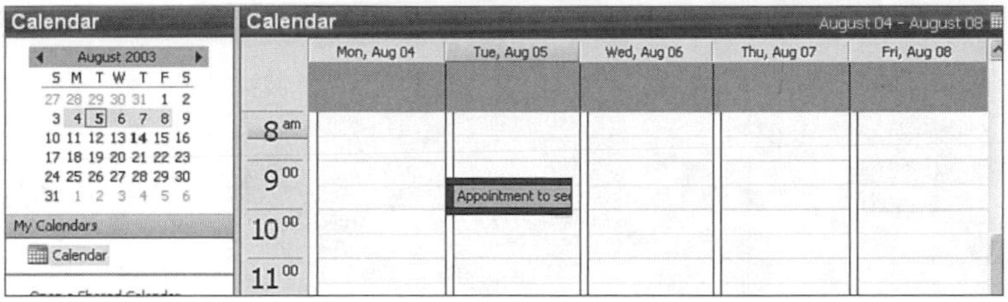

FIGURE 7.3

The Work Week view of the calendar shows the schedule for your workweek but always displays sequential days even if your workweek isn't continuous.

Week view, shown in Figure 7.4, shows the selected week with Saturday and Sunday displayed in a compressed size. Weekend days are always shown compressed in Week view, there is no way to change the view of weekend days as you can in Month view.

FIGURE 7.4

The Week view of the calendar shows the current week highlighted with a colored bar in the Date Navigator and always compresses Saturdays and Sundays.

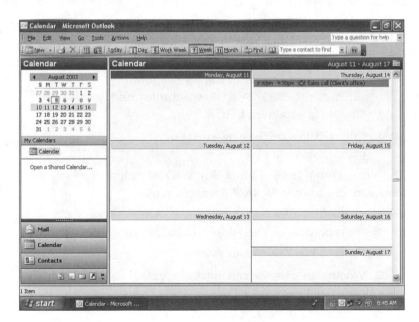

Month view, shown in Figure 7.5, shows an entire month at a glance.

FIGURE 7.5

The Month view of the calendar shows the current month highlighted with a colored bar in the Date Navigator and, by default, compresses weekend days.

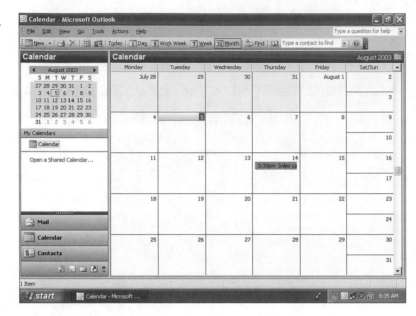

Follow these steps to change the compression of weekend days in Month view:

1. Right-click in the Calendar and select **Other Settings** to open the Format Day/Week/Month View dialog.

2. Check the **Compress weekend days** checkbox in the Month area to show Saturday and Sunday in compressed format. Uncheck the checkbox to show Saturday and Sunday in expanded format.

3. Click **OK** to save the new weekend compression settings.

The other settings in the Format Day/Week/Month View dialog, shown in Figure 7.6, enable you to configure the following:

- Fonts of times and text displayed in Day view
- Fonts in Week and Month view
- Whether to show the end times of appointments and meetings in Week and Month view
- Whether to show start and end times as clocks in Week and Month view
- Whether to display dates with appointments, meetings, or events in boldface in the Date Navigator

note

A bug in Outlook shows the wrong days in Work Week view if your workweek isn't sequential. For example, if your workweek is Monday, Tuesday, Thursday, Friday, and Saturday, Work Week view shows Monday through Friday and doesn't show Saturday.

FIGURE 7.6

The Format Day/Week/ Month View dialog enables you to set display fonts, compression of weekend days, and the time scale shown in Day view.

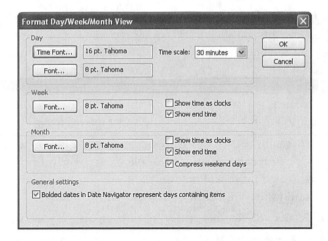

The option for showing start and end times as clocks shows the times using dial-face clocks, as shown in Figure 7.7. This display style, which is available only in Week or Month view, takes up less space than text times, which leaves more space for the subject text of the calendar item. Compare the appointment shown in Figure 7.4 with the same appointment shown in Figure 7.7 to see the difference between the two time display styles.

FIGURE 7.7

The clock-style display of times makes room for additional text from the subject of the calendar item.

Table Views for the Calendar

Most often you will want to use one of the Day/Week/Month views in Calendar folders. The format, which is similar to paper calendars and planners, enables you to see your appointments, meetings, and events in a way that makes it easy to see how your time is allotted. However, calendar table views are useful when you are printing calendar information and when you want to analyze or display similar types of calendar items. You will learn about printing information from a table view in Chapter 15, "Printing Outlook Information."

The following table views are available by default; you can also create or modify other table views:

- **Active Appointments**—Shows appointments that haven't come due yet. No past appointments are shown, except for recurring appointments where at least one of the appointments is still in the future. The recurrence pattern determines when each appointment occurs—for example, on the first day of each month. Recurring appointments are shown grouped by the recurrence pattern. Recurring appointments show the starting date and time of the first of the recurring appointments and also show the recurrence pattern.

- **Events**—Shows all events, even those that occurred in the past. Events are grouped by their recurrence—for example, none, yearly, or monthly. Recurrence is used for repeating events, meetings, and appointments that occur at regular intervals, such as a yearly sales conference.

- **Annual Events**—Shows all events that happen once a year, such as birthdays.

- **Recurring Appointments**—Shows only appointments that are set to happen more than once.

- **By Category**—Shows all appointments, events, and meetings grouped by their categories.

Any table view can be arranged by specific fields. For example, the By Categories view arranges items by categories. To set the arrangement of items in a table view, select **View**, **Arrange By** and select the arrangement you want from the list. Other useful arrangements for calendar items are by **Date**, **Subject**, and **Importance**.

One useful arrangement that isn't available as a default arrangement is By Location. To add a location arrangement to a table view, select **View**, **Arrange By**, **Current View**, **Customize Current View** to open the Customize View dialog. Select **Group By**, and in one of the Group Items By drop-downs, select **Location**. You can set up to four groupings for any view. To save your changes, click **OK** twice. Figure 7.8 shows a By Categories view that has an added Location grouping.

FIGURE 7.8

Table views such as this view grouped by categories and then by location are useful for seeing related calendar items grouped together.

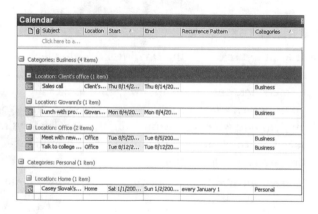

Making an Appointment

Now that you are familiar with moving around in the calendar and viewing calendar items, the next step is learning how to create appointments, meetings, and events.

Creating Quick Appointments

If you are using the By Categories table view of a Calendar folder, you can create a quick appointment by clicking in the **Quick Appointment** row in the Subject field. Enter a subject for the appointment and then fill in any other desired fields that are shown in that table view. The start and end times for the appointment are automatically filled in for you. The start time is set to the next hour after the current time, and the end time is set 30 minutes after the start time. The information in any fields that are displayed in the table view, such as start and end times, can be changed in the Quick Appointment row without opening the new appointment. Select **Enter** to save the new appointment.

The Quick Appointment row in a By Categories view is shown in Figure 7.9. To add more information to the appointment after it is created, open the appointment by double-clicking it and fill in the information in the appointment form.

FIGURE 7.9

Quick appointments automatically set a start time at the next hour after the current time and set the end time to 30 minutes after the appointment starts.

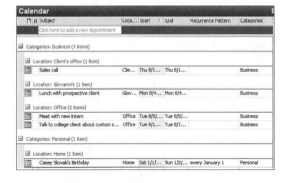

Setting up Detailed Appointments

To create a new appointment using the appointment form, select **Actions**, **New Appointment** (see Figure 7.10). Enter a **Subject** and **Location** for the appointment. The **Start time:** is automatically set to the currently selected time in the calendar. If you are using a calendar view that doesn't show the times, the new appointment's start time is set to the start of your workday. The **End time** is set to 30 minutes after the start time.

FIGURE 7.10
You can color-code appointments with labels, and you can also set their importance.

Changing the Time and Date

To change the time of an appointment, use the Date and Time drop-downs to select a date and a time for the start and end of the appointment. Your schedule is shown as Busy by default for a new appointment; the available settings for your time are Free, Tentative, Busy, and Out of Office. These settings are used for free/busy scheduling for meetings; you will learn more about using free/busy scheduling in Chapter 21.

You can fill in any time fields in Outlook by using the time drop-downs, but you also can type a time directly in the drop-downs. For example, you can type 3:12 PM, which is a time not included in the drop-downs. You can select a time in the drop-downs and then manually change the selected time, such as selecting 3:00 PM and then changing the minutes to 12.

Setting Up a Reminder

Check the **Reminder** checkbox if you want a reminder of this appointment. Be sure to select how long before the appointment to display the reminder in the reminder time drop-down. To change the reminder sound from its default, select the sound to play for the reminder by clicking in the speaker icon. Any .WAV file can be used for a reminder sound.

tip

You can drag an e-mail that is about a meeting or appointment to a Calendar folder to AutoCreate a new appointment item. The e-mail subject becomes the appointment subject, the e-mail text is included in the appointment, and the appointment includes any attachments in the e-mail.

You can also drag other items, such as tasks and appointments, into a Calendar folder to AutoCreate appointments.

tip

You also can use short-hand when entering a time; for example, you can enter **1** and Outlook will convert it to 1:00 PM. If you enter **6** and the current time is 10:00 AM, the 6 is converted to 6:00 PM. The conversions from shorthand occur when you tab from the time field.

Making Items Private

Private items aren't shown if you share your calendar with other people. To mark an item private, check the **Private** checkbox. This feature provides you with a means of keeping some information private, such as medical or dental appointments.

Organizing with Color-Coded Labels

Labels are used to color-code appointments, meetings, and events. Ten labels are available for Outlook Calendar items, in addition to the default of No Label.

Each label is assigned a color, which cannot be changed. You can change the label description, however. To edit the descriptions for labels, right-click an appointment and select **Label**, **Edit Labels**. Highlight the description you want to change and enter a new description. Click **OK** to save the new label descriptions.

Scheduling Meetings

As you learned earlier, meetings are appointments or events to which other people have been invited. Resources for a meeting, such as a conference room or slide projector, are also "invited" to the meeting. A meeting is automatically created when you schedule an appointment or event with other people, and a meeting request is sent to the other attendees and resources for the meeting.

Replying to a Meeting Request

When you receive and open a meeting request, it has buttons to send Accept, Tentative, or Decline responses to the person scheduling the meeting. There is also a Propose New Time button that you can use if you want to propose a new time for the meeting. These buttons are similar to the Voting buttons you learned about in Chapter 4, "Advanced E-mail Techniques."

If you click the Propose New Time button, a free/busy dialog opens in which you can check other attendees' schedules and propose a new time for the meeting. You will learn more about using free/busy scheduling in Chapter 21.

When you click one of the Accept, Tentative, or Decline response buttons, you are offered a choice of editing the response before sending it, sending the response without editing it, or not sending a response at all. Editing a response enables you to add comments or other information to your response before it is sent to the meeting organizer. Not sending a response prevents the organizer of the meeting from tracking your response and from knowing if you will or won't attend the meeting.

If you respond to a meeting request using the Accept or Tentative buttons, the meeting is automatically added to your schedule. The time is marked as Busy or

Tentative, depending on which button you selected. You don't have to do anything to get Outlook to process meeting requests after you respond to them; the processing is done when Outlook is idle and waiting for input. Outlook automatically deletes the meeting request after processing it. You can see the deleted meeting request in your Deleted Items folder.

Tracking Attendees for a Meeting You've Scheduled

When you receive responses to your meeting request, they are automatically processed when Outlook is idle, or you can force them to be processed by opening the responses. Responses are tallied in the InfoBar of the meeting form, and a Tracking tab is added to show the response status for each attendee. Figure 7.11 shows the Tracking tab for a meeting.

FIGURE 7.11

Meeting attendees' status is tracked in the Tracking tab of the meeting form, where accepted, tentative, and declined responses are displayed.

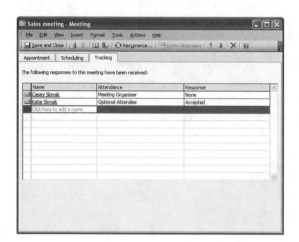

You will learn more details about planning a meeting, viewing group schedules, and checking attendees' free/busy status in Chapter 21.

Creating Events

As you learned earlier in this chapter, events are appointments that are scheduled to last an entire day. You can do the following with them:

- To create a new event, select **Actions**, **New All Day Event**. The event form is identical to an appointment form, except there are no time drop-down fields because an event lasts all day.

- To convert an appointment into an event, uncheck the **All day event** checkbox.

- To convert an event into an appointment, check the **All day event** checkbox.

The other differences between appointments and events are the default reminder times before the appointment or event, and the default setting for your time. Appointments use a default reminder time set in the Calendar preferences; events use a default reminder time of 18 hours before the event. Appointments show your time as Busy by default; events show your time as Free.

Using Calendar Reminders

When a reminder comes due, it is displayed in a window (see Figure 7.12), and a sound is played, unless you disable either of these actions.

FIGURE 7.12

Reminder windows display all current reminders and enable you to dismiss the reminder or snooze it to have it display again.

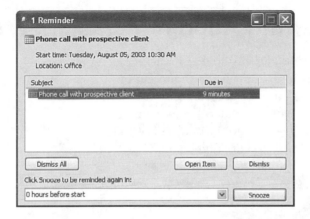

To enable or disable the sound for reminders or the reminders display in the Reminder window, do the following:

1. Select **Tools**, **Options**.
2. Select the **Other** tab; then select **Advanced Options**, **Reminder Options**. The Reminder Options dialog is shown in Figure 7.13.
3. Check or uncheck the **Display the reminder** and **Play reminder sound** checkboxes to enable or disable the reminder window and sound.
4. Select **Browse** to open the Reminder Sound File dialog. There, you can select any .WAV file as your reminder sound and select **Open** to use that .WAV file if you want to use a different sound than the default Reminder.WAV file.
5. Click **OK** to save your changes .

> **tip**
>
> To see all reminders that are currently active, select **View**, **Reminders Window** to open the Reminders dialog. The Reminders dialog enables you to select any active reminder and snooze or dismiss it. You also can open the item that has the selected reminder or dismiss all selected reminders.

FIGURE 7.13

In the Reminders Options dialog, you can enable or disable the display of reminders and set whether to play a sound when a reminder comes due.

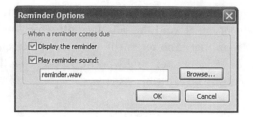

Setting Up Recurring Appointments, Meetings, and Events

Appointments, meetings, and events that occur at regularly scheduled intervals are referred to as *recurring* items. Examples of recurring calendar items are a meeting that is scheduled every Friday, a birthday (which occurs once a year), and an appointment that is scheduled for the first day of every month.

The scheduled frequency of the calendar item is called the *recurrence pattern*. Recurrence patterns can also have exceptions, such as once every day except for Sunday. In the following sections, you will learn how to set recurrence patterns for calendar itemsAppointments,.

Recurring meetings and events are created exactly the same way recurring appointments are created, and setting daily and yearly recurrence patterns is similar to creating weekly and monthly recurrence patterns.

Creating Recurrence Patterns

Any appointment,Appointments, meeting, or event can have a recurrence pattern applied to it.

Recurrence patterns can be set for daily, weekly, monthly, or yearly intervals. The following examples show how to create recurring appointments with weekly and monthly intervals.

To create a new recurring appointment, start by doing the following:

1. Select the **Calendar** button in the Navigation Pane to make the Calendar the current folder.

2. Select **Actions**, **New Appointment** to open a blank appointment form.

3. Enter any necessary information in the appointment form and select **Recurrence** from the toolbar or **Actions**, **Recurrence** to open the Appointment Recurrence dialog, as shown in Figure 7.14.

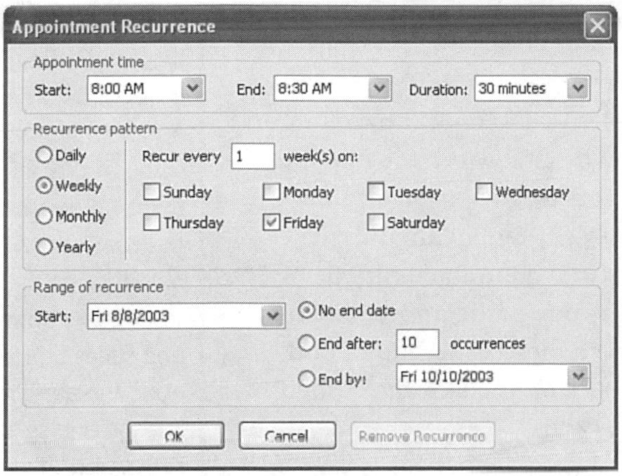

FIGURE 7.14

Recurrence pattern settings change depending on whether daily, weekly, monthly, or yearly recurrence is selected.

The settings available for the Appointment time and Range of recurrence sections are the same regardless of which type of recurrence pattern is used. The start, end, and duration settings are taken from the settings on the appointment form. If you change these settings in the Appointment Recurrence dialog, they are also changed in the appointment.

For this example, leave the default appointment settings as they are. Set them to use the beginning of your workday as the start time and set the duration to 30 minutes.

The Range of Recurrence settings are the start date and the number of recurrences for the appointment. The default start date is today's date. To change the date, select the desired start date in the **Start** drop-down. The following settings are available for the number of recurrences:

> After the recurrence pattern is created, the time and date fields for the appointment are no longer available in the appointment form. To change the appointment times or recurrence pattern, open the Appointment Recurrence dialog, make the changes, and click **OK** to save them. To remove the recurrence pattern, select **Remove Recurrence**.

- **No end date**—Creates a recurring appointment that never ends.
- **End after**—Ends after a number of occurrences. The default setting is 10 occurrences. To change the setting, enter a number in the number entry field.

■ **End by**—Creates a recurring appointment that ends on a specific date. The default date is 10 weeks after the start date. To change the end date, select a new ending date in the **End by** drop-down.

The recurrence pattern for a weekly recurring appointment enables you to select how often and on which day or days of the week the appointment occurs. To create an appointment that occurs every other week, change the **Recur every** number to **2** in the number entry field. The initial setting for the day of the appointment is the current day. To change the setting or add additional days, check or uncheck the desired days in the day checkboxes.

For this sample appointment, leave the settings as they appear and click **OK** to create the recurrence pattern. This appointment will recur every week on the current day of the week and never stop recurring.

Select **Save and Close** on the toolbar to save the weekly recurring appointment, or select **File**, **Close** and then **No** to close the appointment form without saving the appointment.

> **caution**
>
> If you edit the times or dates of recurring appointments where some of the appointments in the series are in the past, you will change the date/time of the past appointments. To edit one appointment of a recurring series that started in the past, open the appointment you want to change and select **Open this occurrence** and then click **OK**. If you select **Open the series**, any changes you make will change the entire recurring series of appointments.

The next example of a recurring appointment is a monthly recurring appointment. To create one, open a new appointment form by selecting **Actions**, **New Appointment** and enter any necessary information in the appointment form. Open the Appointment Recurrence dialog by selecting **Actions**, **Recurrence** and select the **Monthly** option button. The Appointment Recurrence dialog should now look like the one shown in Figure 7.15.

For this appointment, create a recurrence pattern where the appointment occurs on the third Monday of every other month:

1. Select the second option button for the recurrence pattern.
2. Select **third** in the first drop-down. The available choices are first, second, third, fourth, or last.
3. Select **Monday** in the day drop-down. Note the other choices available; you can select a specific day of the week, day, weekday, or weekend day.
4. In the number entry field, change **1** to **2**.
5. Click **OK** to save the recurrence pattern.

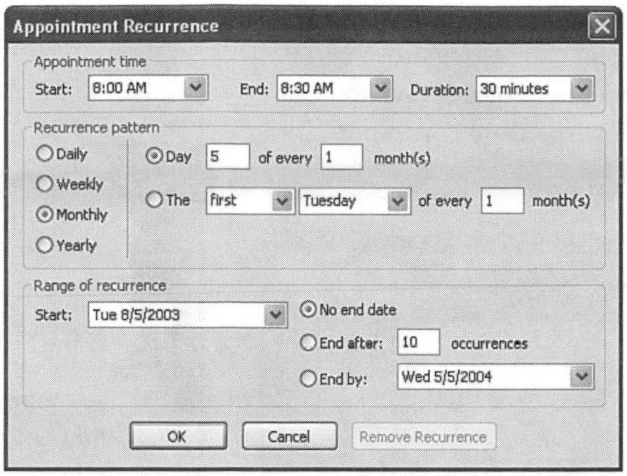

FIGURE 7.15

Recurrence pattern settings for monthly recurrence patterns enable you to select a day of the month or a specific day within the month.

The InfoBar for the appointment now lists the recurrence as occurring every third Monday of every two months.

Select **Save and Close** on the toolbar to save the weekly recurring appointment, or select **File**, **Close** and then **No** to close the appointment form without saving the appointment.

Customizing Recurrence Patterns

Outlook doesn't have settings for creating recurrence pattern exceptions, but you sometimes can create a recurrence pattern with an exception by using a different setting for the recurrence pattern. For example, to create a daily recurrence pattern that occurs every workday except Tuesday, you can use a weekly recurrence pattern. Check every workday and make sure Tuesday is not checked as the day on which the appointment occurs.

Setting exceptions for most weekly, monthly, or yearly appointments usually isn't possible. Take, for example, the day U.S. taxes are due to be filed. This date is usually April 15. The exception is if April 15 falls on a Saturday or Sunday. In that case, taxes are due on the following Monday. There is no way to create this exception in Outlook.

Viewing Tasks in the Calendar

The standard view of the Calendar folder shows the Date Navigator and the selected calendar view. You can also display tasks from your to-do list in the Calendar folder, to present a view that shows things to do in addition to appointments, meetings, and events. The to-do list display is called the TaskPad.

To display the TaskPad in the Calendar, select **View**, **TaskPad**. The Date Navigator moves to the right side of the calendar display, and the TaskPad opens below the Date Navigator, as shown in Figure 7.16.

FIGURE 7.16

The TaskPad view is configurable to show tasks with or without due dates and can be set to show different sets of tasks.

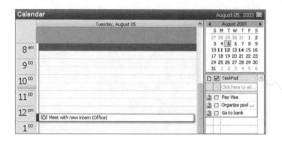

To change which tasks are displayed in the TaskPad, select **View**, **TaskPad View**.

Sending Calendar Information

There are three ways to make calendar information available to other people who don't share your calendar. You can send the calendar information as an Outlook item to someone else who uses Outlook, you can send the information using the iCalendar Internet calendar standard, or you can publish your calendar information as free/busy information on the Internet or a local network. You will learn about publishing free/busy information in Chapter 21.

To send an Outlook appointment, meeting, or event to another Outlook user as an Outlook item, select the item you want to send and select **Actions**, **Forward**. A new e-mail message is opened with the calendar item included as an attachment to the e-mail message. The subject of the e-mail is set to the subject of the calendar item with the forwarding indicator FW: placed at the beginning of the subject. The recipient of the e-mail can open the attachment and save it to add the item to his or her calendar.

To send an Outlook Calendar item using an Internet standard, select **Actions**, **Forward as iCalendar**. An iCalendar item is created as a file with an .ics extension and attached to a new e-mail. The iCalendar item is a text file that can be opened and examined using Notepad or any other text editor. Outlook understands reading this format as well as creating it; opening an iCalendar item creates an Outlook calendar item.

You can also save calendar items using Internet standards as files in the Windows file system. To do so, open an Outlook calendar item, select **File**, **Save As**, and select either **iCalendar Format (*.ics)** or **vCalendar Format (*.vcs)**. The iCalendar format is a later format and can transmit more information than the older vCalendar format. After you select the desired format, select **Save** to save the item as a file.

It's hard to tell when to send a calendar item using the iCalendar format or the vCalendar format. Most modern e-mail software understands the iCalendar format, so try that first. If the recipient tells you his or her software didn't understand the iCalendar format, resend the item using the older vCalendar format.

note

Send Outlook items only to other Outlook users. Other e-mail software cannot understand Outlook items. If the person you want to send an appointment to doesn't use Outlook, send the appointment in the iCalendar format.

Setting Calendar Options

To set calendar options, select **Tools**, **Options** and go to the **Preferences** tab. The calendar options you can set include the default time before an appointment for reminders, the start and end times of your work day, the days of the week you work, and the background color for your calendar display.

Setting Reminder Preferences

Reminders for appointments and meetings are so important that their settings are right on the Preferences tab. Figure 7.17 shows the reminder settings.

Here, you can do the following:

- To enable reminders as a default for all appointments and meetings, check the **Default reminder** checkbox.

- Select the default time a reminder should activate before an appointment or meeting in the time drop-down. The default reminder time for all-day events is always 18 hours before the event begins.

tip

You can also enter a time directly in the time input text box. The input text box understands shorthand such as *m* for minutes, *h* for hours, *d* for days, and *w* for weeks.

FIGURE 7.17

FIGURE 7.17

The calendar reminder options are located on the Preferences tab and set the defaults for all newly created appointments and meetings.

Setting Calendar Options

Select **Calendar Options** on the Preferences tab to open the Calendar Options dialog, as shown in Figure 7.18.

FIGURE 7.18

The Calendar Options dialog enables you to set your workweek as well as set other calendar options.

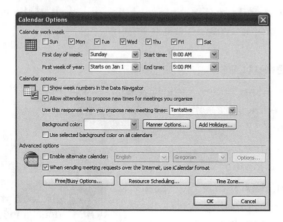

Setting the Calendar Workweek

In the Calendar work week section, select the days for your workweek. Outlook supports setting any days as workdays, but the workweek runs from the starting day to the ending day. Outlook doesn't support gaps in the workweek. For example, if you work from Monday to Saturday, but Thursday isn't a workday, the workweek is still considered to run continuously from Monday to Saturday. The days displayed in Calendar folders for the Work Week view are determined by this setting.

Select the first day of the week and your workday's starting and ending times in the drop-downs. Select the first week of the year from the drop-down; your choices are

- Starts on January 1
- First 4-Day week
- First full week

The First week of the year setting determines which week number is used for the current week. In the Calendar options section, this setting is applied when you check the checkbox to show week numbers in the Date Navigator.

You will learn about the settings for meetings, planner options, free/busy options, and resources scheduling in Chapter 21.

Choosing a Background Color

The background color for your default calendar is selected in the Background color drop-down. By checking the **Use selected background color on all calendars** checkbox, you can make this the default color for all calendar folders.

Adding Holidays to the Calendar

Holidays are automatically installed in Outlook for your selected regional settings. To add holidays for other countries, select **Add Holidays** and check the countries whose holidays you want to add to your calendar. Holidays are also available for Christian, Islamic, and Jewish religious holidays. After you finish adding all the holidays you want, click **OK** to add the new holidays.

Setting an Alternate Calendar

In the Advanced Options section of the Calendar Options dialog, you can enable an alternate calendar, which appears alongside the standard date display in the Calendar folder. When you check the **Enable alternate calendar** checkbox, alternate calendars such as Japanese, Chinese, and Arabic become available. Alternate calendars may have settings such as Lunar, Zodiac, and Gregorian available, and some settings such as English and Arabic Hijiri also have adjustment options provided. If you want to enable an alternate calendar, experiment with the settings in the alternate calendar drop-downs so that the alternate calendar uses the format you want.

Selecting Time Zones

Select **Time Zone** in the lower right of the Advanced options section to set up your primary Outlook time zone and an alternate time zone, as shown in Figure 7.19. You can use alternate time zones to track times in other areas of the world and times when you are traveling. The local time of appointments, meetings, and other time-related items is adjusted when you select an alternate time zone.

Each time zone can have a label identifying the time zone and can be adjusted for daylight saving time based on the daylight saving time dates in the selected time zone. Time zones are selected in the Time zone drop-downs.

FIGURE 7.19

The Time Zone dialog enables travelers to set up alternate time zones.

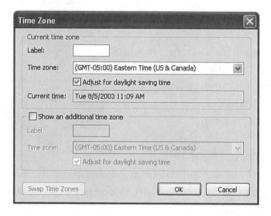

> **caution**
>
> Always check to make sure that the Outlook time zone matches the Windows time zone set in the Control Panel's Date and Time application. You use the Time Zone tab in the Date and Time Properties to select your Windows time zone. If the Windows and Outlook time zones don't match, received e-mails may have the wrong time, and meetings and other events sent over the Internet will have time errors.

If you have more than one time zone defined, you can switch from one to the other as the current time zone by selecting **Swap Time Zones**. When you are finished with the Time Zone settings, click **OK** to save your settings and return to the Calendar Options dialog.

THE ABSOLUTE MINIMUM

In this chapter, you learned about Outlook's calendar features. To review, you now know how to

- Navigate in the calendar by day, week, month, and year.

- Choose and customize the calendar views that are available to display calendar items.

- Create appointments, meetings, and events and schedule them to occur at regular intervals.

- View tasks in the calendar and send calendar information to other people.

- Set preferences and other options for working with the calendar.

With the skills you acquired in this chapter, you can now work efficiently with the Outlook calendar. In the next chapter, you will learn how to work with tasks.

IN THIS CHAPTER

- Working with tasks.
- Editing tasks.
- Assigning and accepting tasks.
- Handling recurring tasks.
- Sharing Tasks folders.

8

TASKS

Outlook tasks are like that to-do list you've been keeping on paper, but with some significant advantages over a paper task list. For one thing, your Outlook tasks are much harder to lose than that paper to-do list. In this chapter, you will learn how to create, use, and assign Outlook tasks.

Working with Tasks

Tasks are chores you have to complete, such as writing a report for work or school, writing a chapter for a book, and mowing the lawn. Just like real tasks, Outlook tasks can be assigned to other people. Of course, the person to whom you assign the task must accept it; otherwise, the task is still your responsibility.

Tasks can recur at regular intervals—for example, paying the rent or mortgage every month before the first day of the following month. You learned about recurring appointments in Chapter 7, "The Calendar," and setting up recurring tasks is similar to setting up recurring appointments.

Many task properties are common to most Outlook items, such as a Notes area for text and to show attachments and a subject, and areas for categories and Contacts links.

Tasks also have the following properties that are useful for managing your to-do list:

- **Start Date**—This property indicates the date the task is started. You don't have to start a task when you create it, and assigning a task a Start Date is optional.

- **Due Date**—This property indicates the date when the task is due to be completed. Tasks do not have a time field, so they become overdue the day after they were due.

- **Status**—This property indicates the current task status, such as Not Started or Completed.

- **Priority**—This setting can be Low, Normal, or High.

- **% Completion**—The range is from 0 to 100%. % Completion is linked to some Status settings; for example, Not Started is linked to 0% Completion.

- **Reminder**—Tasks can be set to display reminders.

- **Private**—The Private checkbox prevents the task from being visible to other people when a Tasks folder is shared with others.

- **Owner**—The owner of a task is assigned when the task is created, and cannot be changed unless the task is assigned to someone else and the person accepts the assignment. In that case, the person assigned the task becomes its owner.

- **Total Work, Actual Work, Mileage, Billing Information**—These text fields can be used for any purpose.

You will learn more about these properties as you work with tasks in this chapter.

Tasks Folders

You can work with tasks in a Tasks folder or in the TaskPad in Calendar folders. You learned about the TaskPad in Chapter 7.

To navigate to a Tasks folder, select the **Tasks** button in the Navigation Pane or select a Tasks folder in the Folder List. You can also navigate to the default Tasks folder by selecting **Go**, **Tasks**.

Figure 8.1 shows an Outlook Tasks folder in the Detailed List view. In the next section, you will learn about the different task views.

FIGURE 8.1

The Detailed List view shows completed tasks using a strikethrough font.

Tasks Folder Views

Outlook provides 10 default views for Tasks folders. You can create new views or customize the default views. (You will learn how to create new views or customize existing views in Chapter 14, "Outlook Views.") The default views provided for the Tasks folder are described in Table 8.1.

Table 8.1 Outlook Tasks Folder Views

View	Shows
Simple List	Table view of all tasks showing completion status, task subject, and due date.
Detailed List	Table view of all tasks showing priority, attachment status, task subject, task status, due date, percentage of completion, and categories.
Active Tasks	Table view of tasks showing priority, attachment status, task subject, task status, due date, percentage of completion, and categories *sorted by due date and showing only tasks that are not completed.*
Next Seven Days	Table view of tasks showing priority, attachment status, task subject, task status, due date, percentage of completion, and categories *sorted by due date and showing only tasks due in the next seven days.* Completed tasks are shown.

Table 8.1 (continued)

View	Shows
Overdue Tasks	Table view of tasks showing priority, attachment status, task subject, task status, due date, percentage of completion, and categories but *showing only tasks that are overdue. Sorted by due date and then by priority.*
By Category	Table view of all tasks showing priority, attachment status, task subject, task status, due date, percentage of completion, and categories *grouped by categories and sorted by due date.* If no category has been assigned a task, it will be grouped in the None category.
Assignment	Table view of tasks showing priority, attachment status, task subject, owner, due date, and task status *showing tasks that have been assigned to other people. Sorted by owner and then by due date.*
By Person Responsible	Table view of all tasks showing priority, attachment status, task subject, person who requested the task, owner, due date, and status *grouped by task owner and sorted by due date.*
Completed Tasks	Table view of all tasks showing priority, attachment status, task subject, person who requested the task, owner, due date, and status *sorted by due date.*
Task Timeline	Timeline view of all tasks showing the start and end dates and task subjects. Start and end dates are shown as bars on the timeline.

Figure 8.2 shows a Task Timeline view indicating at a glance the tasks for a period of time and how much time each task is estimated to require from start to finish.

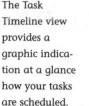

FIGURE 8.2

The Task Timeline view provides a graphic indication at a glance how your tasks are scheduled.

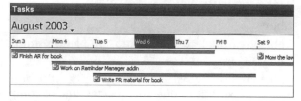

Creating New Tasks

To create a new task no matter what folder you are in, select **New** in the Standard toolbar and then select **Task**. You also can create a new task by pressing **Ctrl+Shift+K**.

What folder new tasks are added to depends on where in Outlook you are when you create the task.

- If you are in a Tasks folder the task is added to that folder.

- If you aren't in a Tasks folder the task is added to your default Tasks folder.

A new task item is created with no start date or due date. When you set a due date for a task, a reminder is automatically set for that task. The reminder defaults to the start of your work day. You learned how to set your work day in the "Setting Calendar Options" section in Chapter 7.

Figure 8.3 shows a task item for a task that is in progress.

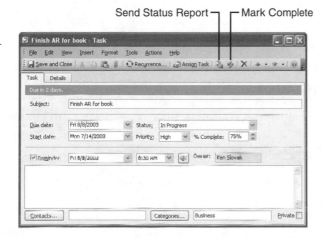

FIGURE 8.3

The InfoBar in the open task shows when the task is due.

Many of the table views of a Tasks folder also enable you to create a new task by clicking in the **Click here to add a new Task** row, as shown in Figure 8.4.

Tasks you create by clicking in the New Task row are not opened to show a task form; you simply add whatever information you want in the fields available in that view. If you want to add additional information to the task, you can open the task for editing after it is created.

You can also create a new task when you are in a Contacts folder. If a contact is selected in a folder view or is open, select **Actions**, **New Task for Contact**. This technique creates a new task with a link to that contact already entered in the Contacts field of the new task. You learned about linking items to contacts in the "Viewing Contact Activities" section of Chapter 6, "Contacts and Address Books." Tasks created in this way are always created in your default Tasks folder.

FIGURE 8.3

FIGURE 8.3

Clicking in the
Click here to
add a new Task
row is an easy
way to create a
new task with-
out opening a
task form.

			Subject	Status	Due Date	% Complete	Categories
			Click here to add a new Task				
			Work on SpamCatcher addin for 1st milst...	Waiting ...	Sat 8/23/2003	50%	Business
			~~Write PR material for book~~	~~Completed~~	~~Sat 8/9/2003~~	~~100%~~	~~Business~~
		!	Finish AR for book	In Progr...	Fri 8/8/2003	75%	Business
			Mow the lawn	Not Sta...	Sat 8/9/2003	0%	Personal

Editing Tasks

When you open a task for editing, it opens to the Task tab, as shown in Figure 8.5.
New tasks have no start and due dates, have a status of Not Started, a Normal priority, and are 0% complete. The task owner is automatically filled in and cannot be
changed unless you assign the task to another person and he or she accepts the task.
You will learn about assigning tasks in the next section of this chapter.

FIGURE 8.5

The Task tab of
a task item con-
tains the task
properties you
will use most
frequently.

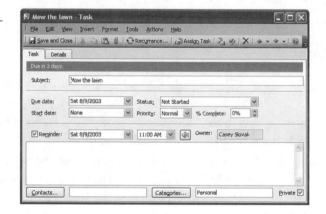

Adding a Subject, Status, and Priority

Use the Subject line to add a subject for the task. If you do not include a subject, you
will see a task in the various views, but you won't be able to tell what the task is
without opening it.

You use the Status and Priority drop-downs to assign a status and priority to a task.
These fields have lists of possible values, which are the only ones you can use. The
default values in the Status and Priority lists cannot be changed. The values available for the status are as follows: Not Started, In Progress, Completed, Waiting on
someone else, and Deferred. The available Priority fields are Low, Normal, and High.

Setting the Task Progress Options

To change the task completion percentage, select the up or down arrows next to the % Complete field. The increments for % Complete are 0%, 25%, 50%, 75%, and 100%. Setting 0% Complete automatically changes the status to Not Started. Setting 25%, 50%, or 75% completion changes the status of the task to In Progress, and setting 100% completion changes the status of the task to Completed. You can also type a number in the % Complete field to set a % Complete value to any value between 0% and 100%; for example, you can type **10** in the field to set a value of 10% completed.

The linking of the Status and % Complete fields works both ways. If you set the status to Not Started, the % Complete field becomes 0% completed. If you set the status to Completed, the % Complete field becomes 100% completed. Setting the status to In Progress, Waiting on Someone Else, or Deferred does not change the % Completed value.

Other ways you can mark a task complete include

- Right-clicking on a task in a folder view and selecting **Mark Complete**
- Clicking in the Status field when it's displayed as a checkbox
- Selecting Complete when Status is displayed as a pop-up list

Setting Dates for Starting and Completing a Task

Most tasks have at least a start or due date, but such a date is not required. Tasks without start or due dates are usually ones that you can start and finish at any time, such as a task for cleaning the attic. If you enter a start or due date for a task, you can select the arrow next to the field to open a drop-down date picker, as shown in Figure 8.6.

Using the date picker to enter a start or due date is the same as using the date picker to enter a start or end date for an appointment, which you learned about in Chapter 7. Click a date, or if the date isn't shown in the date picker, select the left or right arrows in the date picker to change the month shown. Selecting a date closes the date picker and enters that date in the Start Date or Due Date fields.

You can also enter a start or due date directly in the field by entering a date in your standard date format or by typing in a date offset, just as in appointment date fields. You can use one of the many date offsets; Outlook is good about figuring out what the offset really means. The following list shows some of the shortcuts you can enter for date offsets:

- **1d**—Means 1 day from today.
- **1w**—Means 1 week from today.
- **1m**—Means 1 month from today.
- **1y**—Means 1 year from today.

FIGURE 8.6
Using the date
picker makes it
easy to select a
start or due
date.

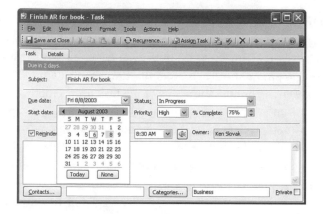

Setting a Reminder for a Task

You can set reminders on tasks, just as you can do
with appointments. For example, you can use task
reminders to remind you to start a task, remind
you about completion milestones for a task, or
remind you when a task is due. Check the
Reminder checkbox to enable a reminder on a
task item, and use the Reminder date picker and
time picker to set when you want the reminder to
fire. Select the **Alarm** icon between the Reminder
Time and Owner fields to open a dialog from
which you can select the sound to play when the
reminder fires.

Reminders for tasks
fire only when the task is
in the default Tasks folder. In
other folders, a task with a
reminder that is due turns red.

Adding Notes and Attachments to a Task

You can enter notes about a task in the Notes field of a task item and can link a task
to one or more contacts by selecting the contact or contacts from the address book
that is displayed when you select the **Contacts** button. You can categorize the task
by typing a category in the Categories field or by selecting the **Categories** button to
open the Categories dialog. To set the privacy of the task, check the Private checkbox
if you want to mark the task as private in a corporate workgroup setting.

You can insert attachments in the Notes field of a task by selecting the appropriate
option from the Insert menu in an open task item. This menu enables you to attach
a file or an Outlook item as an attachment to a task.

Filling in the Details Tab for a Task

The Details tab contains two free-form text fields for entering information: Mileage, and Billing Information. You can use these fields, which can't be renamed, for any information you want (see Figure 8.7). The Companies field is another field where you can enter any information you want.

Two other fields, Total work and Actual work, are free-form time fields. You can use them to track times, and they understand the same shorthand time entries as the ones you learned about in "Setting Dates for Starting and Completing a Task," earlier in this chapter. Company names entered in the Companies field are not checked against companies for your contacts; they are just free-form text.

The Update list field and Create Unassigned Copy button are enabled only for assigned tasks, which you will learn about in the next section.

The Date completed field is linked to the % Complete and Status fields on the Task tab. If you mark a task 100% complete or set its status to Completed, the Date completed field changes to the date the Status or % Complete field was changed to in order to indicate the task was completed. If you use the date picker drop-down to set a completion date for the Date completed field, the Status and % Complete fields change to indicate the task is complete. You can also enter a formatted date or date offset to set a Date completed setting.

FIGURE 8.7

The Details tab of a task contains a number of free-form fields that can contain any text and similar time fields.

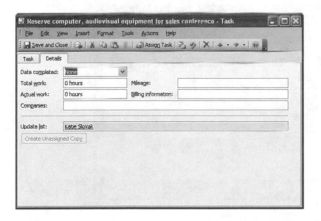

Assigning and Accepting Tasks

You can create a task and assign it to someone else, which is useful not only for business environments where you are part of a workgroup, but also when you are collaborating in any setting with other people. For example, you might be planning a sales conference for your company, and one person is in charge of booking a meeting center and caterer, another person is in charge of computer and audiovisual equipment, and another is in charge of inviting attendees and keeping an attendance roster. The Assigned Tasks feature enables you not only to assign these tasks to other people, but also to receive status reports they send about the tasks so that you can make sure everything is moving smoothly with the sales conference planning.

Assigning a Task to Someone Else

You can assign a task to someone else either by selecting **Actions**, **New Task Request** when in a Tasks folder or by assigning a pre-existing task to someone else. To assign a task that already exists to someone else, open the task and select **Actions**, **Assign Task**. You can also use the **Assign Task** icon on the Standard toolbar in an open task item to assign a task to someone else.

> **tip**
>
> Tasks don't have a time field for their start or due dates. Tasks are due only on a specific day, not at a specific time during the day.
>
> One way to simulate a due time is to use either the Total work or Actual work field.

When you assign a task to someone else, a Task Request form is opened, as shown in Figure 8.8. The Task Request contains all the data in the task item, as well as some additional fields.

FIGURE 8.8

A Task Request form enables you to request updates and status reports on progress toward completion of the task.

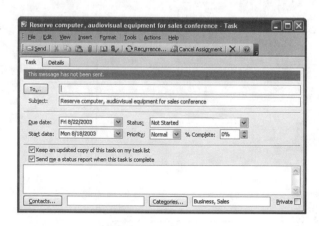

If you decide not to assign the task to someone else, select the **Cancel Assignment** icon on the Standard toolbar in an open Task Request form or select **Actions**, **Cancel Assignment**.

The To field in a Task Request works exactly the same way the To field works in an e-mail item. Use it to enter an e-mail address to send the task assignment to, or select the **To** button to open the Select Task Recipient dialog where you can select a recipient for the task assignment.

The other fields in a Task Request form are checkboxes for keeping an updated copy of the assigned task on your task list and for receiving a status report when the task is completed. If you leave the Keep an updated copy of this task on my task list checkbox unchecked when you assign the task, you will not have a copy of the assigned task and you will not be updated with changes in the task's status. You can still receive a status report when the task is completed even if you don't keep a copy of the assigned task.

After you finish setting the Task Request properties, send it to the person you are assigning it to by selecting the **Send** icon on the Standard toolbar.

Receiving a Task Assignment

When you receive a task assignment in your Inbox, it has two buttons labeled Accept and Decline at the top, as shown in Figure 8.9.

FIGURE 8.9

A received task assignment has voting buttons for accepting or rejecting the task.

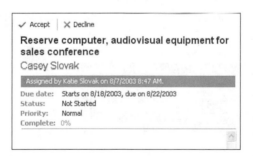

```
✓ Accept   ✕ Decline

Reserve computer, audiovisual equipment for
sales conference
Casey Slovak
Assigned by Katie Slovak on 8/7/2003 8:47 AM.
Due date:   Starts on 8/18/2003, due on 8/22/2003
Status:     Not Started
Priority:   Normal
Complete:   0%
```

Clicking either the Accept or Decline button opens the Accepting Task or Declining Task dialog where you can choose to send the response immediately or to open the response so you can edit it. The Accepting Task dialog is shown in Figure 8.10. The only difference in the Accepting Task and Declining Task dialogs is the title.

If you accept the Task Request, a new task is created in your default Tasks folder and the Task Request is deleted. The task created by accepting the task assignment is shown in a By Person Responsible view in Figure 8.11. If you decline the assigned task, no new task is created and the Task Request is deleted. If a task is declined, the original owner remains the owner of the task. The message accepting or declining the assigned task is saved in your Sent Items folder.

FIGURE 8.10

The Accepting Task dialog enables you to add comments and attachments to the response before sending it.

FIGURE 8.11

Accepting a task assignment creates a new task in your Tasks folder.

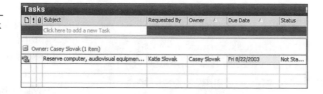

If the person who assigned the task chose to keep a copy of it in his or her Tasks folder, that person will receive an updated copy of the task when it is accepted or declined. The copy of the task is also updated automatically when the status and % Completion properties change. The copy of assigned task will also show when it was accepted and by whom, as you can see in Figure 8.12. Even if you don't keep a copy of the assigned task, you will receive notification when the person assigned the task accepts or declines it.

FIGURE 8.12

Your copy of an assigned task shows when it was accepted and by whom.

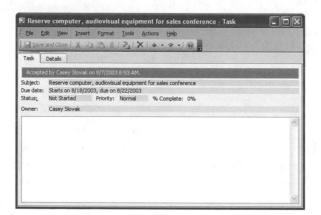

Figure 8.13 shows the copy of the original assigned task kept by the task's creator. The retained copy of the task shows when the last update on the assigned task was received, its current status, Priority and % Complete information, and the owner of the task, who is the person who accepted the assigned task.

If you assign a task to someone else and keep a copy of it in your Tasks folder, you can create an unassigned task from the assigned task by selecting the **Create Unassigned Copy** button in the Details tab of the opened copy of the task. If you create an unassigned copy of the task, the unassigned copy is disconnected from the assigned task, and you will no longer receive updates for the task you assigned. This feature is useful if you no longer want to receive updates when the task's status changes.

FIGURE 8.13

When the assigned task's status changes, your copy is updated automatically.

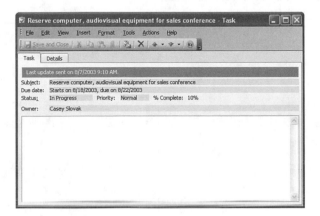

Sending a Task Status Report

At any time after you accept a task, you can choose to send status reports to other people. Open the task and select **Actions**, **Send Status Report** to send a report to the person who assigned the task or to anyone else. When you open the status report, it is already addressed to the person who assigned the task, but you can add other recipients for the status report or remove the original recipient and send the report to anyone you choose.

Figure 8.14 shows the task status report as it is received by the person who created and assigned the task.

Status of a Completed Task

If you have accepted a task assignment and open the task and view the Details tab, you will see that the Update List field now shows the person who assigned the task as a recipient of updates. If the person who assigned the task checked the setting to receive a status report when the task is complete,

tip

You can also send a status report from an updated task that was assigned to someone else. If you assign a task and receive a status report on that assigned task, you can send a report on the updated task to another person. This capability is useful if you want to update a manager on the task's status without having the new owner of the task directly report to that manager.

he or she will automatically receive a status report at that time; you do not have to manually send a status report to let that person know the task was completed.

If the person who assigned the task chose to keep a copy of it in his or her Tasks folder, the completed task will automatically be marked complete in his or her Tasks folder when you mark the task complete in your Tasks folder.

FIGURE 8.14

A task status report informs the person who assigned the task how work on the task is progressing.

Task Status Report: Reserve computer, audiovisual equipment for sales conference

Casey Slovak

To: Katie Slovak

I started it this morning, there should be no problems reserving the equipment.

Casey

Subject:	Reserve computer, audiovisual equipment
for sales conference	
Start date:	Mon 8/18/2003
Due date:	Fri 8/22/2003
Status:	In Progress
% Complete:	10%
Total work:	0 hours
Actual work:	0 hours
Requested by:	Katie Slovak

Handling Recurring Tasks

You learned about recurrences in Chapter 7 when you learned how to create recurring appointments. Recurring tasks are similar to recurring appointments. Recurring tasks are scheduled at regular intervals: daily, weekly, monthly, or yearly. An example of a recurring monthly task is paying a utility or phone bill every month.

Unlike recurring appointments, recurring tasks are visible only one at a time. All instances of a recurring appointment are shown in the calendar, but only one instance of a recurring task is shown in the Tasks folder or the TaskPad in the calendar at a time. Recurring tasks can be assigned to other people the same way individual tasks are assigned to other people.

To create a recurring task, create a new task or open an existing task, and select **Actions**, **Recurrence** to open the Task Recurrence dialog. Another way to open the Task Recurrence dialog in an open task is to click the **Recurrence** icon on the Standard toolbar. Figure 8.15 shows the Task Recurrence dialog with daily recurrence selected.

FIGURE 8.15

Using the Task
Recurrence dia-
log is similar to
setting a recur-
rence for an
appointment.

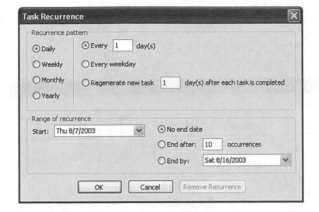

Table 8.2 shows the settings available for tasks that recur on a daily basis.

Table 8.2   Daily Recurring Task Settings

Setting	Effect
Every 1 day	Enter the interval in days for the task to recur.
Every weekday	No interval entry is required; the task recurs every weekday. (You learned how to define weekdays in the Calendar Options dialog in Chapter 7.)
Regenerate New Task	Enter an interval for the task to be regenerated after the original task is marked complete. This option creates a new task with the original recurrence settings after the previous task is marked complete.
Start	Select a start date for the recurring task. Recurring tasks must have a start date.
No end date	No entry is required; the task recurrence never ends.
End after X occurrences	Enter the number of recurring task events to create.
End by	Select a date the set of recurring tasks ends.

You can select only one of the recurrence pattern settings and one of the range settings. Click **OK** to create a recurring task with the selected settings.

Setting a Weekly, Monthly, or Yearly Recurrence Pattern

The settings for weekly, monthly, and yearly recurring tasks are similar to the settings for daily recurring tasks. Figure 8.16 shows the available settings for a task that
recurs on a weekly basis.

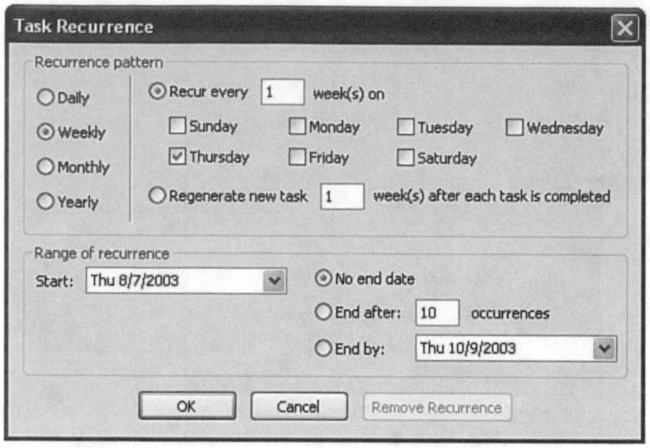

FIGURE 8.16

A weekly recurrence pattern can be used for tasks that recur more than once during the week.

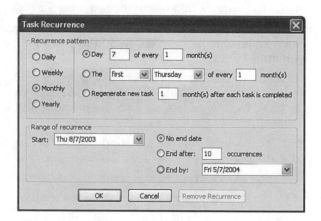

The weekly recurrence settings enable you to select on which day of the week the task recurs. Select one or more days of the week on which the task recurs or select to regenerate the task at a weekly interval after the preceding task is marked complete.

Settings for monthly recurring tasks are shown in Figure 8.17.

FIGURE 8.17

A monthly recurrence pattern can be used to set a task to recur at intervals of more than one month.

Monthly task recurrence settings enable you to set the task to occur on a specific day of the month every month, at an interval such as the last weekday of every month or the third Friday of every three months, or to regenerate the task at a monthly interval after the preceding task is marked complete.

Settings for tasks that recur on a yearly basis are similar to monthly recurring task settings. The available settings for yearly recurring tasks are shown in Figure 8.18. Yearly tasks can recur on a specific date such as July 3, or using a setting such as the first Monday of every August.

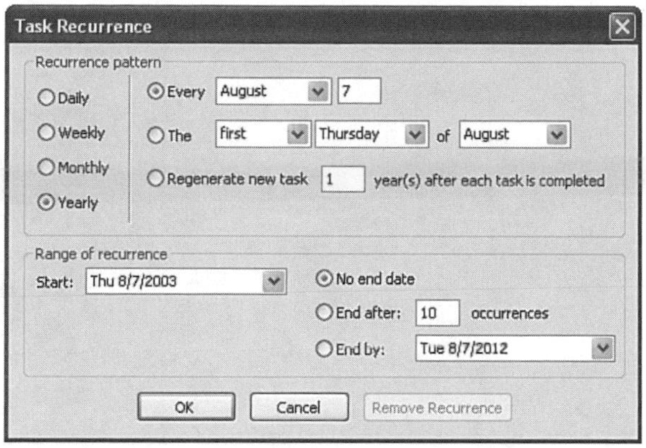

FIGURE 8.18

The Task Recurrence dialog with a yearly recurrence pattern.

Skipping or Canceling Recurring Tasks

You can skip an occurrence of a recurring task by opening the task and selecting **Actions**, **Skip Occurrence**. If you skip an occurrence of a recurring task, the following task in the series is generated. If a recurring task is set to occur a specific number of times, skipping an occurrence of the task counts as one of the task occurrences.

To cancel a recurrence pattern for a recurring task, open the task and then open the Task Recurrence dialog. Next, select the **Remove Recurrence** button and then click **OK** to clear the recurrence pattern for that task and convert it into a task that occurs only one time.

THE ABSOLUTE MINIMUM

In this chapter, you learned about Outlook tasks. To review, you now know how to

- Create and edit tasks.
- Set a reminder alert for a task.
- Assign tasks to other people and accept task assignments.
- Send a task status report.
- Create recurring tasks with daily, weekly, monthly, or yearly recurrences.

With the skills you acquired in this chapter, you can now use Outlook tasks to organize your to-do list electronically. In the next chapter, you will learn how to work with the Outlook Journal and Notes.

IN THIS CHAPTER

- Using the Journal to track your activities.
- Using Journal entries to time your work.
- Organizing the Journal using categories.
- Using and organizing Outlook Notes.

9

THE JOURNAL AND NOTES

The Journal is your Outlook diary, which is used for tracking and timing activities such as sending and receiving e-mails, working in Microsoft Office applications, and making phone calls. Outlook Notes are the electronic equivalent of paper "sticky" notes and are used to jot down information. In this chapter, you will learn how to use both as part of your Outlook information management tools.

Using the Journal

The Outlook Journal is the equivalent of an electronic diary. Some of its uses are to track your work with other Office applications, log phone calls, log e-mails to and from selected recipients, and time various activities.

Journal entries can be forwarded, just like any other Outlook item. Select **Actions**, **Forward** to open an e-mail message with the selected Journal entry attached to the e-mail. The **Forward** action is also available on the context menu when you right-click a Journal entry.

By default, the Journal folder isn't shown in the list of buttons in the Navigation Pane. To navigate to the Journal folder, open the Folder List in the Navigation Pane and select the Journal folder. Another way to navigate to the Journal folder is to select **Go**, **Journal**.

The first time you select the Journal folder, the dialog shown in Figure 9.1 is displayed.

> **tip**
>
> To show the Journal button in the Navigation Pane, select the **Configure Buttons** icon, shown as a double right arrow; select **Add or Remove Buttons;** and then select **Journal** on the button's fly-out menu.

FIGURE 9.1

The Enable Journaling dialog opens the Journal Options dialog if you select Yes.

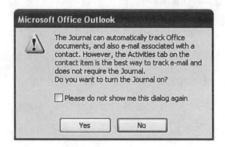

You can enable the Journal from this dialog and also set the dialog so that it is never shown again. If you select Yes, the Journal Options dialog is opened so that you can select which activities are journaled. You can also open the Journal Options dialog by selecting **Tools**, **Options** and clicking the **Journal Options** button.

Journaling Your Activities

The settings in the Journal Options dialog for automatic journaling are divided into two groups. The first group is for automatic journaling of various activities; the second group is for automatic journaling of work with files for various applications, as shown in Figure 9.2.

FIGURE 9.2

The Journal
Options dialog
enables you to
set contacts and
applications to
be journaled.

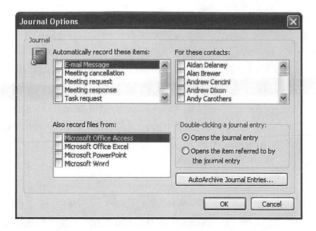

The activities you can journal automatically are

- E-mail messages
- Meeting cancellations
- Meeting requests
- Meeting responses
- Task requests
- Task responses

These activities are journaled only for selected contacts. Check the activities you want journaled and then check the contacts you want to enable for journaling of the selected activities. You must individually check each contact; there is no provision for checking all contacts at once. If you create new contacts you want journaled, return to this dialog and check those contacts to enable them for automatic journaling.

To enable journaling of each file you work with in an Office application, check that application in the list of applications. The applications you can journal include

- Microsoft Access
- Microsoft Excel
- Microsoft PowerPoint
- Microsoft Word
- Microsoft Project
- Microsoft Visio

Other applications may also be available in the application list if those programs are written to support Outlook journaling or if add-ins are available to add journaling to those applications. One example of an application that can provide journaling through an add-in is AutoCAD, the well-known computer-assisted design program.

Select how you want a Journal entry to open when double-clicked in a folder view. The default setting, Opens the Journal entry, opens the Journal entry with a link to the Office file in the body of the Journal item. Selecting the option **Opens the item referred to by the journal entry** opens the Office file when the Journal item tracking work in that file is double-clicked.

The AutoArchive Journal Entries button opens a dialog for setting archive options for the Journal folder. You will learn about archiving in Chapter 13, "Archiving Data."

When you are satisfied with the settings in the Journal Options dialog, click **OK** to save the journaling settings. After setting the activities and applications to journal, you need to exit Outlook and start it again to activate the automatic journaling.

Creating Journal Items

When you work in an application that supports journaling and Outlook isn't open, the application writes your activities in the application to a Journal log file. When you start Outlook, the Journal log file is read and new Journal entries are automatically created. Journal entries for supported applications track the start and end times you worked with the file and attach a link to the journaled file in the Journal item.

Figure 9.3 shows a Journal entry automatically created for work with a Microsoft Word file.

FIGURE 9.3

A Journal entry for a Microsoft Word file showing when the file was worked on.

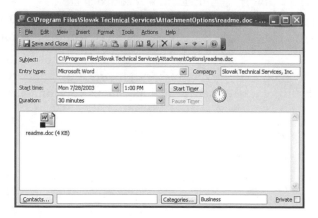

The Journal entry shown in Figure 9.3 has a shortcut attachment to the Word file that opens the Word document. To open that attached file shortcut, either double-click it or right-click it and select **Open** from the context menu.

To manually create a new Journal entry, select **Actions**, **New Journal Entry** when you are in a Journal folder.

Automatic journaling for contacts works only for e-mails; meeting cancellations, requests, and responses; and task requests and responses. You can manually open a new Journal entry already linked to a contact in two ways:

- Select a contact in a Contacts folder and select **Actions**, **New Journal Entry for Contact**. This action creates a Journal entry with the contact name in the Subject field and the contact's company name in the Company field. The contact is linked to the Contacts field of the Journal entry, and the current time is placed in the Start Time field.

- Select a contact in a Contacts folder and select **Actions**, **Call Contact** and one of the call options on the Call Contact fly-out menu. When the New Call dialog opens, check the **Create new Journal Entry when starting new call** checkbox, as shown in Figure 9.4. The Journal entry is created when the call is started and already has the contact and company names filled in, with a link to the contact in the Contacts field. The time the call was started is placed in the Start Time field.

note

You can link manual Journal entries to contacts by selecting the **Contacts** button in an open Journal entry and selecting one or more contacts in the Select Contacts dialog. Click **OK** to close the Select Contacts dialog and add the link. Journal entries linked to a contact can be viewed in the contact's Activities tab using the Journal or All Items views.

FIGURE 9.4

The New Call dialog enables you to create a Journal entry already filled in with the call time and contact information.

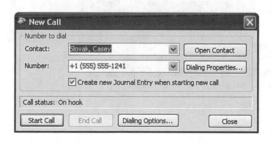

When you create a new Journal entry, the default entry type is a phone call. Click in the **Entry type** drop-down to display a list of the Journal entry types you can select. The new Journal entry displays the current date and time as the **Start time**. You can use the date and time pickers to select a different starting date and time, or you can type a start date and time in the Date and Time fields.

The list of Journal entry types you see depends on which applications you have installed and whether custom Journal entry types have been created. The list of entry types is kept in the Windows Registry, and advanced users or custom applications can create new Journal entry types for you.

Organizing Journal Items

You can use categories to group your Journal entries. If you create a custom category named Wedding, for example, you can use the By Category view to group all your wedding Journal entries together. This way, you can easily see all the phone calls, faxes, conversations, and other activities you have journaled, grouped in one place. To change to a By Categories view, select **View**, **Arrange By**, **Current View**, **By Category**. Figure 9.5 shows a timeline view of a Journal folder using a By Categories view to group all the journaled activities together.

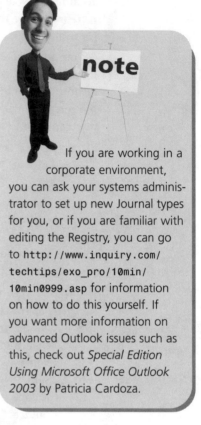

If you are working in a corporate environment, you can ask your systems administrator to set up new Journal types for you, or if you are familiar with editing the Registry, you can go to http://www.inquiry.com/techtips/exo_pro/10min/10min0999.asp for information on how to do this yourself. If you want more information on advanced Outlook issues such as this, check out *Special Edition Using Microsoft Office Outlook 2003* by Patricia Cardoza.

FIGURE 9.5

The By Category view uses categories to group Journal entries, making it easy to see related Journal entries.

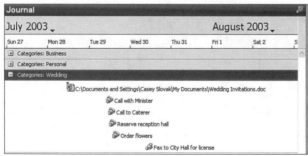

Timing Things

In many types of jobs, such as sales, you need to track how much time you spend on various activities, such as the time spent on business calls or answering e-mails. Journal entries are ideal for this purpose because they have Start Timer and Pause Timer controls that can be used to track elapsed time.

To time an activity using a Journal entry, open a new or existing Journal entry and select the **Start Timer** button. Minimize the Journal entry and start the activity you want to time. You can also make notes about a phone conversation or other activity in the notes field of the Journal item to document the activity or to remind you of details about the activity. To stop the timer, select the **Pause Timer** button. When you save and close the Journal entry, the elapsed time you worked on the activity is automatically written to the Duration field of the Journal entry.

A Journal entry form with the timer controls is shown in Figure 9.6.

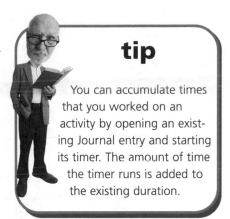

tip

You can accumulate times that you worked on an activity by opening an existing Journal entry and starting its timer. The amount of time the timer runs is added to the existing duration.

FIGURE 9.6

Timer controls on a Journal entry enable you to track elapsed time spent on an activity.

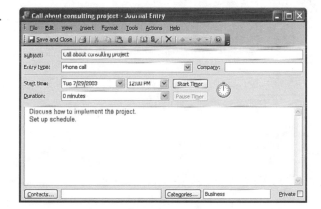

Using Outlook Notes

Outlook Notes are the equivalent of those paper sticky notes that can be found everywhere sticking to any available surface. Notes are used to jot down information or ideas you want to save, and provide a place to store information that doesn't belong in e-mails or other Outlook items. I use Notes to store information I want to remember for books, articles, and projects, and for ideas to research.

To create an Outlook Note like the one shown in Figure 9.7, select **Actions**, **New Note** when you are in a Notes folder. You also can create a Note by dragging an e-mail into a Notes folder, which autocreates a new note. The Note contains the sender, recipient, subject, and text of the original e-mail.

FIGURE 9.7
Outlook Notes
are useful
for storing
information.

7/29/2003 1:34 PM

The Notes Menu

Notes provide space for you to enter any text and have a time/date stamp showing when the Note was created or last modified. If you click the page icon at the top left of an open Note, a menu opens, as shown in Figure 9.8. From this menu, you can set the Note's color, its Contacts field to link the Note to a contact, and its Categories field.

FIGURE 9.8
You can use the
Notes menu to
set a Note's color
and categories
and to link a
Note to contacts.

Changing Color and Adding Categories

A Note is usually yellow, although you can change the default color in the Notes options, which you will learn about later in this chapter. To change a Note's color, open the Notes menu and select **Color**, and then select one of the following colors:

- **Blue**
- **Green**
- **Pink**
- **Yellow**
- **White**

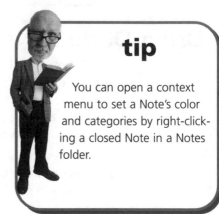

tip

You can open a context menu to set a Note's color and categories by right-clicking a closed Note in a Notes folder.

Using colors with Notes can help you to organize them into groups. You can set the view of a Notes folder to By Color to view the Notes grouped by color, as shown in Figure 9.9.

FIGURE 9.9

Notes grouped by color.

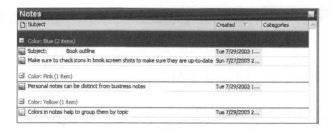

You can also use categories to group your Notes. If you create Notes that are assigned to the Business and Personal categories, you could use the By Category view to group all your business and personal Notes together.

To set a Note's categories, open the Notes menu and select **Categories** to open the Categories dialog, shown in Figure 9.10. Check one or more categories and click **OK** to add the categories to the Note.

FIGURE 9.10

Notes can be grouped by assigning them categories.

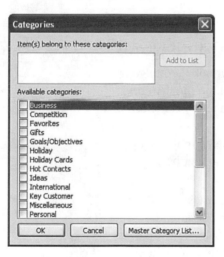

Linking Notes to Contacts

Notes can be linked to contacts, which enables viewing all Notes related to the contact in the contact's Activities tab. To link a Note to a contact, follow these steps:

1. Open the Notes menu by clicking on the page icon at the top left of an open Note.

2. Select **Contacts** to open the Contacts for Note dialog, shown in Figure 9.11.

FIGURE 9.11

Notes can be linked to contacts so all Notes related to the contact can be viewed in the Activities tab of the contact.

3. Select **Contacts** and choose one or more contacts from the Select Contacts dialog.

4. Click **OK** to add the selected contacts to the Note's Contacts field.

5. Click **Close** to close the Contacts for Note dialog.

You can view notes linked to a contact in the contact's Activities tab by selecting the Notes or All Items views.

Moving, Copying, and Forwarding Notes

You can copy or move any Outlook item to your Windows desktop by right-clicking the item and dragging it to the desktop. When the context menu opens, select whether to copy or move the item to the desktop. If you move the item, it will exist only on the desktop; it will no longer be available in the Notes folder.

Copying items to the desktop is most useful with Notes. If you copy a Note to the desktop, it becomes almost like a paper sticky note, an ever-present reminder about something. If the text of the Note is short enough, all of it is displayed, as shown in Figure 9.12.

Notes can be forwarded, just like any other Outlook item. To do so, select **Actions**, **Forward** to open an e-mail message with the selected Note attached to the e-mail. The **Forward** action is also available on the context menu when you right-click a Note.

note

The context menu opened by right-clicking on a Note does not enable you to set the Note's Contacts field. The only way to set a Note's Contacts field is to click the paper icon at the top left of an open Note.

tip

Notes that are placed on the desktop will appear even if Outlook isn't open. Opening a Note on the desktop to read it will start Outlook so that the Note can be opened.

FIGURE 9.12

A Note can be placed on the Windows desktop where it is always available.

Setting Notes Options

To set the default appearance of Notes, select **Tools**, **Options** and click the **Notes Options** button to open the Notes Options dialog, shown in Figure 9.13.

Select the default color, size, and font used for Notes; then click **OK** to create all new notes with those settings.

One other Notes option is available, located in a different location in the Options dialog. Select **Tools**, **Options** and click the **Other** tab and then **Advanced Options**. In the Appearance options section, check **When viewing Notes, show time and date** to display the time and date a Note was created or modified. The date and time are displayed at the bottom of the Note when it is opened.

FIGURE 9.13

In the Notes Options dialog, you can set the default color, size, and font of Outlook Notes.

THE ABSOLUTE MINIMUM

In this chapter, you learned about the Outlook Journal and Notes. To review, you now know how to

- Journal and time your activities.

- Automatically journal work with other Office applications.

- Organize Journal entries using categories.

- Use Outlook Notes to jot down information.

- Organize Notes using colors and categories.

With the skills you acquired in this chapter, you now know how to work with Outlook Journal items and Notes. In the next chapter, you will learn how to work with Outlook folders.

PART IV

MAKING OUTLOOK WORK FOR YOU

IN THIS CHAPTER

- Understanding Outlook's default folders.

- Learning how to create folders and sub-folders.

- Learning to move, copy, and rename folders.

- Knowing how to delete folders.

- Understanding how to recover deleted folders and items with Exchange server.

10

USING FOLDERS

Throughout this book, you have been working with items in different Outlook folders such as Inbox and Contacts, and now you will learn how to work with the folders themselves. In this chapter, you will learn how to create, copy, move, and delete folders to organize how you work with Outlook.

Working with Outlook's Default Folders

Outlook automatically creates a set of default folders for your default data file. This data file is either a PST file or an Exchange mailbox. Each of these default folders holds certain types of items and is used for a specific purpose. You can also create your own folders, which will be described in the section "Creating Folders and Subfolders," later in this chapter. Table 10.1 shows the default folders and what they are used for. You can't delete, rename, or move Outlook's default folders.

Table 10.1 Outlook Default Folders

Folder Name	Folder Use
Outlook Today	Special display folder
Calendar	Appointments, meetings, and events
Contacts	Contact items and distribution lists
Deleted Items	Temporary storage for deleted items and folders
Drafts	Saved e-mails that have not been sent
Inbox	Incoming items
Journal	Journal entries
Junk E-Mail	E-mail items flagged as junk or spam
Notes	Outlook notes
Outbox	Items waiting to be sent
Sent Items	Sent e-mail items
Tasks	To-do list items

Outlook also creates three default search folders, and you can create your own search folders. Search folders are described in Chapter 5, "Search Folders." The three default search folders are

- For Follow Up
- Large Mail
- Unread Mail

Each folder can contain only certain types of Outlook items. If you place an e-mail item in a Calendar folder, it is automatically converted into an appointment. If you drag an e-mail to a Contacts folder, a new contact is created, with the e-mail address filled in. The name is also filled in if it's available in the original e-mail item. This process of Outlook converting items into the default type for the folder is called the *AutoCreate* function.

All Outlook folders are defined by the type of item they contain, as you can see in the list that follows. You can create many different Calendar or other types of folders and name those folders whatever you want, but they can contain only items specific to that folder type. You cannot create other types of folders in Outlook. Certain programs can create special folders in Outlook, but this procedure is not something you can do yourself.

- Calendar Items
- Contact Items
- Journal Items
- Mail and Post Items
- Note Items
- Task Items

Creating Folders and Subfolders

Outlook folders are a lot like the folders in the Windows file system. A folder in Outlook can have subfolders under it, and subfolders can also have their own subfolders. The main differences between Outlook folders and Windows folders are that Outlook folders can contain only certain types of items, based on the folder type, and all Outlook folders are within the Outlook data store and are not available outside the Outlook data file.

You can create very complex arrangements of folders that suit your needs and the way you want to store things in Outlook. Figure 10.1 shows an arrangement of folders and subfolders in the Folder List.

Custom folders are a great way to organize items in Outlook. Figure 10.1 shows a Family E-mails folder that is on the same level as Outlook's default folders. Other custom folders are shown as subfolders of some of the default folders—for example:

- Casey's Appointments is a subfolder of the Calendar folder.
- Church Contacts and Personal Contacts are subfolders of the Contacts folder.

You can also create subfolders for custom folders that you create. Hierarchies of folders and subfolders help you organize items in logical groupings.

If you're planning a wedding, for example, you might set up a mail folder named Wedding to

tip

You can also open the Create New Folder dialog by selecting **New, Folder** in the Standard toolbar, or by right-clicking on a folder in the Navigation Pane and selecting **New Folder.** By default, a new folder of the same type as the folder you right-clicked will be created. It will reside as a subfolder to the selected folder.

hold all correspondence related to the wedding. Under that folder you might create a Wedding Tasks folder, a Wedding Calendar folder, and a Wedding Notes folder to organize a to-do list, appointments and meetings, and notes about the wedding. Everything related to the wedding would be grouped in these folders so that you can easily find it when needed. Figure 10.2 shows the set of folders used to organize the wedding planning.

FIGURE 10.1

Custom folders and subfolders shown in this Folder List. The Calendar and Contact subfolders have custom names but still contain only the item type for which they are created.

To create a new folder, follow these steps:

1. Select **File**, **New**, **Folder** to open the Create New Folder dialog, as shown in Figure 10.3.

2. Type a name for your new folder in the **Name** text box.

3. Select a folder type from the **Folder contains** drop-down list. Your choices are

   - Calendar Items
   - Contact Items
   - Journal Items
   - Mail and Post Items
   - Note Items
   - Task Items

4. Select where you want to place the folder. The folder you select will be the parent folder for the new subfolder. To create a new top-level folder, select **Personal Folders** (or **Mailbox** if you are using Exchange).

5. Click **OK** to create the new folder or **Cancel** to close the Create New Folder dialog without creating a new folder.

FIGURE 10.2

The Wedding
folders.

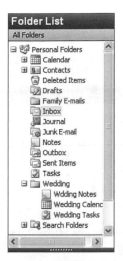

tip

You can have more than
65,000 folders and subfolders in Outlook, so for all
practical purposes, there is
no limit to the number of
folders you can create.

FIGURE 10.3

The Create New
Folder dialog
enables you to
choose the types
of items your
folder will con-
tain and select
where in the
Folder List the
custom folder
should appear.

Moving, Copying, and Renaming Folders

If you create a folder and later decide you want to place it in a different location,
you can move the folder to wherever you want it relocated. You can also copy a
folder and all its contents to a new location, and you can rename a folder if you
decide you don't like its original name. However, you can't move, copy, or rename
any of the default Outlook folders.

To move or copy a folder, follow these steps:

1. Select the folder as the current folder. You can select the folder in the
   Navigation Pane's Folder List or in one of the groupings such as Mail in the
   Navigation Pane.

2. Select **File**, **Folder**, **Mo_v_e _foldername_** or **_C_opy _foldername_**, where _foldername_ is the name of the folder you want to move or copy. Figure 10.4 shows the Folder menu.

3. The Move Folder and Copy Folder dialogs are identical, except for their titles. Copying a folder to a new location leaves the folder you are copying in its original location and creates a copy of the folder and all its contents in the new location. The Move Folder dialog enables you to move the selected folder and its contents from its current location to the new location that you specify (see Figure 10.5).

tip

After you create a folder, if you decide that it is the wrong type, you must delete it and create a new folder. You can't change the folder type for an existing Outlook folder.

FIGURE 10.4

The Folder menu gives you immediate access to all the ways you can manipulate folders in Outlook.

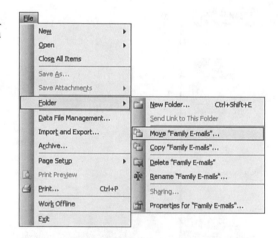

FIGURE 10.5

The Move Folder dialog enables you to specify a new location for the selected folder.

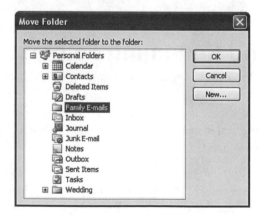

4. Select where you want the new folder to be placed and then click **OK** to move (or copy) the folder to its new location, or select **Cancel** to cancel the move or copy operation. The source folder (the folder you are moving or copying) is placed under the target folder (the location you select) as a subfolder of the target folder.

5. If you want to move or copy the folder to a location under a folder that doesn't exist yet, click the **New** button to open the Create New Folder dialog and create the new folder. Click **OK** to create the new folder and close the Create New Folder dialog and return to the Move Folder or Copy Folder dialog. After you create the new folder, you can select it as the target for the folder move or copy operation.

To rename a folder, choose **File**, **Folder** to open the Folder menu, or open the folder context menu as shown in the preceding steps and select **Rename foldername**. Type a new name for the folder and press **Enter** to rename the folder or **Escape** to cancel the renaming process.

tip

You can also right-click on a folder in the Folder List or in a folder group in the Navigation Pane and select **Move foldername** or **Copy foldername** to open the Move Folder or Copy Folder dialog.

tip

Another way to move or copy a folder is to right-click the folder in the Navigation Pane and drag it to the location where you want it copied or moved. A context menu will open, giving you the choice of moving or copying the folder to the new location when you release the right mouse button.

Deleting and Undeleting Items and Folders

When you delete an item, it is placed in the Deleted Items folder. When you delete a folder, it is placed as a subfolder of the Deleted Items folder. The exception to this rule occurs when you delete an item or folder using the key combination **Shift+Delete**. This is known as a *hard delete*, and items deleted this way usually cannot be recovered.

You can delete something in many ways in Outlook. The following list shows different ways you can delete an item or folder:

- Press the **Delete** key.
- Click the delete symbol in the Standard toolbar.
- Select **Edit**, **Delete**.

- Press the key combination **Ctrl+D**.
- Right-click on an item or folder and select **Delete** from the context menu.
- In an open item, select **File**, **Delete** or press the key combination **Ctrl+D**.

If you change your mind about deleting an item or folder, you can select it and drag it back to where you want it if it is still in the Deleted Items folder. If you empty the Deleted Items folder manually or automatically when you close Outlook, the items and folders in the Deleted Items folder are gone forever in most cases.

Recovering Deleted Folders and Items with Exchange Server

You can recover folders or items that have been deleted and removed from the Deleted Items folder only if you are using Exchange server and the administrator has enabled deleted items recovery for your mailbox. Deleted items recovery keeps a record of items deleted for a period set by the administrator—for example, five days. During that period, a deleted item can be recovered, even an item that was hard-deleted using **Shift+Delete**.

To use deleted items recovery, follow these steps:

1. Navigate to the Deleted Items folder by clicking the **Mail** button in the Navigation Pane and selecting the **Deleted Items** folder.

2. Select **Tools**, **Recover Deleted Items**. The Recover Deleted Items dialog opens, as shown in Figure 10.6.

3. Select the folder, item, or items you want to recover and click the **Recover Selected Items** icon shown in Figure 10.6. If you want to recover everything that can be undeleted, click the **Select All** icon. If you click the **Purge Selected Items** icon, any selected items are purged completely and are gone forever.

4. The Recover Deleted Items dialog will close, and the recovered folder, item, or items will be placed in the Deleted Items folder.

tip

Some people use the Deleted Items folder as a storage and archiving location, which is a very bad idea. It's far too easy to clear out the Deleted Items folder (or forget you enabled the feature to clear the folder when Outlook closes) and then realize you needed an item that was just permanently deleted.

If you want to store items, either create a custom folder for storage (you could name it Storage) to keep the items online or use Outlook's archiving to move the items offline. Store items offline when you don't need to use them very often and store them online when you need frequent access to them. Archiving is covered in Chapter 13, "Archiving Data."

FIGURE 10.6

The Recover
Deleted Items
dialog.

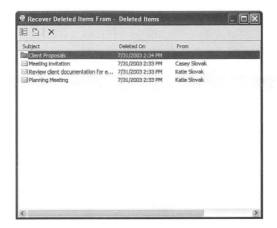

THE ABSOLUTE MINIMUM

Outlook uses folders to organize items of the same type in one location. Using the default Outlook folders, creating custom folders, and organizing folders in a meaningful hierarchy are basic to working with Outlook. In this chapter, you learned how to

- Use the default Outlook folders.

- Create new folders and locate them where you want using the Create New Folder dialog.

- Organize folders in hierarchies.

- Move, copy, and rename folders.

- Delete items and folders.

- Recover deleted folders and items if you are using Exchange Server with deleted item recovery enabled.

In the next chapter, you will learn how to customize the Navigation Pane, which enables you to organize groups of folders and navigate around the Outlook folder structure.

- Learning how to use the Navigation Pane.
- Understanding Favorite Folders.
- Working with the Shortcuts Pane.

11

CUSTOMIZING THE NAVIGATION PANE

In previous chapters, you used the Navigation Pane to move from folder to folder and display different folders. You even learned a little about customizing the Navigation Pane when you learned how to add the Journal button in the Navigation Pane in Chapter 9, "The Journal and Notes." In this chapter, you will learn more about using and customizing the Navigation Pane and how it can make working in Outlook easier.

Working with the Navigation Pane

The Navigation Pane is Outlook's all-purpose navigation tool. It enables you to move from folder to folder and display groups of folders such as Mail or Calendar folders. The Navigation Pane is also used to show shortcuts you create to folders and to display folder views and commands for working with folders. Figure 11.1 shows the Navigation Pane displaying the Folder List, which shows all your Outlook folders.

FIGURE 11.1

The Navigation Pane displays folder groups and can be configured to show folder views.

This illustration of the Navigation Pane shows the Outlook folders in the Folder List at the top of the Navigation Pane, the available views for the current folder below the Folder List, the Mail and Calendar folder group buttons, and the Navigation Pane button bar at the bottom of the Navigation Pane.

When you click a Navigation Pane button that represents a certain type of folder, all folders that contain that type of Outlook item are shown in the Navigation Pane. For example, clicking the Calendar button reveals all Calendar folders—the default Outlook Calendar folder as well as any custom Calendar folders you have created. There are also special Navigation Pane buttons for shortcuts and the Folder List, which shows all your Outlook folders. Customizing the Shortcuts pane is described later in this chapter.

Table 11.1 shows the available Navigation Pane buttons.

Table 11.1 Navigation Pane Buttons

Button	Displays
Mail	E-mail and search folders, Favorite Folders
Calendar	Calendar folders
Contacts	Contacts folders
Tasks	Tasks folders
Notes	Notes folders
Folder List	All folders
Shortcuts	Folder shortcuts
Journal	Journal folders

The button bar in the Navigation Pane displays all the visible buttons that aren't shown as larger, separate buttons. The greater the screen area Outlook has to work with, the more buttons it displays in the Navigation Pane. When it has less screen area available, Outlook displays fewer separate buttons and puts more of the visible buttons on the button bar. So, one way to display more buttons in the Navigation Pane is to maximize the Outlook window.

> **tip**
>
> All the available Navigation Pane buttons may not be shown as separate buttons or be on the button bar. By default, the Journal button isn't shown. You can configure which buttons you want to be shown. You will learn how to customize which buttons are shown in the Navigation Pane later in this chapter.

To change the number of buttons shown in the Navigation Pane, follow these steps:

1. Click to open the **Configure Buttons** menu at the bottom of the Navigation Pane. You open the Configure Buttons menu by clicking the last button on the button bar (which looks like a double right arrow above a down arrow).

2. The Configure Buttons menu opens, as shown in Figure 11.2.

3. Click **Show More Buttons** to show one more button in the Navigation Pane. Click **Show Fewer Buttons** to show one less button in the Navigation Pane.

4. Repeat these steps for each button as needed until the Navigation Pane shows the number of buttons you want.

FIGURE 11.2

The Configure
Buttons menu
enables you to
show more or
fewer buttons,
set Navigation
Pane options,
and make but-
tons visible.

The Configure Buttons menu has two additional commands, **Navigation Pane Options** and **Add or Remove Buttons**, which are similar in that both set which buttons are visible in the Navigation Pane. **Navigation Pane Options** is more powerful because it enables you to set the order of the buttons as well as which buttons are visible.

To open the Navigations Pane Options dialog shown in Figure 11.3, select **Navigation Pane Options**.

FIGURE 11.3

The Navigation
Pane Options
dialog enables
you to select
which items
appear as but-
tons and in
which order.

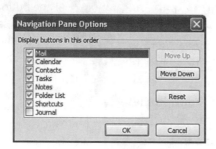

To work with the Navigation Pane Options dialog, you can do the following:

- Check the checkbox next to a button name to display that button in the Navigation Pane.

- Uncheck the checkbox next to a button name to hide that button from the Navigation Pane.

- Check the **Journal** button to display it in the Navigation Pane. (By default, the Journal button is not checked, and the Journal button is hidden.)

- **Move Up** moves the selected button up one place in the display list and the button display order in the Navigation Pane.

- **Move Down** moves the selected button down one place in the display list and the button display order in the Navigation Pane.

- **Reset** returns the button display to its default state.

- Click **OK** to save your changes or **Cancel** to cancel your changes. If you click the Close box in the upper-right corner of the dialog, your changes are canceled.

The final item on the Configure Buttons menu is **Add or Remove Buttons**. Using this menu item, shown in Figure 11.4, you can check and uncheck buttons the same way you would in the Navigation Pane Options dialog. You can show or hide any of the buttons, but you can't change the display order from the Add or Remove Buttons menu.

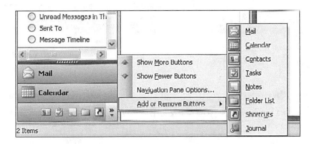

FIGURE 11.4

The Add or Remove Buttons menu is used to show or hide Navigation Pane buttons.

Navigation Pane buttons provide one more feature: a context menu. Right-click any button in the Navigation Pane, and a context menu opens. From it, you can display the Navigation Pane Options dialog. You can also open a new Outlook window based on the button, which enables you to switch back and forth between different views of your Outlook data.

To open another Outlook window using the context menu, select **Open in New Window**. Figure 11.5 shows the Calendar folder opened in a new window in front of the Inbox folder. You can easily switch between the windows by selecting a window in the Windows taskbar. You can even display the same folders in more than one window and use different folder views in each window to view your data in different ways at the same time.

FIGURE 11.5

Opening
another Outlook
window makes it
easy to display
multiple views
of the same
folder or view
more than one
folder at a time.

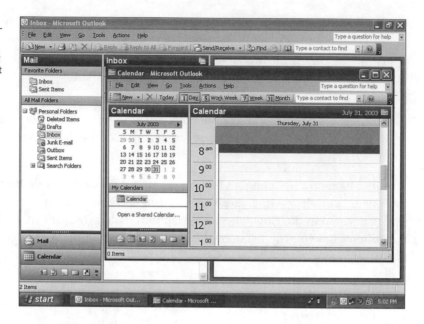

Favorite Folders

Favorite Folders are shortcuts to mail folders that are shown when you display the
Mail folders group in the Navigation Pane. By default, the Inbox and Sent Items
folders are the only folders shown in Favorite Folders. Favorite Folders may seem useless if you have very few custom folders, but if you have many subfolders, they provide an easy way to navigate to deeply buried folders. Instead of having to expand
deeply nested folders and subfolders to find the one you want to view, you can go
right to the folder you want if it's in Favorite Folders. The Favorite Folders area is
shown in Figure 11.6, with a folder nested three levels down from the Inbox added to
Favorite Folders for immediate access.

Working with Favorite Folders

To work with the Favorite Folders area of the Navigation Pane:

- To add a folder to the Favorite Folders, drag the folder to the Favorites Folder
  area of the Navigation Pane, or right-click the folder in the All Mail Folders
  area of the Navigation Pane and select **Add to Favorite Folders**. Only
  e-mail folders can be added to Favorite Folders.

- To remove a folder from the Favorite Folders, right-click the folder in the
  Favorite Folders area of the Navigation Pane and select **Remove from
  Favorite Folders**.

FIGURE 11.6

The Favorite Folders area of the Navigation Pane is used to make e-mail folders located anywhere in Outlook easily reachable with one mouse click.

- To move a folder up in the list of Favorite Folders, right-click the folder in the Favorite Folders area of the Navigation Pane and select **Move Up in List**.

- To move a folder down in the list of Favorite Folders, right-click the folder in the Favorite Folders area of the Navigation Pane and select **Move Down in List**.

Favorite Folders Versus Public Folder Favorites

Public Folder Favorites is available only if you are using Exchange server, so if you are a home user or a business user of Outlook whose company doesn't use Exchange server, you can skip this section.

Exchange public folders are usually visible in Outlook only when you show the Folder List in the Navigation Pane. Public folders are shown in the Folder List as a separate group of folders than the folders in your Exchange mailbox. You

caution

Never delete a folder from Favorite Folders using the **Delete** key or other deletion method. By doing so, you delete the actual folder and all its contents.

tip

You also can drag a folder up or down in the Favorite Folders list to change its position in the list.

must perform a series of steps to make a public e-mail folder visible when you show the Mail folder group, so you don't have to switch to the Folder List to view both your own and public e-mail folder.

To make a public e-mail folder visible in the Mail folder group, you must add it the Favorite Folders area. This process can become confusing because you must add a public folder to Public Folder Favorites before you are able to add it to the Navigation Pane's Favorite Folders area.

- Public Folder Favorites is used to make public folders available when you are working in offline mode. It also is used to enable you to add a folder to Favorite Folders.

- Favorite Folders is a group of folders in the Navigation Pane's Mail folder group. Only e-mail folders can be added to Favorite Folders.

To add a public e-mail folder to Favorite Folders to make it visible in the Mail folder group, follow these steps:

1. Display the Folder List in the Navigation Pane.

2. Scroll down the list of folders until Public Folders is visible.

3. Expand Public Folders by clicking on the plus sign (+) to the left of Public Folders.

4. Navigate to the public e-mail folder you want to add to Favorite Folders.

5. Right-click the folder and select **Add to Favorites**.

6. Click **Add** to add the folder to Favorites in Public Folders.

7. Expand Favorites in Public Folders and right-click the folder you just added.

8. Select **Add to Favorite Folders**.

note

You will learn more about working with Exchange public folders in Chapter 21, "Collaborating with Outlook and Exchange." You learned how to set up Exchange public folders for offline use in the "Send/Receive Groups" section of Chapter 2, "Outlook from the Beginning."

The contents of a public folder in Favorite Folders aren't available when you are working in offline mode unless the public folder has been synchronized for offline use.

Shortcuts

You probably have noticed that most of the display options in the Navigation Pane are predefined and can't be changed. The Shortcuts area in the Navigation Pane is the place where you can place shortcuts to any group of Outlook folders you want. Unlike Favorite Folders, shortcuts can point to any type of folder.

Shortcut Groups are used to organize folder shortcuts into related groups. Shortcut Groups can include any type of folder shortcut, such as a group containing shortcuts to E-Mail, Tasks, and Calendar folders. If you are working on a project, you can create a Shortcut Group for the project and add shortcuts to any folders that store data for the project, including Exchange public folders if you are using Exchange. Navigating to any of the folders in the group is easy because all the folders are listed together.

The Shortcuts pane in the Navigation Pane was called the Outlook Bar in earlier versions of Outlook. If you upgraded from an earlier version of Outlook, your user-defined Outlook Bar Groups were imported as Shortcut Groups.

Figure 11.7 shows the Shortcuts pane, with the default Shortcuts Group containing links to Outlook Today and Microsoft Office Online, the Microsoft Office Web site.

FIGURE 11.7

The Shortcuts area in the Navigation Pane provides another way of navigating among your folders.

If you don't see shortcuts when you go to the Shortcuts area, click the plus sign (+) to the left of a group name to expand a Shortcut Group. To hide the shortcuts in a Shortcut Group, click the minus (–) sign to the left of the group name.

Working with Shortcut Groups

You can add, remove, and rename Shortcut Groups. You can also arrange the list of Shortcut Groups so the groups are listed in the order you want. In this section, you will learn to work with Shortcut Groups.

To add a new Shortcut Group, do the following:

1. Click the **Add New Group** link just below the Shortcuts area.

2. A new group is added to the list of Shortcut Groups, with the default name New Group.

3. Change the Shortcut Group name to a name that describes the new group.

4. Press **Enter** to save the new Shortcut Group.

> **tip**
>
> Any Shortcut Group moved to the top of the list becomes the new default Shortcut Group. All new shortcuts added using the **Add New Shortcut** link are added to the default Shortcut Group.

You can rename a Shortcut Group at any time, which you will learn to do later in this section.

To move a Shortcut Group up or down within the list of Shortcut Groups, follow these steps:

1. Right-click the Shortcut Group name and select either **Move Up in List** or **Move Down in List**.

2. Repeat step 1 until the Shortcut Group is positioned where you want it in the list of groups.

To remove a Shortcut Group, follow these steps:

1. Right-click the Shortcut Group name and select **Remove Group.**

2. Click **Yes** to remove the group and all its shortcuts.

To rename a Shortcut Group, do the following:

1. Right-click the Shortcut Group name and select **Rename Group.**

2. When the group name becomes selected, you can type a new name for the group.

3. Press **Enter** or click somewhere out of the group name entry field to save the new name.

Working with Shortcuts

Shortcuts can be added to or removed from any Shortcut Group. You can rename shortcuts, which doesn't change the name of the folder to which the shortcut points, and you can arrange the shortcuts in a group so the shortcuts are listed in the order you want. In this section, you will learn to work with shortcuts.

To add a new shortcut to the default Shortcut Group, which is the group at the top of the Shortcut Group list, follow these steps:

1. Select the **Add New Shortcut** link just below the Shortcuts area.
2. In the Add to Navigation Pane dialog, shown in Figure 11.8, select the folder to add to the group.

FIGURE 11.8

The Add to Navigation Pane dialog enables you to add a shortcut to a folder to the Shortcuts area.

3. Click **OK** to add the new shortcut, or click **Cancel** or the Close box to cancel the creation of the new shortcut.

To add a new shortcut to a specific Shortcut Group, follow these steps:

1. Right-click the Shortcut Group to which you want to add a shortcut.
2. Click **Add New Shortcut** to open the Add to Navigation Pane dialog, shown in Figure 11.8.
3. Select the folder to add to the group.
4. Click **OK** to add the new shortcut, or click **Cancel** or the Close box to cancel the creation of the new shortcut.

To rename an existing shortcut, do the following:

1. Right-click the shortcut and select **Rename Shortcut**.

2. Type a new name for the shortcut and press **Enter** to save the new name. The name for a shortcut does not have to be the same as the name of the folder to which the shortcut points.

To remove a shortcut from a Shortcut Group, do the following:

1. Right-click the shortcut and select **Delete Shortcut**.

2. Click **Yes** to remove the shortcut from the group. This action does not delete the original folder to which the shortcut pointed.

To move a shortcut up or down within the list in the Shortcut Group, follow these steps:

1. Right-click the shortcut name and select either **Move Up in List** or **Move Down in List**.

2. Repeat step 1 until the shortcut is positioned where you want it in the list of shortcuts.

You also can move a shortcut's position in a Shortcut Group by clicking the shortcut and dragging it to the desired position in the list of shortcuts.

THE ABSOLUTE MINIMUM

In this chapter, you learned about customizing the Navigation Pane. To review, you now know how to

Customize the Navigation Pane by displaying more or fewer buttons.

Show and hide the available Navigation Pane buttons.

Set the order in which buttons are displayed in the Navigation Pane.

Add folders to your Favorite Folders.

Create, remove, and rename Shortcut Groups and shortcuts.

Set the order shortcuts and Shortcut Groups are displayed in the Shortcuts pane.

With the skills you acquired in this chapter, you can customize the Navigation Pane to be more productive for the way you work in Outlook. In the next chapter, you will learn how to find things in all that data you've been collecting in Outlook.

IN THIS CHAPTER

- Understanding how to find items in Outlook.

- Learning how to use Find for simple searches.

- Learning how to use Advanced Find for more advanced searches using criteria.

- Knowing how to save and reuse advanced searches.

12

FINDING THINGS ANYWHERE

Using Outlook to manage your information is great, but you have to be able to find things when you need them; otherwise, all that information is useless. Outlook provides two different features to help you find things: Find and Advanced Find. In this chapter, you will learn how to use Outlook's Find and Advanced Find features.

Finding Things in Outlook

The first point to learn about finding things in Outlook is the difference between Find and Advanced Find. Find enables you to perform simple searches in one or more folders, with the search based on the text in the subject and address fields of items or in the subject field, address field, and text of items.

tip

After running Find or Advanced Find, you can open items returned by the Find operation by double-clicking the item you want to open.

Advanced Find enables you to construct advanced searches that can find items based not only on their text but also on the contents of various fields in the items. Some examples of advanced searches are finding messages based on when e-mails were received or finding contacts that work for a specific company.

The criteria used for a Find or Advanced Find can be saved as Search Folders, which creates a new Search Folder that is constantly updated based on the search criteria. You learned about Search Folders in Chapter 5, "Search Folders." The criteria for an Advanced Find can also be saved as an Office Saved Search (OSS) file, which can be loaded and used again at any time.

Using the Find Pane

To open the Find pane, select **Tools**, **Find**, **Find**. The Find pane appears above the folder title bar, as shown in Figure 12.1.

The Find pane includes the following features:

- **Look for**—This text box provides an area for you to enter the text you want to search for in the contents of a selected folder or folders. Outlook searches the subject and address fields, and and optionally the text of all items for matches with the search text you enter. Search text is not case sensitive, meaning if you enter the search text **profession**, both *profession* and *Profession* will be found.

- **Search In**—This drop-down shows the current Outlook folder as the default search location. You can click the arrow in the drop-down to choose additional settings for the search location.

- **Find Now**—This button starts a search.

- **Clear**—During the search, this button changes to Stop, which you can use to stop the search. After the search is completed, you can use the Clear button to clear the current search text and all the items that have been found with the search phrase.

- **Options**—This drop-down provides a way to save your search results as a new Search folder and also provides access to the Advanced Find feature. It also enables you to use only the subjects of Outlook items for the search text or both subject and text in items. (Search folders were discussed in Chapter 5, "Search Folders.")

- **Close**—This button closes the Find pane without saving or preserving the search text or results.

tip

You can easily reuse previous search text you entered in the Look for box. Click the arrow in the Look for drop-down list and select the text to use again.

note

A Find pane search returns results that include all the search text you enter. The search isn't based only on the search text words appearing consecutively. For example, if you enter **Outlook 2003**, the results include not only items with the words *Outlook 2003* but also items with *Outlook 02/11/2003*.

Searching Other Folders

The Search In button enables you to search in folders other than the current folder and to add additional folders to your search. Click the arrow on the Search In button to display the Search In menu. Your choices are the currently selected folder, All Mail Folders, Mail I Received, Mail I Sent, and Choose Folders, as shown in Figure 12.2. In this example, the Sent Items folder has been selected in the Folders list and appears at the top of the Search In drop-down.

The All Mail Folders selection searches in all mail folders, including Inbox, Drafts, Sent Items, and any other mail folders you use or have created. The Mail I Received selection searches in all mail folders only in items that were sent to you. The Mail I Sent selection searches only items that you sent to someone else. These predefined selections provide commonly selected options and make these options easier to use for searching than if you had to define them yourself.

FIGURE 12.2

You can select other folders and add folders to your search using the Search In menu.

The Select Folder(s) dialog, opened from the Search In menu and shown in Figure 12.3, enables you to specify folders to search. This dialog enables you to check any folder or group of folders for searching.

FIGURE 12.3

The Select Folder(s) dialog enables you to search in specific folders.

In the Select Folder(s) dialog, you can check as many different folders in the Folders tree view as you want. Outlook searches the contents of each checked folder for your search text. You can check the **Search subfolders** checkbox at the bottom of the dialog to easily select a folder and all its subfolders in one action. Use the **Clear All** button to clear all selected folders so that you can search a different group of folders. Click **OK** to use the checked folders in the search.

tip

If you are using Exchange server and search in an Exchange Public Folder, you can search only in the currently selected public folder. You cannot search on subfolders of Public Folders and a folder in your mailbox at the same time. This is a limitation of Exchange.

Selecting Additional Search Options

The Options drop-down, shown in Figure 12.4, provides selections for either searching in the subject and address fields and text of messages or searching only in the subject and address fields as well as for saving searches you created as Search Folders. It also provides a shortcut to the Advanced Find dialog. (Advanced Find is covered later in this chapter.)

FIGURE 12.4

The Options drop-down enables you to set search options and provides access to a shortcut to Advanced Find.

If Search All Text in Each Message is checked, Outlook looks for the search text in the subject and address fields and body text of messages. If this option is not checked, Outlook searches only the subjects and address fields of messages for the search text.

Save Search as Search Folder saves your search text and whether to search all text or just subject and address fields as the search criteria for a new Search Folder. All the folders included in the original search are searched by the Search Folder. Selecting this option opens the dialog shown in Figure 12.5.

FIGURE 12.5

Enter a name and click OK to save your search as a new Search Folder.

Enter a name for the saved search and click **OK** to create a new Search Folder. The saved search is a dynamic search; if you put additional messages that meet the search criteria in one of the folders being searched, those additional items appear in the Search Folder also. Figure 12.6 shows a search saved as a Search Folder named Outlook 2003, with the results of the search grouped in the Search Folder by the folders in which the items are located.

FIGURE 12.6

Saved searches can be saved as new Search Folders, which are dynamically updated as items that meet the search criteria are received.

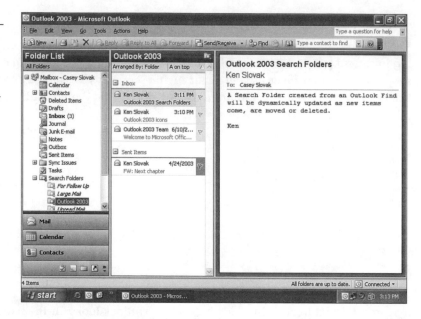

Using Advanced Find

Find is great when you want to search for text in Outlook items, but it doesn't do the job if you want to search for items with certain values in specific fields or need to create more complex searches. If you need to create a complex search, use the Advanced Find dialog. An example of a complex search would be a search for all e-mail messages that were received this month that have attachments and have a High importance.

To open the Advanced Find dialog, select **Tools**, **Find**, **Advanced Find**.

The Advanced Find dialog enables you to create complex searches, but it is also more difficult to use than the Find pane (see Figure 12.7). Take a few minutes to become familiar with the different options available for creating searches by looking at all the drop-downs and tabs.

The Look for area tells Outlook what types of items to look for in your search. The default choice is Messages; the other options are Any type of Outlook item, Appointments and Meetings, Contacts, Files (Outlook/Exchange), Journal entries, Notes, and Tasks. The Files (Outlook/Exchange) option searches for files stored in Outlook and Exchange folders as Office documents. It does not search for files attached to messages.

The In area shows where the search will be performed, and the Browse button opens the familiar Select Folders dialog, enabling you to select one or more folders in which to search. The Find Now button starts the search, and the Stop button stops an ongoing search. New Search clears the existing search conditions to prepare for new search criteria.

FIGURE 12.7

Advanced Find enables you to create complex searches for Outlook items.

The name of the first tab in the Advanced Search dialog is based on the type of item for which you are searching. If you change the type of item you are searching for, the name of the first tab changes to match the type of item for which you are searching.

As mentioned previously, the first tab of the Advanced Find dialog is named for the type of item for which you are searching. The second and third tabs are labeled More Choices and Advanced. You can enter search criteria in more than one of these tabs. All the criteria you enter on all three tabs are used to find only items that meet all the criteria. Later in this chapter, I'll show you how to use multiple values of particular criteria on the Advanced tab to perform a search that looks for items that match one or more of the search criteria.

The First Tab in Advanced Find

In this section, the first tab is referred to as the Messages tab. If you are searching for Contacts, the tab is named Contacts. To be consistent, I will use Messages in the examples in this chapter. Just remember that if you are searching for different types of items, the name of the tab will be different, and different search criteria will appear on the tab.

The Messages tab provides several of the most frequently used search criteria predefined for easy use. You can choose to enter search criteria in one or more of the fields on this tab. Remember that if you enter criteria in more than one field, only items that meet all the criteria are found.

Search for the word(s) looks for the words you enter, with the In area selecting whether the words appear in the subject only, subject and message body, or in frequently used text fields (including the subject and message body).

tip

To search only for specific phrases without including extra text, use quotation marks around your search text. This technique works only in Advanced Find; it doesn't work in the Find pane.

Clicking the **From** button opens the Outlook Address Book dialog, where you can select one or more contacts. The search returns only items sent by those contacts. Similarly, clicking the **Sent To** button enables you to find only items sent to one or more specific contacts.

Checking the **Where I am** checkbox enables the drop-down where you can select from the following choices: the only person on the To Line, on the To line with other people, and on the CC line with other people.

The final criterion in the Messages tab is **Time**, where you can select none, received, sent, due, expires, created, or modified, as well as specific Time criteria. The Time criteria you can use are anytime, yesterday, today, in the last 7 days, last week, this week, last month, or this month. The Time criteria enable you to limit your search to the time frame in which you are interested. If you want to enter different Time criteria than those provided on the Time drop-down list, you can enter them on the Advanced tab.

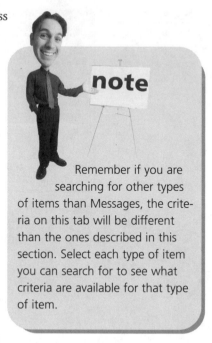

note

Remember if you are searching for other types of items than Messages, the criteria on this tab will be different than the ones described in this section. Select each type of item you can search for to see what criteria are available for that type of item.

The More Choices Tab

The More Choices tab, shown in Figure 12.8, enables you to enter selection criteria that are based on Outlook Categories, items that are read or unread, items with and without attachments, and items of selected importance and specific size. You also can set whether your search text is case sensitive.

FIGURE 12.8

The More Choices tab enables you to search on commonly used Outlook fields.

Clicking the **Categories** button opens the Categories dialog, where you can select from existing categories or enter new ones for your search. If you have used categories previously in the Advanced Find dialog, you can select from those categories by clicking the arrow in the Categories drop-down and selecting one from the list.

The other options that can be selected include

- **Only items that are**—This area enables you to select from items that are either unread or have been marked as read.

- **Only items with**—This checkbox enables you to select from items that have either one or more attachments or no attachments.

- **Whose importance is**—This is the place where you can limit your search to items whose importance is set to either Normal, High, or Low.

- **Match case**—This checkbox enables you to select whether the search should match the case of words that have been entered in one of the other tabs. Searches where case is not matched, for example, will return results for the word *Outlook* whether it is entered as **Outlook** or **outlook**. Case matching, also known as *case sensitivity*, would return only items where the word is entered as **Outlook**, with a capital *O*.

- **Size**—Here, you can choose to search for items of different sizes. The choices are the default doesn't matter, equals (approximately), between, less than, and greater than. If you select any of the size options other than doesn't matter, one or both of the Size entry text boxes are enabled. Between is the only size option that enables both Size entry text boxes. You can enter the size to look for in kilobytes if a Size option is enabled. The size of any attachments in an item are counted toward the overall size of the item.

> **note**
>
> Some options on the More Choices tab are not enabled for use, depending on the type of item for which you are searching. For example, the checkbox for importance settings is available only for e-mail, calendar, and task items.

The Advanced Tab

The Advanced tab, shown in Figure 12.9, is the most flexible and powerful tab for entry of search criteria. On the Advanced tab, you can enter search criteria for any Outlook field, including user-defined fields. (User-defined fields are covered in Chapter 20, "Customizing Outlook Forms.")

FIGURE 12.9

The Advanced tab provides the most powerful options for entering search criteria.

To begin using the Advanced tab, click the **Field** button. Doing so opens a list of commonly used groups of Outlook fields, with each list expanding to enable selection of the fields within that group. Some of the group selections are Frequently-used fields, Address fields, Date/Time fields, and All Mail fields. Many other groups are available as well. Expand them all and see which fields are available in each field group. The Field groups are the same as those in the Field Chooser you use to create custom views, which are covered in Chapter 14, "Outlook Views."

When a field is selected, it appears in the condition selection area, and the Condition and Value drop-downs are enabled. Different field types provide choices of appropriate conditions and values.

For example, selecting Flag Color from the Frequently-used Fields group provides the conditions equals, not equal to, exists, and does not exist, and values for the different flag colors—Purple Flag, Orange Flag, Green Flag, Yellow Flag, Blue Flag, and Red Flag.

Selecting E-mail Account from the All Mail Fields group provides the conditions contains, is (exactly), doesn't contain, is empty, and is not empty. The Value area for this field type is a blank text entry area. Experiment with different fields and field types to see which choices are available for different Outlook fields.

When you are satisfied with the field selection, condition, and value, you can add it to the search criteria by clicking the **Add to List** button. To remove search criterion from the criteria list, highlight the criterion you want to remove and click **Remove**.

Here's an example of creating a search for e-mail messages that have a Red Flag and High importance. To create this search, do the following:

1. Click **New Search** to clear any previous search conditions.

2. Click **Field**, **Frequently-used fields**, **Flag Color**.

3. In the **Value** drop-down, select **Red Flag** (scroll to the bottom of the list to find Red Flag).

4. Click **Add to List**.

5. Click **Field**, **Frequently-used fields**, **Importance**.

6. In the **Value** drop-down, select **High**.

7. Click **Add to List**.

8. To run the search looking for e-mail messages with a Red Flag and High importance, click **Find Now**.

Searching for One or More Values in a Field

All the different criteria entered on the three Advanced Find tabs are used for the search. Each condition must be met for an item to be returned by the search. A common need, however, might be to search for items that have one of a number of different values for a field.

If you want to search for items that have either a Red Flag or a Purple Flag, you first set up search criteria for finding items with a Red Flag. Then, after adding that setting to the search criteria, enter search criteria for the Flag Color field, but this time set the value to Purple Flag and then add that to the search criteria list. Items with either a Red or Purple Flag will be found. You can use this technique with as many conditions and fields as you want to search for items with one or another desired value in a field. For each field that has multiple conditions in the search criteria list, Outlook will return items with any of those values.

> **tip**
>
> You can easily forget that you have criteria entered in another tab in Advanced Find. I recommend clicking the **New Search** button before you start entering search criteria to make sure all previously entered search criteria have been cleared.

Saving and Reusing Advanced Searches

After you set up a search the way you want it and are satisfied with the results of the search, you can save it if you think you might want to run the search again. After all, if you can make things easy for yourself, why create the same search over and over again, possibly forgetting to enter search criteria and having to do all that work again?

You can save a search in Advanced Find in two different ways. If the search is only in mail folders, you can save it as a Search folder, as you saw earlier with saved searches in the Find pane. You can also save a search using Advanced Find as a file on your hard drive, even if folders of mixed types are used in the search.

To save a search in Advanced Find as a Search Folder, select **File**, **Save Search as Search Folder** from the Advanced Find File menu. Enter a descriptive name for the new Search Folder and click **OK** to save it. Your search is always available and is kept dynamically updated as new items are added to the folders being searched.

To save a search in Advanced Find as a file, select **File**, **Save Search** in the Advanced Find File menu. The familiar Office Save dialog opens, and you can select a name and location for your saved search. I recommend giving each saved search a descriptive name, such as *Items With Attachments Search*, so you know what it is for and saving all your searches in one location on your hard drive so you can locate them easily later. Saved searches have an .oss (Office Saved Search) extension. Click **OK** to save the search as a file.

To reuse a search you have saved as a file, select **File**, **Open Search** and navigate to your saved search location. Click **OK** to open the saved search. Opening a saved search clears any search criteria currently in Advanced Find and loads the saved search criteria. If you want to preserve criteria already in Advanced Find, make sure to save the current criteria before you open a saved search.

THE ABSOLUTE MINIMUM

In this chapter, you learned how to find Outlook items anywhere in Outlook, even if the items are located in different folders. Now you know how to

- Use the Find pane to locate items with specific text in the subject and address fields and item text or just the subject and address fields.

- Use the Advanced Find dialog to locate items using advanced search criteria or to search for values in multiple fields.

- Open items returned by the searches by double-clicking the items in the Find pane or the Advanced Find dialog.

- Save searches for reuse as Search Folders or as files.

In this chapter, you learned how to find things in Outlook. In the next chapter, you will learn about archiving Outlook data to move older items from your default data file to other Outlook data files.

IN THIS CHAPTER

- Learning about archiving Outlook items.
- Understanding when and how to archive.
- Learning how to configure archive settings.
- Learning how to work with archived data.
- Learning how to back up Outlook data.

13

ARCHIVING DATA

Over time, you collect more and more items in your Outlook folders, and finding things becomes harder and slower. You can move things to storage folders, but that's just a temporary fix. In this chapter, you will learn how to use archiving, which moves items to a different data file based on how old the items are and where they are located. You will also learn how to back up Outlook data and settings, which doesn't remove the date from the Outlook data file.

About Archiving

Some people save every e-mail message they've ever received because they might need them, but they never look at any of the older messages. Some businesses, such as financial service companies and law firms, save every e-mail message because of legal or business requirements but rarely refer to those messages. These e-mail messages as well as tasks, appointments, and other Outlook items don't need to be located in your default Outlook data file; they just have to be available somewhere if you do need them. The best solution is *archiving* items that you don't need to access very often.

When items are archived, they are removed from your default data file and either moved to a different data file or deleted. Items are archived automatically by Outlook, which is called *AutoArchiving*, unless you turn off archiving. You also can archive items manually whenever you want in addition to using AutoArchiving.

PST files in Outlook 2003 can be as large as 20GB using the default settings, so it might not seem to be very important to use archiving to remove items from your data file. However, as PST files grow larger, they take longer to load, and finding things in them takes longer. The same performance limitations apply to Exchange mailboxes as PST files, and many Exchange mailboxes also have size limits set by the Exchange administrator. If your mailbox's size goes over its limit, you can't receive any e-mail or create any new items until you reduce its size below the limit. For these reasons, archiving is an important function in Outlook.

> **tip**
>
> Outlook requires read/write access to open a PST file. If you store an archive PST file on a CD, you must copy it to a hard drive and clear the read-only property of the PST file before Outlook can open it.
>
> To clear the read-only property for a PST file, locate it using Windows Explorer or Windows Search, right-click on the filename, and select **Properties**. Then uncheck the **Read-only** attribute and click **OK**.

Outlook creates a default archive data file named `archive.pst`, located in the hidden `C:\Documents and Settings\<profile name>\Local Settings\Application Data\Microsoft\Outlook` folder. You also can create additional archive data files located anywhere you want. Some people put their archive data files on removable hard drives, hard drives located on a network, backup tapes, or even on CDs.

You can use as many archive data files as you want; you can even have separate archive data files for each of your Outlook folders. You can create a new archive data file each year and give it a name that includes the year, such as `Archive2003.pst`. You also can create archive data files for each of your business clients and archive everything related to them in separate PST files. This makes it easy to know which archive to look in when you want to find something.

Outlook archiving settings are very flexible and can be highly customized. You can set default archive settings and globally apply them to all your folders. You can also individually create archive settings for any folder, which override the default global settings for the folder. You can even select certain folders to be protected from archiving so items in those folders are always available in online storage.

tip

If you intend to share archive PST files with users of earlier versions of Outlook, you are still subject to the 2GB size limit of Outlook 97 to Outlook 2002 PST files. Make sure to create an archive PST file that is compatible with earlier versions of Outlook, which you will learn to do later in this chapter.

Knowing When to Archive

Outlook has default archive settings for the default folders in your data file. You can change these settings, as you will learn later in this chapter in the "Examining Archive Settings" section. Archive settings are based on the age of items, which is called their *aging period*. When items reach their aging period, they are automatically archived, a process Outlook calls *AutoArchive*. You can also manually archive folders based on the ages of items in the selected folders, as you will learn later in this section.

The default aging periods for folders are shown in Table 13.1.

Table 13.1 Folder Aging Periods

Aging Period	Folder
2 months	Sent Items, Deleted Items
3 months	Junk E-mail, Outbox
6 months	Inbox, Calendar, Tasks, Notes, Journal, Drafts
3 months	Contacts (Contacts folders are never AutoArchived)

Custom folders default to a six-month aging period.

Even though all types of folders have default aging periods, many folders have archiving turned off by default. Only the Calendar, Deleted Items, Journal, Sent Items, and Tasks folders are enabled for archiving by default. Custom folders always have archiving disabled by default.

The way Outlook determines the age of an item varies based on the item type. Table 13.2 shows the method used for determining the age of different Outlook item types.

Table 13.2   Item Aging Methods

Item Type	Method Used
E-mail, Post	Sent/received date or last modification date/times, whichever is later.
Calendar	Appointment, event, or meeting date or last modification date/time, whichever is later. Recurring items are not automatically archived.
Task	Completion date or last modification date/time. Tasks that are not marked complete are not automatically archived. Tasks assigned to other people are archived only if marked complete.
Note	Last modification date/time.
Journal	Creation date or last modification date/time.
Contacts	Archived manually only, based on creation date or last modification date/time.

If AutoArchiving is enabled globally, which it is by default, archiving occurs for items that are older than the aging period in folders where archiving is turned on. AutoArchiving occurs at regular intervals—by default, once every 14 days. If Outlook is not running when AutoArchiving is due to occur, the archiving will occur the next time Outlook starts after the AutoArchive due date.

You can run manual archiving whenever you want. Archiving items manually does not change the next scheduled AutoArchive date.

To archive items manually, select **File**, **Archive**. The Archive dialog opens, as shown in Figure 13.1.

If a folder is selected when the Archive dialog opens, the folder and all its subfolders are selected for archiving. The archive settings for the folder type are automatically set based on the folder type, but you can change the settings for the archiving operation. You can also select the option to archive all folders based on their AutoArchive settings. You will learn about these settings in the next section.

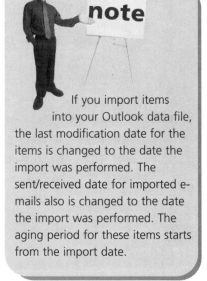

note

If you import items into your Outlook data file, the last modification date for the items is changed to the date the import was performed. The sent/received date for imported e-mails also is changed to the date the import was performed. The aging period for these items starts from the import date.

FIGURE 13.1

The Archive dialog is used for manual archiving and is the only way to archive a Contacts folder.

All items that are older than the date shown in the calendar drop-down will be archived. In this drop-down, you can select a date as the threshold date for archiving items.

You can use the default archive data file for the manual archiving operation, or you can use a different archive data file. To select a different archive data file or create a new one for this archive, click the **Browse** button and navigate to the folder you want to use. To create a new archive file, enter a new filename, and the new archive file will be created when archiving starts. After you set the properties for the manual archive operation, click **OK** to archive the selected folders.

tip

To manually archive all folders and subfolders based on custom settings set for that archive operation, select Personal Folders (or the Mailbox folder if you are using an Exchange mailbox) in the folder list in the Archive dialog.

The checkbox setting titled **Include items with "Do Not AutoArchive" checked** is probably a mystery because most Outlook users have never seen this property anywhere. It is the NoAging property and is shown in the Outlook user interface as Do Not AutoArchive.

So how do you set this property if it's not usually shown anywhere? The easiest way to set this property for an item is to open the item and select **Properties** from the **File**, menu of the open item. The Properties dialog for an open item is shown in Figure 13.2. Check the **Do not AutoArchive this item** checkbox and click **OK** to save this setting for the item.

FIGURE 13.2

Using the
Properties dialog
for an open item
is the easiest
way to set the
Do Not
AutoArchive
property for the
item.

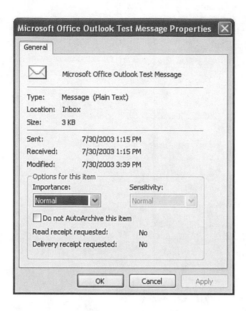

You also can customize a table view of a folder to
show the Do Not AutoArchive field for any folder
except a Contacts folder. You will learn how to customize folder views in Chapter 14, "Outlook
Views." If you add this field to the folder view, you
can check the Do Not AutoArchive field for items
without opening the items. This field is not available for contact items, however, so you must open
each contact item to change the Do Not
AutoArchive property.

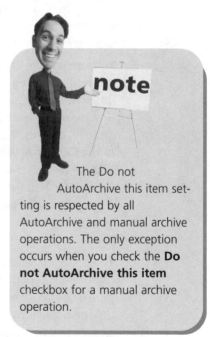

The Do not
AutoArchive this item setting is respected by all
AutoArchive and manual archive
operations. The only exception
occurs when you check the **Do
not AutoArchive this item**
checkbox for a manual archive
operation.

Examining Archive Settings

Automatic archiving (AutoArchive) is enabled in
two stages. First, you set the global settings for
archiving, and then you set custom settings for any
folder whose default settings are not what you
want.

AutoArchive Global Settings

To display the AutoArchive global settings, select **Tools**, **Options**, select the **Other**
tab, and then click the **AutoArchive** button.

You can also display the AutoArchive global settings by right-clicking any folder (except Contacts) in the Navigation Pane and selecting **Properties**, selecting the **AutoArchive** tab, and then clicking on the **Default Archive Settings** button. The folder must be enabled for AutoArchiving for the **Default Archive Settings** button to be enabled.

The global AutoArchive settings dialog is shown in Figure 13.3.

FIGURE 13.3

The global AutoArchive settings dialog enables you to set AutoArchive settings used throughout Outlook.

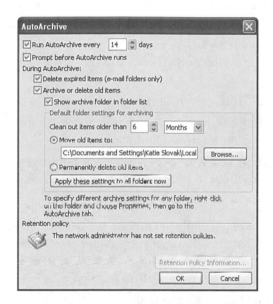

By default, AutoArchiving is set to run every 14 days. You can change this interval or completely disable AutoArchiving by unchecking the Run AutoArchive setting.

The During AutoArchive section of the AutoArchive dialog contains the following settings:

■ **Delete expired items (e-mail folders only)**—You can set e-mail items to expire after delivery by opening the item's Options dialog. In an open item, select **View, Options** to open the Options dialog. You can also open the Options dialog by right-clicking an item in a folder and selecting **Options** from the context menu.

caution

Outlook will run AutoArchiving without prompting unless you check the setting to prompt before running AutoArchive.

- **Archive or delete old items**—If expired items are not deleted, they are archived according to this setting. If this setting isn't checked, AutoArchiving is performed only for expired e-mail items based on the **Delete expired items (email folders only)** setting.

- **Show archive folder in folder list**—If this option is checked, the default archive data file is shown in the Folder List in the Navigation Pane. This setting makes it easy to work with archived items if you have only one archive folder.

- **Clean out items older than**—Here, you can select an aging period that applies globally to all folders that do not have customized folder archive settings.

- **Move old item to**—This setting selects the default archive data file.

- **Permanently delete old items**—This setting deletes all items and does not move them into the default archive data file.

- **Apply these settings to all folders now**—This button is used to apply the global AutoArchive settings to all folders that do not have custom folder archive settings.

The Retention Policy section applies only to Outlook profiles working with Exchange Server. Companies can set item and document retention policies that override settings you apply. You can view the Retention Policy settings, but unless you are an Exchange administrator, you cannot change these settings.

Click **OK** to save the global AutoArchive settings.

AutoArchive Folder Settings

To display the AutoArchive settings for a folder, right-click the folder in the Navigation Pane, select **Properties**, and then select the **AutoArchive** tab. Contacts are not automatically archived, so Contacts folders do not have an AutoArchive tab. The folder AutoArchive settings dialog is shown in Figure 13.4.

Most of the settings in the folder AutoArchive settings dialog are similar to the settings in the global AutoArchive settings dialog, so you can refer to the preceding section to refresh yourself on those settings. The folder-specific settings are as follows:

- **Do not archive items in this folder**—If this setting is checked, the folder will not be AutoArchived. It can be manually archived even if AutoArchive is disabled, as you learned earlier in this chapter.

- **Move old items to**—This setting normally uses the default archive data file, but you can set the folder archive to use a different folder. Any folder can have its own archive data file, which enables you to maintain separate archives for special folders or groups of folders.

FIGURE 13.4

The folder AutoArchive settings dialog enables you to set archiving settings for the folder that are different than the global AutoArchive settings.

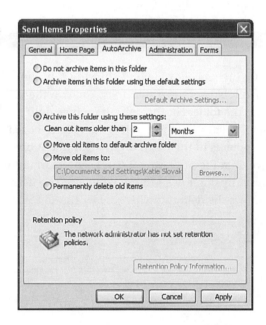

Working with Archived Data

Archiving keeps your Outlook data store running as fast as possible, and keeps it within corporate mailbox limits if you are using an Exchange Server mailbox.

Several different strategies are used for archiving:

- Archive all items from all folders to a default archive data store. This strategy keeps all your items together but leads to huge archive data stores where finding things is just as hard as if you had never archived.

- Set up archive data files based on time periods. One common strategy is to set up a new archive data file for each year, such as Archive2003.pst. This strategy keeps things organized, but over time you build up quite a few archive data files and you might have to search through a number of archives to find something.

- Set up folder-based archive data files, such as CalendarArchive.pst. This strategy keeps all items of a certain type together, so finding an old e-mail, task, or other item you are looking for is fairly easy.

■ Set up project-based archive data files; for example, the set of Wedding folders mentioned in Chapter 10, "Using Folders," could be archived to a `WeddingArchive.pst` file.

■ Use a combination of the strategies outlined here to set up an archiving system that suits the way you want to work.

I recommend using a default archive data file and showing it in the Folder List. This makes the archived data available online at all times. You can then set up AutoArchiving properties for the folders in the default archive data store to archive items out of the default archive data store into other data stores based on year and project. I usually like to keep items in the main archive for about one year and then move them to other archive data files; this way, I can keep the main archive from becoming too cluttered. I usually don't need immediate access to items older than one year old. Figure 13.5 shows the default archive folder in the Folder List.

FIGURE 13.5

Showing the Archive data file in the Folder List makes it easy to work with archived items.

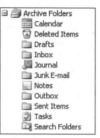

Archived data is no less valuable because it is not in your primary Outlook data store. If the data is worthless, it should be deleted and not archived. Because this data is still valuable, you should back it up as often as you back up your primary Outlook data store. If you lose a hard drive to a lightning strike or other calamity, you will miss your archive data as much as any other data, even if you don't need to access it very often.

Backing Up Outlook Data and Settings

Backing up Outlook data is different from archiving the data. Archiving moves or deletes data from your Outlook data store, whereas backing up the

note

Items that are archived from subfolders retain the folder structure they originally had. Even if no items are archived from a parent folder, it is created in the archive data file to retain the original folder structure.

data makes a copy of the data in another Outlook data file. Outlook settings such as your profile and e-mail account information also can be backed up, which is different from backing up your Outlook data.

Backing up your Outlook data and settings is very important because hard drives can fail and computers can be damaged by electrical power surges, power failures, and lightning strikes. You can use a surge suppressor strip and an uninterruptible power supply (UPS) to minimize electrical problems, but you can never completely eliminate all possible causes for computer data loss. It's better to be prepared for a disaster than to lose your data.

Backing Up Outlook Data

Your default PST file is usually named `Outlook.pst` and is located in a folder that is hidden from view by Windows. This folder is `C:\Documents and Settings\<profile name>\Local Settings\Application Data\Microsoft\Outlook`.

If you don't use tape or other backup software, the easiest way to back up your Outlook data is to find your PST file and make a copy of it to a removable hard drive, a network hard drive, or some other removable storage medium. Backups should be made regularly, at least once a week or more often depending on how valuable your data is to you. You never know when a disaster will happen and make it necessary to retrieve your backup data.

tip

To make the Local Settings folder visible, open Windows Explorer, select **Tools**, **Folder Options,** and then select the **View** tab. On the View tab, select the **Show Hidden Files and Folders** option and click **OK**.

Backing Up Outlook Settings

Microsoft Office 2003 includes a Save My Settings Wizard that you can use to back up Outlook settings as well as settings from other Office applications. To start the Save My Settings Wizard, select **Start**, **All Programs**, **Microsoft Office**, **Microsoft Office Tools**, **Microsoft Office 2003 Save My Settings Wizard**. Make sure to close Outlook and all other Office applications before you run this wizard.

Figure 13.6 shows the opening screen of the Save My Settings Wizard. Follow the directions in the Save My Settings Wizard to either save your settings or restore previously saved settings.

FIGURE 13.6

The Save My Settings Wizard enables you to save and restore settings for Outlook and other Office 2003 applications.

THE ABSOLUTE MINIMUM

In this chapter, you learned about archiving your Outlook data. To review, you now know how to

- Set up global and folder-level AutoArchive settings.
- Use the Do Not AutoArchive property.
- Perform a manual archive operation.
- Work with archived data.
- Back up your Outlook data and settings.

With the skills you acquired in this chapter, you can remove aged items from your Outlook data store and store them in archive data stores, working with the items as needed. In the next chapter, you will learn how to work with and customize Outlook views.

- Learning about different types of views.
- Understanding how to customize views.
- Learning how to work with the Customize View dialog.
- Knowing how to copy and distribute views.

14

OUTLOOK VIEWS

You have been using Outlook views for as long as you've been using Outlook, even if you didn't know it. The view determines what information is displayed when you view a folder and how the information is displayed. In this chapter, you will learn how to make selecting views easier, how to modify existing views, and how to create new custom views.

Identifying the Types of Views

Outlook views organize your data in different ways. You have already become familiar with these types of views without even knowing it, just by opening various Outlook folders:

- **Table**—Views in E-mail and Tasks folders
- **Card**—Views of Contacts folders
- **Timeline**—Views of Journal folders
- **Icon**—Views of Notes folders
- **Day/Week/Month**—Views in Calendar folders

Every folder has standard views available for it when it is created—for example, the familiar Messages view of the Inbox. You can customize the existing views and create new views whenever you want to change the way your Outlook data is displayed.

Folders can display any of the types of views, even if those view types aren't included in the standard views for a folder. For example, you could create an Icon view for the Inbox, but it would be of limited value because it would display e-mail icons for every e-mail item in the folder and show only part of the subject of each message. Table 14.1 shows the standard views available in each type of Outlook folder.

The standard views for folders include different types of views. In e-mail folders, the Messages, Last Seven Days, and Sent To views are all variations of table views. Message Timeline is a timeline view. Other types of folders also use different types of views among their standard views.

Table 14.1 Outlook Standard Views

Folder Type	Views
E-mail	Messages, Messages with AutoPreview, Last Seven Days, Unread Messages in This Folder, Sent To, Message Timeline
Calendar	Day/Week/Month, Day/Week/Month with AutoPreview, Active Appointments, Events, Annual Events, Recurring Appointments, By Category
Contacts	Address Cards, Detailed Address Cards, Phone List, By Category, By Company, By Location, By Follow-up Flag

Folder Type	Views
Tasks	Simple List, Detailed List, Active Tasks, Next Seven Days, Overdue Tasks, By Category, Assignment, By Person Responsible, Completed Tasks, Task Timeline
Notes	Icons, Notes List, Last Seven Days, By Category, By Color
Journal	By Type, By Contact, By Category, Entry List, Last Seven Days, Phone Calls

Every one of the standard views is constructed from one of the five basic types of views: Table, Timeline, Card, Day/Week/Month, or Icon. Filtering, sorting, grouping, and formatting are what make each view different. You will learn about the basic view types in the following sections, and the "Customizing Views" section in this chapter will show you how to customize existing views and create new ones.

I recommend you become familiar with all the standard views so you know what and how each one displays your data. You might even discover that you prefer a different view than the one that's the default. To examine the standard views for most Outlook folders, scroll down in the Navigation Pane to the Current View section and click each different view. Figure 14.1 shows the Current View section of the Navigation Pane for the Tasks folder.

> **tip**
>
> Folders normally don't display the Current View section of the Navigation Pane. To show this section of the Navigation Pane, select **View, Arrange By, Show Views in Navigation Pane**. Enabling the Current View section for one folder enables it for all folders of that type; for example, enabling it for the Inbox enables it for all e-mail folders.

FIGURE 14.1

The Current View section of the Navigation Pane.

Table Views

Table views display data in rows and columns, in the same way a worksheet in Excel displays data. Each row represents one Outlook item, and each column is a field from the item. Figure 14.2 shows the Inbox in an expanded Table view with the Reading Pane turned off. This view shows more fields for each item than you see when the Reading Pane is turned on.

FIGURE 14.2

A Table view of the Inbox displays information in rows and columns.

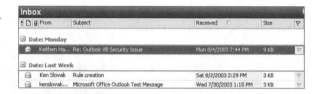

Most of the standard views are table-type views. The differences among the various table-type views for a folder are in which fields are shown, how the data in the folder is filtered, and how it is grouped.

Card Views

Card views are defined only in Contacts folders by default; however, you can define your own Card views for any type of folder. Cards look similar to the familiar Rolodex cards used for storing address and phone information on paper contact filing systems. Figure 14.3 shows a Detailed Address Card view of contacts.

FIGURE 14.3

Even though you can define Card views for other folders, they are most useful and informative when used in Contacts folders.

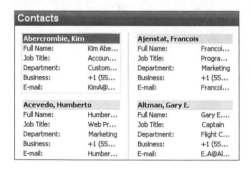

Timeline Views

Timelines show items organized by date, with columns in the timeline representing periods of time and rows representing data items from those time periods. Figure 14.4 shows a Timeline view of e-mail messages in the Inbox folder.

FIGURE 14.4

Timeline views show items ordered by the time they were received or created.

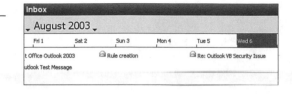

Timelines are particularly useful when you want to organize your data by time period, and are used mostly in Journal and Tasks folders.

Icon Views

An Icon view is defined only in the Notes folder. This viewing format is most useful for displaying limited information in a limited amount of space. Icon views display only the subject of an item and an icon indicating the item type. This view is useful in Notes, where the first line of text in the Note becomes the subject (see Figure 14.5). It is less useful for other types of items where important information is kept in many different fields.

Timeline views arrange items using different time intervals depending on whether they show a Day, Week, or Month view. Day view uses hours as the interval; Week and Month views use days as the time interval.

FIGURE 14.5

Icon view of the Notes folder shows the first line of text in Notes.

Day/Week/Month Views

Not surprisingly, Day/Week/Month views are used primarily for Calendar folders. They can be displayed showing one day in detail or a week's or month's worth of data (see Figure 14.6).

Day/Week/Month views are limited in the number of fields they can show, showing only fields related to time or date, recurrence, and some text information such as subject and location. The amount of text information shown depends on whether a Day, Week, or Month view is displayed.

Now that you are familiar with all the different types of views, it's time to learn how to customize them to display the data you want shown in the way you want it displayed.

Customizing Views

You can customize a view in two main ways. The first way is to change some of the view settings, such as changing how items are arranged or grouped in the view. The second way is to perform a full customization of the view. Like everything else in Outlook, both types of customization can be accomplished in a number of ways.

The settings you can change in a view without fully customizing the view are as follows:

- Showing and hiding the Reading Pane
- Arranging items by different fields
- Grouping items by different fields
- Expanding and collapsing groups
- Sorting items
- AutoPreviewing items

tip

You can change the relative sizes of the Reading Pane and a folder display pane by moving the mouse cursor over the border between the panes until it turns into a double bar with arrows and dragging the pane border to the right or left to change the pane's size. You can also change the relative sizes of other panes, such as the Navigation Pane in the same way.

Changing the Reading Pane size is a global change. If you change the Reading Pane size in one folder, the change will be reflected in all folders where the Reading Pane is displayed.

In the following sections, you will learn how to change different view settings. In "Working in the Customize View Dialog," you will learn how to fully customize views and create new views.

Showing and Hiding the Reading Pane

E-mail folders are the only type of folder that shows the Reading Pane by default. You can show the Reading Pane on the right side or bottom of the window, or you can turn it off completely in any folder by selecting **View**, **Reading Pane** and then clicking **Right**, **Bottom**, or **Off**. Figure 14.7 shows how to set the Reading Pane for display on the right in a Contacts folder.

FIGURE 14.7

The Reading Pane can be shown on the right or on the bottom of the folder view.

Both positions for the Reading Pane have advantages and disadvantages:

- **Right**—Provides more space for reading the selected item without having to scroll in the Reading Pane but shows fewer fields from each item in the view

- **Bottom**—Shows more fields from each item in the view but shows less of the text in the selected item

Choosing the Arranged By Option

How items are displayed in a view is based on the Arranged By selection for the view, groups that the items are sorted into, and the field on which the display is sorted. The default view of an E-mail folder arranges items by date, sorted by newest item on top.

To change the way items are arranged in a folder where the Reading Pane is displayed, click the **Arranged By** column header to open a menu that enables you to easily change the field by which items are arranged. Figure 14.8 shows the arrangements available in the Arranged By menu.

You can also open the Arranged By menu by selecting **View**, **Arrange By** in any folder. The list of fields in the Arranged By menu is available only in table-type views.

Using Show in Groups

You are already familiar with grouping items from the Messages view of the Inbox. Items in the Messages view are grouped by date, which is the date the item was sent or received. Items in a view are displayed in an order determined first by any groups and then within the groups by the Arranged By setting.

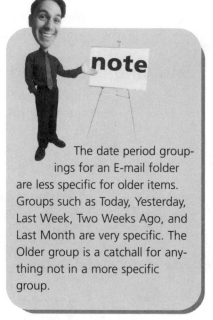

note

The date period groupings for an E-mail folder are less specific for older items. Groups such as Today, Yesterday, Last Week, Two Weeks Ago, and Last Month are very specific. The Older group is a catchall for anything not in a more specific group.

To toggle the display of groups, select **View**, **Arrange By**, **Show in Groups**.

Expanding and Collapsing Groups

You can expand or collapse a selected group or all groups from the Expand/Collapse Groups submenu of the View menu, as shown in Figure 14.9. The **Collapse This Group** and **Expand This Group** commands are enabled only if a group heading is selected.

FIGURE 14.8

The Arranged By menu enables you to quickly change how items in a folder are arranged.

FIGURE 14.9
Expanding and
collapsing
groups using the
menu com-
mands.

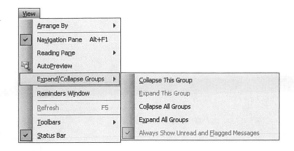

If you want to expand or collapse one group, it
often is easier to use the icons that appear next to
the group name in the view. Collapsed groups
show either a plus sign or a down-arrow icon, and
expanded groups show either a minus sign or an
up-arrow icon. Clicking an icon expands or col-
lapses that group. The menu command is easier to
use than the icons if you have a large expanded
group where the icon is scrolled out of view.

Click the **Always
Show Unread and
Flagged Messages** menu item to
show unread and flagged items
even in groups that are collapsed.
This option does not work in the
standard Messages view. To test
how it works, use the
Conversation view in a folder that
has groups of conversations with
some unread or flagged items.

Sorting Items

To quickly sort items in a table view by a field, click in the column header for that
field. A second click toggles the sort from ascending order to descending order, or
vice versa.

The sort field and sort order are indicated by an arrow in the field. An up-pointing
arrow indicates an ascending sort, and a down-pointing arrow indicates a descending sort, as shown in Figure 14.10.

FIGURE 14.10
Contacts shown
sorted in
descending order
on the Full
Name field.

Using the AutoPreview Feature

AutoPreview displays three lines of text under each item from the Notes field.
AutoPreview is available only in table-type views. Figure 14.11 shows AutoPreview
in the Inbox folder.

FIGURE 14.11

AutoPreview enables you to see a few lines of each message.

Customizing Using the Context Menu

Another way to customize the view is to right-click a column header in any Table view where the Reading Pane is not displayed. Figure 14.12 shows the customizing context menu displayed when you right-click a column header in a Table view.

FIGURE 14.12

The context menu enables you to perform many view customizations without using the View menu.

This menu has many commands that are useful for quickly customizing a view. Many of these commands are available from the <u>V</u>iew menu, but they are often buried many levels below that menu. The context menu is the most convenient way to access the following commands if you are displaying a Table view:

- **Arra<u>n</u>ge By**—Opens the Arrange By submenu. It's also used to turn groups on and off and to open the Customize dialog.

- **Sort <u>A</u>scending**—Sorts the view on the field that was right-clicked. Older, smaller, or lower data in the field is shown first.

- **Sort Des<u>c</u>ending**—Sorts the view on the field that was right-clicked. Newer, larger, or higher data in the field is shown first.

- **<u>G</u>roup By This Field**—Groups items by the contents of the specified field. For example, you can group the Contacts folder by Company while using a Table view.

■ **Group By Box**—Opens the Group By Box showing the fields used for grouping and the grouping hierarchy. Figure 14.13 shows a view of the Contacts folder using a Phone List view with Categories and Company groupings. Contacts are first grouped by Category and then by Company within each Category Group.

FIGURE 14.13

The Group By box enables you to set up a grouping hierarchy using drag and drop.

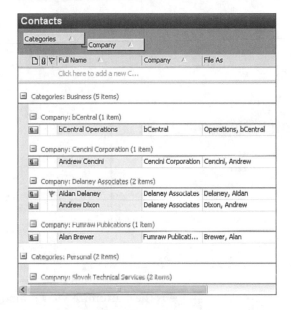

■ **Remove This Column**—Removes the selected field from the view. The field is not removed from the items, and all data in the field is retained. You can also remove a field from a Table view by dragging it from the row of column headers and dropping it anywhere except on the row of column headers. If you drop it at another place in the row of column headers, the position of the field in the columns is changed.

■ **Field Chooser**—Opens the Field Chooser dialog, which enables you to add fields to Table views (see Figure 14.14). See "Using the Field Chooser" later in this chapter for more information on using this feature.

■ **Alignment**—Opens a submenu, enabling you to left-, right-, or center-align the data for the selected field.

■ **Best Fit**—Sets the width of the selected field to the size needed for the item whose data takes up the most space in that field.

■ **Format Columns**—Opens the Format Columns dialog, shown in Figure 14.15. You will learn how to use the Format Columns dialog later in this chapter, in the section "Using the Format Columns Dialog."

FIGURE 14.14

The Field Chooser enables you to add additional fields to a view and to create and delete custom fields.

FIGURE 14.15

The Format Columns dialog enables you to set field format, width, label, and alignment.

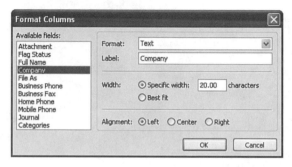

- **Customize Current View**—Opens the Customize View dialog, which provides access to all view customizations. The customizations available in the Customize View dialog are covered in the "Working in the Customize View Dialog" section.

Using the Field Chooser

To use the Field Chooser, drag a field from the list of available fields to the row of column headers and drop the field where you want it located. If a field is not available in the field list, click the arrow for the drop-down at the top of the Field Chooser and select the category of fields that contains the desired field. The list of field types contains fields that are used in the types of items in the folder as well as fields for other item types. Even though you can add a mismatched field, such as an e-mail field to a Contacts view, the field won't contain any data and usually can't be used to add data.

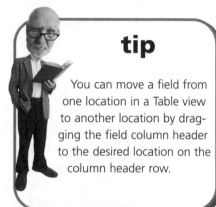

tip

You can move a field from one location in a Table view to another location by dragging the field column header to the desired location on the column header row.

You click the **New** and **Delete** buttons in this dialog to create and delete custom fields in the current folder. You will learn about custom fields in Chapter 20, "Customizing Outlook Forms."

Working in the Customize View Dialog

You can open the Customize View dialog, shown in Figure 14.16, by selecting **<u>View</u>**, **<u>Arrange By</u>**, **Custo<u>m</u>**. Or you can click the **Arranged By** column header shown when the Reading Pane is displayed to open the Arranged By menu and then select **Custom**. The title of the Customize View dialog always shows the name of the current view, and any changes you make to the view apply only to that view in the current folder.

FIGURE 14.16
The Customize View dialog.

Choosing the Fields in a View

Click the **<u>F</u>ields** button at the top of the Customize View dialog to open the Show Fields dialog, shown in Figure 14.17. This dialog provides similar functions to the Field Chooser and adds two additional functions, described in the following paragraphs.

The Maximum number of lines in multi-line mode option sets the number of lines displayed in views where the Reading Pane is shown. The Messages view of the Inbox shows the default two lines, for example. The first line displays an icon indicating the read/unread status of an item, the name of the person who sent the item, and the date the item was received. The second line shows the subject and an icon indicating whether attachments are included with the item. Increasing this number shows additional fields, such as size of the item.

To add fields to the view from the available fields list, select one or more fields and click the **Add** button. To remove fields from the view, select one or more fields in the Show these fields in this order list and click the **Remove** button. If the fields you want to add to the view aren't listed in the available fields list, click the arrow at the right of the **select available fields from** drop-down and select the field group that contains the fields you want.

FIGURE 14.17

The Show Fields dialog enables you to control which fields are displayed in a view.

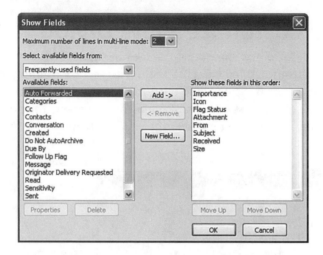

To change the order fields are shown in the view, select a field and click the **Move Up** or **Move Down** button.

You use the New Field, Properties, and Delete buttons for custom fields in the folder, and you will learn about their uses in Chapter 20. The Properties and Delete buttons are enabled only when a custom field is selected.

To save your changes in the Show Fields dialog, click **OK** to return to the Customize View dialog.

Grouping

Click the **Group By** button near the top of the Customize View dialog to open the Group By dialog, shown in Figure 14.18.

If the current view has groupings applied, the Automatically group according to arrangement checkbox is checked. To apply your own groupings to a view, uncheck this checkbox. You can apply up to four groupings in a view.

Select the field to group on from the drop-down list for each grouping. Then select whether to arrange items in that group in ascending or descending order and whether to show the field in the view for each grouping.

If the fields you want to group on are not shown in the drop-down list, select the appropriate field group in the **Select available fields from** drop-down.

FIGURE 14.18
The Group By dialog enables you to set up multiple grouping options for items in the current view.

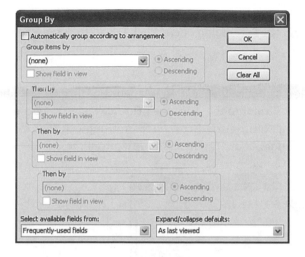

The Expand/collapse defaults drop-down for the view enables you to set the view to As last viewed, All expanded, or All collapsed when you select the view in a folder. You can later expand or collapse groups by choosing an option from the **View** menu or by clicking the **expand/collapse** icon to the left of a group name in the folder pane.

Click the **Clear All** button to clear all groupings you've created, while leaving the Group By dialog open; click **OK** to save your grouping settings.

Sorting

Click **Sort** in the Customize View dialog to open the Sort dialog (see Figure 14.19).

FIGURE 14.19
The Sort dialog enables you to sort your items on multiple fields.

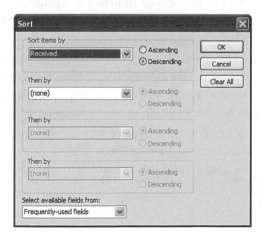

Unlike sorting by clicking a field column header, using the Sort dialog enables you to sort by up to four fields. Selection of fields to sort on and sort order are the same as in the Group By dialog. Click **Clear All** to clear any sorting changes you've made, while leaving the Sort dialog open. Click **OK** to save your sorting settings.

Filtering

Click **Filter** in the Customize View dialog to open the Filter dialog, shown in Figure 14.20. This dialog is similar to the Advanced Find dialog you learned about in Chapter 12, "Finding Things Anywhere." Refer to Chapter 12 for information on settings on the Messages, More Choices, and Advanced tabs.

FIGURE 14.20

When a filter is set for a view, only items that meet the filter criteria are shown; however, the remaining items in the folder still exist. Change the view or remove the filter to show all items in the folder.

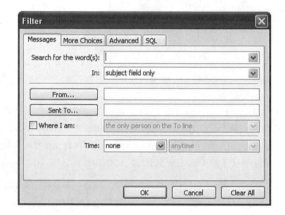

On the SQL tab, you can enter a filter in *DASL syntax*, which is an advanced way to find or filter items based on a schema of field names. *DASL* stands for DAV Searching and Locating, and *DAV* stands for Distributed Authoring and Versioning. That's quite a mouthful, so DASL is much easier to remember.

DASL syntax is an advanced topic based on Internet and HTML standards and is not covered in this book. To see examples of DASL syntax for a filter, however, you can enter one or more filter conditions in the other tabs of the Filter dialog and then click the **SQL** tab to see how the filter conditions are translated into DASL syntax.

When you filter the items in a folder, items that don't match the filter are hidden in the view. The items are still there; they have not been deleted or moved. They are just hidden from view. To see items that don't match the filter, either clear the filter or switch to a different view.

Other Settings

Click the **Other Settings** button in the Customize View dialog to open the Other Settings dialog, as shown in Figure 14.21. This dialog enables you to format the appearance of the folder when using the view.

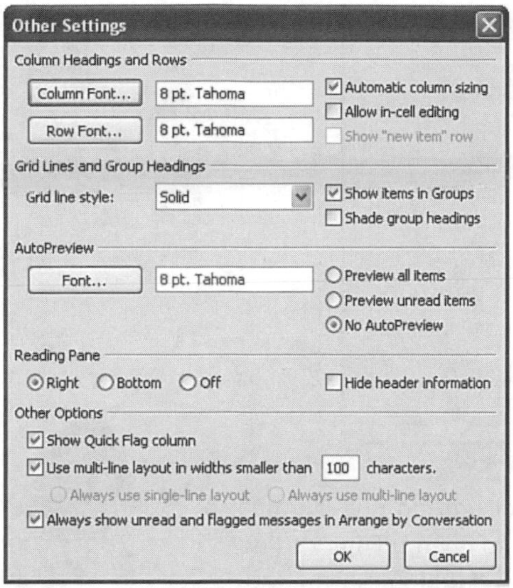

FIGURE 14.21

The Other Settings dialog controls formatting of items in the current view.

The settings you can configure in this dialog are

- Setting font, size, and style of the column headings in the view
- Setting font, size, and style of the rows in the view
- Enabling automatic column sizing to adjust column size to field data size
- Allowing in-cell editing, which enables you to edit data in a field in a view without opening the item for editing
- Showing the "new item" row for quick creation of new items
- Showing gridlines and the style of the gridline between rows
- Showing items in groups
- Shading group headings
- Enabling AutoPreview and setting AutoPreview style
- Showing or hiding the Reading Pane and header information
- Showing the Quick Flag column
- Allowing single or multi-line layout
- Showing or hiding unread and flagged messages in Arrange by Conversation views

Click **OK** to save the changes made in the Other Settings dialog.

Automatic Formatting

Click the **Automatic Formatting** button in the Customize View dialog to open the Automatic Formatting dialog, as shown in Figure 14.22. This dialog enables you to specify formatting rules for items in the view based on conditions you apply in the dialog.

FIGURE 14.22

In the Automatic Formatting dialog, you can specify formatting rules.

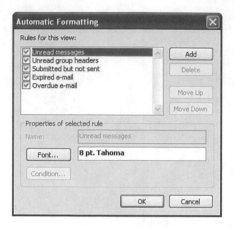

Click **Add** to add a new formatting rule. Name the rule and click **Condition** to open a Filter dialog similar to the Advanced Find dialog. Set the test conditions the item must meet to have the formatting rule applied and click **OK** to save the formatting rule conditions.

Click **Font** to select a font, font style, font size, font effects, and font color for the formatting rule. Click **OK** to apply the font formatting.

Click **OK** again to save the Automatic Formatting rule.

You will learn more about rules in Chapter 19, "Organizing E-mail with Rules."

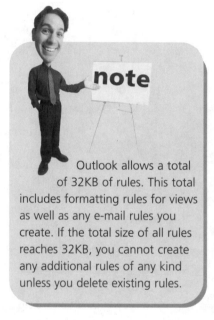

note

Outlook allows a total of 32KB of rules. This total includes formatting rules for views as well as any e-mail rules you create. If the total size of all rules reaches 32KB, you cannot create any additional rules of any kind unless you delete existing rules.

Using the Format Columns Dialog

Click **Format Columns** in the Customize View dialog to open the Format Columns dialog, as shown in Figure 14.15.

The Format Columns dialog enables you to set the display format, label, width, and alignment for the fields in the current view.

The format you can apply to a field depends on the type of field. Text fields can be displayed only as text. Fields that are true or false, such as whether an e-mail has any attachments, can be displayed in several formats.

■ Text fields can be formatted only as text. No other formatting options are available for text fields.

■ Status fields such as attachments can be formatted as Yes/No, On/Off, True/False or Icon. Icon displays an icon such as the paper clip used to indicate an item has an attachment, or a checkbox for fields such as Completed in a task item.

■ List fields such as flags can be formatted as Bitmap with pop-up list or text with pop-up list. Both formats show a pop-up list that contains all the available entries for the list. The flags pop-up list shows all the available Quick Flags in addition to selections for Unflagged and Completed.

■ Numeric fields show standard numeric format depending on the Regional settings in the Control Panel's Regional and Languages application, and various computer formats for numeric display such as 640KB for the size field.

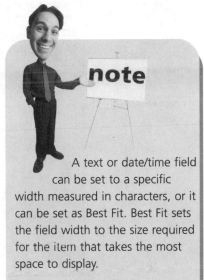

A text or date/time field can be set to a specific width measured in characters, or it can be set as Best Fit. Best Fit sets the field width to the size required for the item that takes the most space to display.

Text or date/time fields can be set to left, right, or center alignment.

■ Date/time fields show various formats for displaying date, time, and date/time with and without the day of the week. Many date/time fields also have a Best Fit format that selects the display format based on the column width in which the field is displayed.

A field's label is shown as the column header. It can be any text you enter and doesn't change the actual name of the field; it just changes what the field is called in that view.

Reset Current View

Click **Reset Current View** to clear any changes made to the current view in any of the Customize View settings and return the view to its previous settings.

Creating a New View

The dialog used to create a new view is buried deep under the <u>V</u>iew menu. To open the Custom View Organizer dialog, shown in Figure 14.23, select **<u>V</u>iew**, **<u>A</u>rrange By**, **Current <u>V</u>iew**, **<u>D</u>efine Views**.

FIGURE 14.23

The Custom View Organizer dialog enables you to create new views and manage existing views.

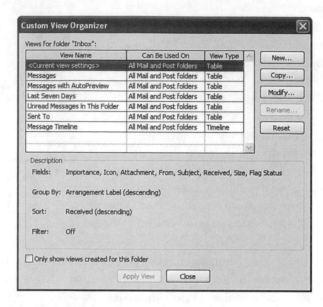

You use the Custom View Organizer dialog to

- Create new views.
- Copy existing views to a new view.
- Modify existing views.
- Rename user-defined views.
- Delete user-defined views.
- Reset existing standard views.

The following sections describe how to use the buttons and functions in the Custom View Organizer dialog.

Using the New Button in the Custom View Organizer

Click **New** to open the Create a New View dialog, as shown in Figure 14.24.

In the Create a New View dialog, enter a name for the new view, select the type of view to create, and designate where the view can be used. Click **OK** to create the new view. The Customize View dialog, shown in Figure 14.16, opens so that you can define the settings for the new view.

At this time, it is very important to set the Can be used on setting in the Create a New View dialog to indicate how you want the new view used. You can use either of the This Folder options if you want the view used only in the current folder. If you think you might ever want to use the view in any other folder of the same type, select the All option.

FIGURE 14.24

The Create a New View dialog enables you to create any type of view in any Outlook folder.

This setting cannot be changed after the Create a New View dialog is closed. If you forget to make a new view available in other folders, you later can copy the view to another new view and make the copy available in other folders.

Using the Copy Button in the Custom View Organizer

Back in the Custom View Organizer dialog, click **Copy** to open the Copy View dialog. Give the new view a name and designate where it can be used. Click **OK** to copy the selected view to a new view. The Customize View dialog shown in Figure 14.16 opens so that you can define the settings for the new view.

Using the Modify Button in the Custom View Organizer

In the Custom View Organizer dialog, click **Modify** to open the Customize View dialog shown in Figure 14.16, where you can modify the settings for the selected view.

Using the Rename Button in the Custom View Organizer

Click **Rename** to open the Rename View dialog when a user-defined view is selected in the list of available views. There, enter a new name for the view and click **OK** to rename the view.

Only user-defined views can be renamed. If a standard view is selected, the **Rename** button is disabled.

Using the Delete and Reset Buttons in the Custom View Organizer

Click **Delete** when a user-defined view is selected in the list of available views to delete the user-defined view. Standard views cannot be deleted. If a standard view is selected, the Delete button becomes the **Reset** button.

Click **Reset** when a standard view is selected in the list of available views to reset the view to its default setting. Some views, such as Detailed List in a Tasks folder cannot be reset, and for those views the **Reset** button is disabled.

Applying Views to Folders

To show only views that were created in the current folder in the list of available views, check the **Only show views created for this folder** checkbox.

When you are finished creating or modifying a view, click **Apply View** at the bottom of the Custom View Organizer dialog to save the selected view and make it the current view.

Click **Close** to close the Custom View Organizer dialog.

Copying and Distributing Views

The best way to make a view available in other folders is to make it available to all similar folders when the view is created, as you learned in the preceding section. If you didn't do this when you created the view, you must copy all the views from the source folder to the target folder to make the view available, or you can copy the view to a new view and apply that view to all similar folders.

To copy all the views in a folder to another folder if you are using an Exchange mailbox, select the folder where you want the view to be available. This folder is the target folder. Then select **File**, **Folder**, **Copy Folder Design** to open the Copy Design From dialog, as shown in Figure 14.25.

FIGURE 14.25

The Copy Design From dialog, which is available only if you are using an Exchange mailbox, makes it possible to copy views from one folder to another.

The Copy Folder Design menu command described in this section is available only if you are using Microsoft Exchange server and are using an Exchange mailbox.

After you've opened the dialog, do the following:

1. In the **Copy design from this folder** list, select the folder that contains the view you want to copy as the source folder.

2. Check the **Forms & Views** checkbox to copy all views and published forms from the source folder to the target folder.

3. Click **OK** to start the copy operation.

You can also check the Permissions, Rules, and Description checkboxes to copy those folder design elements to the target folder from the source folder.

To distribute views to other users, you must first create a new Outlook data file and then copy the folder design of the folder that has the view to the new data store:

1. Select **File**, **New**, **Outlook Data File** to create a new PST file. If you intend to distribute the view to users of older versions of Outlook, select the **Outlook 97-2002 Personal Folders File (.pst)** option. Some view settings in Outlook 2003 do not exist in earlier versions of Outlook, so a view distributed to those versions of Outlook may not look the same or may even cause errors.

2. Enter the name and location of the new PST file in the Create or Open Outlook Data File dialog and click **OK** to create the new PST file.

3. Click **OK** again to accept the default settings in the Create Microsoft Personal Folders dialog.

4. Display the Folder List and select the new Personal Folders file, shown in Figure 14.26. This file will list only Deleted Items and Search Folders folders.

FIGURE 14.26

A new Personal Folders file is used to distribute views to other users.

5. Right-click the folder that has the view you want to distribute to other users and drag it to the new Personal Folders file. Drop the folder on Personal Folders and select **Copy** from the context menu. Rename the copied folder, giving it a descriptive name. For example, if you are copying the Inbox folder, name the new folder `InboxViews`. You learned how to rename folders in Chapter 10, "Using Folders."

6. Close the Personal Folders file with the copy of the source folder by right-clicking **Personal Folders** in the Folder List and selecting **Close "Personal Folders"**.

To use the custom views in a Personal Folders file, follow these steps:

1. Open the Personal Folders file by selecting **File**, **Open**, **Outlook Data File**. Navigate to the file, select it, and click **OK** to open it.

2. Copy the folder to your Outlook data file by right-clicking on the folder and dragging it to somewhere in your data file. Select **Copy** when you drop the folder in its new location.

3. Select the copied folder as the current folder in the Folder List in the Navigation Pane.

4. Select **View**, **Arrange By**, **Current View**, **Define Views** to open the Custom View Organizer dialog.

5. Select the view you want to use and click **Copy**.

6. In the Copy View dialog, give the view a new name and select the **All** option to make the view available in all folders of that type.

7. Click **OK** twice and then click **Close** to make the new view available.

THE ABSOLUTE MINIMUM

In this chapter, you learned about Outlook views. To review, you now know how to

Identify the types of Outlook views.

Customize existing views.

Create new views.

Copy views and distribute them to other Outlook users.

With the skills you acquired in this chapter, you learned many different ways to organize your information in different Outlook views. In the next chapter, you will learn how to print Outlook information.

IN THIS CHAPTER

- Using table and memo formats for printing.
- Printing different types of Outlook items.
- Customizing Outlook printouts.

15

PRINTING OUTLOOK INFORMATION

Even though Outlook makes a great place to store information, sometimes you want to print some of that information. Outlook print styles are used as templates for printing information in different formats. In this chapter, you will learn how to print Outlook information and customize print styles.

Printing Formats

All Outlook print styles are based on either a table or memo format. A table format is arranged in rows and columns, whereas a memo format is formatted like the page of a book. Table formats print each item in its own row, with the information for that item printed in the columns of the row. Table formats can print information from many items on one printed page. Memo formats print each item in a separate area of a page or on its own page, so the trade-off with printing formats is how much detail you want printed versus how many pages are printed. Figure 15.1 shows a print preview of tasks in a table format. Each task is a row, with the tasks sorted by due date. The columns shown are Status (with completion indicated by a check mark), Subject, and Due Date.

FIGURE 15.1

Table format can be used to print information from many items on one page.

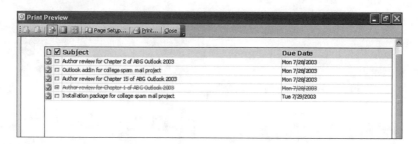

Figure 15.2 shows a print preview of one task shown in memo format. Here, the task fields are shown as if they are in a memo or in a page in a book, with more information from the task shown than in the table view.

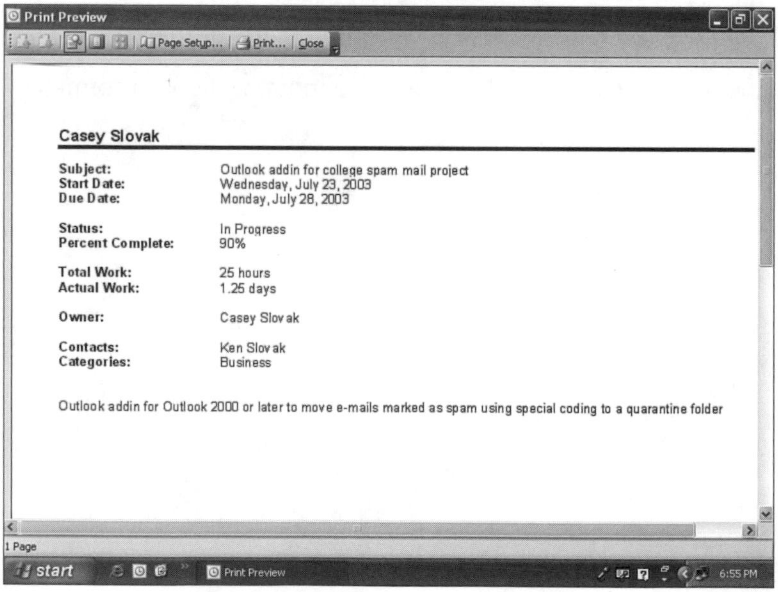

FIGURE 15.2

Memo format prints information from each item with the information formatted like a page in a book.

Printing Outlook Items

Three menu commands on Outlook's **File** menu control printing: **Page Setup**, **Print Preview**, and **Print**. You can also execute the **Print** menu command by pressing the keyboard shortcut **Ctrl+P**.

Table 15.1 shows the functions of each of the printing menu commands.

Table 15.1   Outlook Printing Menu Commands

Menu Command	Function
Page Setup	Selects the print format to use for the printout. Also used to define settings for print formats and create custom print formats.
Print Preview	Shows a screen preview of a printout using the current page setup.
Print	Opens a dialog for selecting print options.

The Page Setup Flyout

The Page Setup flyout is a context-sensitive menu. The print styles available on the menu change depending on the types of items the folder can contain. Figure 15.3 shows the Page Setup flyout commands for a Calendar folder.

FIGURE 15.3
The available print styles for the current folder and view appear in the Page Setup flyout.

The one constant on the Page Setup flyout is the **Define Print Styles** command, which opens the Define Print Styles dialog and enables you to define the default settings for the available print styles. You can also create custom print styles copied from the standard print styles in the Define Print Styles dialog. The Define Print Styles dialog can also be opened from the Print dialog, which you will learn how to use in the "Customizing Styles and Printouts" section of this chapter.

Table 15.2 shows the standard print styles available for each Outlook folder type.

Table 15.2   Standard Print Styles

Folder Type	Print Style
Calendar	Daily, Weekly, Monthly, Tri-fold, Calendar Details, Table, Memo
Contacts	Card, Small Booklet, Medium Booklet, Table, Memo, Phone Directory
E-mail	Table, Memo
Tasks	Table, Memo
Journal	Table, Memo
Notes	Table, Memo

The Page Setup Dialog

The **Page Setup** command on the **File** menu enables you to select a print style for the current printout. When you select a print style, the Page Setup dialog is opened, allowing you to set up print and printer options. The Page Setup dialog has three tabs for setting printout options: Format, Paper, and Header/Footer. Figure 15.4 shows the Format tab of the Page Setup dialog for the Daily style printout of a Calendar folder.

The Format Tab

The Format tab is divided into three sections: Preview, Options, and Fonts.

The Preview section shows a thumbnail image of how the printout will appear on paper. This image shows how the selected style will look when printed but doesn't show details like a print preview does.

tip

Some print styles are available for a folder only when certain views are used for that folder. For example, in a Calendar folder, Table print styles are available only when you use a table view such as By Category. When a table view is used in a Calendar folder, only Table and Memo print styles are available. If you don't see a specific print style available in the Page Setup flyout, change to a different view type.

FIGURE 15.4
On the Format tab of the Page Setup dialog, you can set print formatting options.

The Options section is blank for most print styles, with no available options. Any style listed as Table or Memo will not have printout options available in the Options section of the Format tab. The specialized print styles for Contacts and Calendar folders do have options available in the Options section of the Format tab.

For Contacts styles, the options enable you to set how many columns are printed on each page, whether items start on a new page or immediately follow each other, whether letter headings and contact indexes are included, and how many blank forms are printed at the end of the printout.

For Calendar styles, you can select how many pages are printed per time period, whether to include the TaskPad and a notes area in the printout, and what time periods are included in the printout. The notes area can be either blank or lined and is used for handwritten notes you might want to add to the printout. Some Calendar print styles also enable you to select whether to print weekend days and the arrangement of days from top to bottom or left to right. Note that the Calendar Details style allows printing of files attached to

tip

Any of the print styles that enable you to print attached files print the attachments only to the default system printer. Outlook checks for the default system printer only when it starts, so if you change default printers while Outlook is running, Outlook does not recognize the change. Select a default printer before you start Outlook, or if you decide you want to change the default printer, exit Outlook, change the printer, and then restart Outlook.

calendar items, although the attachments are printed only to the default printer. You cannot select a different printer to use for this printout.

The Fonts section of the Format tab enables you to set the font properties for headings and text in the printout and to select whether to use gray shading in the printout.

The Paper Tab

The Paper tab of the Page Setup dialog is shown in Figure 15.5.

FIGURE 15.5

On the Paper tab of the Page Setup dialog, you can select the paper type and printout orientation.

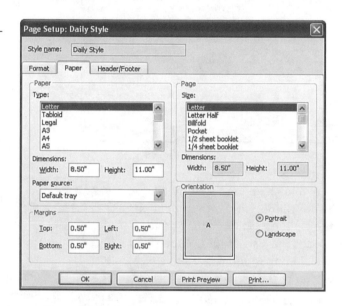

On this tab, you can select paper and page sizes and layouts, page margins, and whether to print in vertical (portrait) or horizontal (landscape) orientation .

The Header/Footer Tab

The Header/Footer tab of the Page Setup dialog is shown in Figure 15.6.

The Header/Footer tab enables you to add a header and/or a footer to the printout. You can select separate font styles for headers and footers, and you can use the icons located below the footer pane to insert the page number, total number of pages, printout date, printout time, and user name in a header or footer pane. You can also type text in the header and footer panes to be printed on each page of the printout. For example, you might want to place the text "Confidential" in 24-point red text as a footer for each page in a printout.

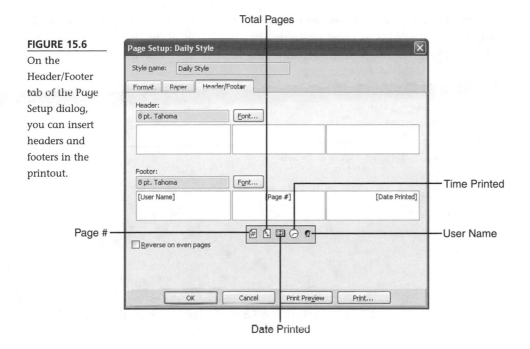

FIGURE 15.6
On the Header/Footer tab of the Page Setup dialog, you can insert headers and footers in the printout.

After you set up your pages for the selected style, click **OK** to save the changes for the current Outlook session. Click **Print Preview** to see how your settings will look when printed, or click **Print** to open the Print dialog.

The Print Preview Dialog

The Print Preview dialog shows you what your printout will look like. Within the printout area of the dialog, the cursor is shaped like a magnifying glass with either a plus or minus sign inside. Clicking the mouse when a plus sign is displayed in the magnifying glass cursor enlarges the preview image and changes the plus sign to a minus sign. Clicking the mouse when a minus sign is displayed in the magnifying glass cursor shrinks the preview image to its original size and changes the minus sign to a plus sign. Zooming in and out like this in the print preview does not change the printed image size; it just changes the display in the print preview dialog.

tip

Print preview is not available for HTML e-mail items from the Outlook **File** menu. However, you can preview plain text or rich text formatted items.

If you use Word as your e-mail editor, you can preview a printout for an HTML message. Open the message and select **File**, **Print Preview** to use Word to preview the printout.

The Print Preview dialog toolbar, shown in Figure 15.7, has icons for paging up and down in previews of multi-page printouts; showing the print preview actual size, on one page, and on multiple pages; opening the Page Setup and Print dialogs, and closing the Print Preview dialog.

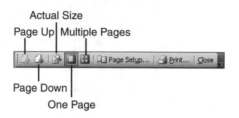

FIGURE 15.7

The Print Preview toolbar in the Print Preview dialog controls how the print preview is shown.

The Print Dialog

The Print dialog is the central location for all actual printing in Outlook (see Figure 15.8).

FIGURE 15.8

On the Print dialog, you can set printer options and start the printout.

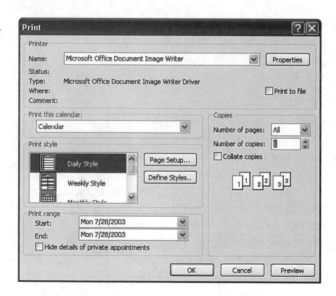

On the Print dialog, you can select a printer, set the printer properties, set the pages and the number of copies to print, select the print style for the printout, and select print ranges to use. If you are printing items that support a Private setting, such as calendar and contact items, you can select whether to hide details of private items.

You also can open the Page Setup, Define Styles, and Print Preview dialogs from the Print dialog to make additional changes prior to printing.

When everything is set up to your satisfaction, click **OK** to begin printing.

Customizing Styles and Printouts

tip

You can use only the default system printer if you want to print attachments with the printout.

Selecting the Memo style in the Print dialog shows an option for printing attachments when e-mail items are being printed. This is the only way to select printing of attachments in e-mail items; the option isn't available in any of the other printing dialogs.

The Define Print Styles dialog, shown in Figure 15.9 for a Calendar folder, enables you to modify the defaults for print styles. You can change the default settings for a standard print style or copy a standard print style to a new style, which enables you to create custom print styles and keep the default settings for the standard print styles.

FIGURE 15.9

The Define Print Styles dialog enables you to edit, copy, and reset default print styles.

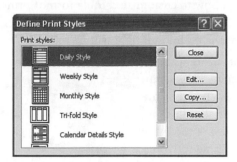

Select an available style for the current folder from the Print Styles list and click **Edit** to open the Page Setup dialog. You learned how to use the Page Setup dialog earlier in this chapter. Any changes you make to a style become the default settings for that style.

Click **Copy** to create a copy of the selected style. Because any changes you make to a print style become the default settings for that style, it's a good idea to make a copy of a print style before you start modifying it. That way, you are changing only the copy and not changing the defaults for the selected style. Make changes to a standard print style only when you want all copies of that style to always start with the changed settings. Both standard and custom styles can be copied.

Click **Reset** to reset a standard print style to its default settings. This button is useful if you have modified a standard print style and want to remove all your changes and return to the original, standard style. You cannot reset a custom print style; you can only change it again or delete it.

When a custom style is selected, the Reset button becomes a Delete button. Click **Delete** to delete the custom style.

The only other customization Outlook allows for printouts applies to table style printouts and is one of those Outlook features that isn't well documented. Table styles print the columns and rows that are shown in a Table view of a folder. If a field is not shown in the table view, data from that field isn't printed. If you want to print data from a field, make sure the field is displayed in the table view before you start your printout. You learned how to add fields to a view in Chapter 14, "Outlook Views."

Customizing a Print Style

In this example, you will learn how to customize a table format print style. The printout will be for the Inbox folder, and you will add an additional field to the Inbox table view so data from the additional field will be printed.

The fields displayed in the Inbox are usually partly concealed by the Reading Pane. If the Reading Pane is not displayed, you can more easily see which fields are shown in the view. The fields displayed in the standard Messages Arranged By Date view of the Inbox are Importance, UnRead, Attachment, From, Subject, Received Date, Size, and Flag. The field you will add to the view in this example is the To field.

The first steps for customizing this printout are closing the Reading Pane and adding the To field to the view as follows:

1. Select **View**, **Reading Pane**, **Off** to close the Reading Pane.

tip

You can turn on the Reading Pane again after you add the additional field to the Inbox view. The printout will print data from the additional field even if it is not visible when the Reading Pane is on.

2. Right-click in the column headings of the view and select **Field Chooser**.

3. In the Field Chooser, scroll down the list of fields, drag the **To** field to the column headings, and drop the field just before the Subject heading.

4. Close the Field Chooser.

Now that the To field is displayed in the view, it will be printed with the other fields in the view.

To create a new, customized table format print style, follow these steps:

1. Select **Page Setup**, **Define Print Styles** to open the Define Print Styles dialog, shown in Figure 15.10.

FIGURE 15.10

Using the Define Print Styles dialog, you can edit, copy, or reset existing print styles.

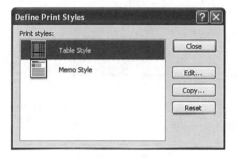

2. Select the Table Style print style and click on **Copy** to open the Page Setup dialog.

3. In the **Style name** entry field, change the name of the new style from Copy of Table Style to Custom Table Style (you can use any name you like).

4. On the Format tab, uncheck the **Print using gray shading** checkbox to remove the shading from the grouping headings.

5. Select the **Header/Footer** tab, shown in Figure 15.11.

6. To change the Header font to 12 point Tahoma, select **Font**. In the Size area, click **12** and then click **OK**.

7. Click in the leftmost text area of the Header section and click on the **Page Number** icon, which is the leftmost icon below the Footer section, to insert the code for printing the page number.

8. Type a space and the word of, then another space, and then click on the second icon from the left to insert the code for **Total Pages**.

9. Click in the rightmost Header section text area and then click the **Date Printed** icon, which is the middle icon.

FIGURE 15.11

The Header/ Footer tab enables you to print headers and footers containing Outlook information as well as text you enter yourself.

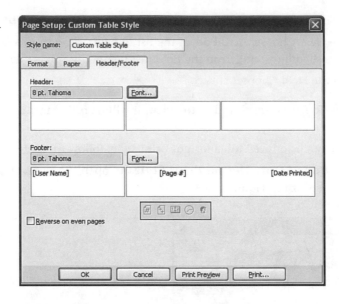

10. Delete the Footer printing codes from all three Footer text areas. The Page Setup dialog should look like the one shown in Figure 15.12.

FIGURE 15.12

The customized table format style uses a custom header, no footer and customized printing settings.

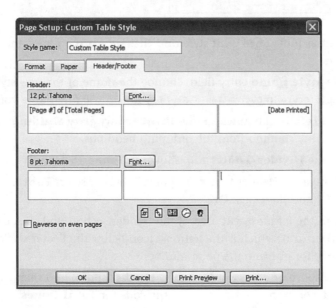

11. Click **OK** to save the new, customized print style and then **Close** to close the Define Print Styles dialog.

The new Custom Table Style print style is now available for use in the Define Print Styles and Print dialogs.

Customizing other print styles is similar to the procedure for customizing a table style. Experiment with different print styles and custom settings to see how you can customize other print styles. If you don't like a custom print style after you design it, select it in the Define Print Styles dialog and click **Delete** to delete it.

Outlook's printing and formatting options are sufficient for many printing needs but are somewhat limited. Outlook printouts certainly don't qualify as what you see is what you get (WYSIWYG) printing. In fact, not much—if anything—has been enhanced in Outlook's printing options since Outlook 97 was originally released.

Additional Printing Options

To further customize printing of Outlook data, you must turn to other applications. You can copy Outlook data to Excel and use Excel to format and print your data, or you can use Word to format Outlook data for printing.

To copy data to Excel, select a table-style view of a folder in Outlook and select all the items you want to print. Press **Ctrl+C** to copy the data, switch to Excel, and then press **Ctrl+V** to paste the data into Excel. After the data is in Excel, you can use Excel's formatting options to format the data for printing.

There are other ways to format Outlook data for printing, such as linking data with Access and designing Access reports to print the data, using third-party libraries for printing, and using program code to merge Outlook field data into Word form fields or bookmarks, but such topics are beyond the scope of this book.

You can also merge Outlook contact data into Word as part of a mail merge. You will learn about mail merging using Word in Chapter 17, "Setting Up a Mail Merge."

If you are interested in learning more about other ways to print and format your Outlook data, see the Web page `http://www.slipstick.com/dev/customprint.htm` on the excellent Outlook resource Web site Slipstick.

THE ABSOLUTE MINIMUM

In this chapter, you learned about printing Outlook items. To review, you now know

What options are available for printing items in Outlook, including how to select a print format.

How to use the printing menu commands.

How to customize print settings.

With the skills you acquired in this chapter, you can print your Outlook data. In the next chapter, you will learn how to import and export Outlook data.

16

IMPORTING AND EXPORTING WITH OUTLOOK

In most cases, if you want to use data from another program in Outlook, you must import the data into Outlook. And the opposite is also true: If you want to use Outlook data in another program, you must export the Outlook data. In this chapter, you will learn how to use Outlook's Import and Export Wizard.

Understanding Import and Export Formats

Outlook can import and export data in a number of different formats and to and from a number of different programs. Some of the import formats may not be available in Outlook unless they are installed as optional components.

Installing Outlook Import Formats

To see which components have been installed, follow steps 1 to 6 in this section. Components that have not been installed are listed as Not Available or Installed on First Use. Appendix A, "Microsoft Office Outlook 2003 Installation," contains instructions for installing all Outlook components, which I recommend.

To add formats that are not already installed, do the following:

1. Make sure you have your Office CD available.

2. Open the **Add/Remove Programs** application in the Control Panel.

3. Select **Microsoft Office 2003** and click the **Change** button.

4. When the setup screen opens, select the **Add or Remove Features** option and click **Next**.

5. Make sure all the applications you want installed are checked and also check the **Choose advanced customization of applications** checkbox. Then click **Next**.

6. Click the plus sign to expand the **Microsoft Office Outlook** tree. Do the same to expand the **Importers and Exporters** tree and then the **Import from Other Formats** tree, as shown in Figure 16.1.

7. Select each importer to install by clicking on the hard drive icon next to the importer.

8. Select **Run from My Computer** for each importer you want to install.

caution

The Change button may not be available if Office was installed using a Windows administrative profile and you are logged in with a user profile. If you do not have a Change button, log out of your current Windows profile and have someone with an administrative profile install the optional import components.

caution

If you uncheck any of the installed Office applications, they will be uninstalled. Be very careful about which Office applications are checked and which are not checked.

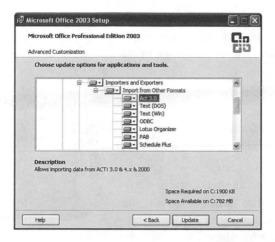

FIGURE 16.1

Some Outlook
importers are
optional compo-
nents and must
be installed to
be available.

9. Click **Update** and follow the Office installer instructions to complete installation of the importers.

Using Import Formats

If all the Outlook import formats are installed, the import formats shown in Table
16.1 are available.

Table 16.1   Outlook Import Formats

Import Format	Versions
Outlook Express	4, 5, 6
Eudora (Pro and Light)	2, 3, 4
ACT!	3, 4, 2000
Comma Separated Values (CSV)	Windows, DOS
Tab Separated Values (TSV)	Windows, DOS
Lotus Organizer	4, 5
Microsoft Access	
Microsoft Excel	
Personal Address Book (PAB)	
Personal Folders File (PST)	
Schedule+	7
Schedule Plus Interchange (SC2)	
VCard (VCF)	
iCalendar and vCalendar (VCS)	

The Outlook Express and Eudora import options are available under the **Import Internet Mail Account Settings** and **Import Internet Mail and Addresses** selections.

You might find that the program you want to import from isn't listed or that you are using a later version of a program that is listed. Try the following to work around either of these issues:

- If a program from which you want to import data into Outlook is not listed in the available import formats, see whether the program can save data in one of the supported import formats.

- If you are using a version of a supported program that is later than the supported versions, see whether that program can save data in an earlier format that is supported by Outlook or in one of the supported import formats.

tip

You can also import VCard and VCS files by double-clicking them in Windows Explorer.

tip

Microsoft Excel and Access provide additional import and export formats that Outlook does not provide. You can use Excel or Access as an intermediate application for imports and exports. First, import or export your data into Excel or Access and then either import into Outlook from Excel or Access, or export or save from Excel or Access into the desired format.

Using Export Formats

Outlook supports the export formats shown in Table 16.2.

Table 16.2 Outlook Export Formats

Export Format	Versions
Comma Separated Values (CSV)	Windows, DOS
Tab Separated Values (TSV)	Windows, DOS
Microsoft Access	
Microsoft Excel	
Personal Folders File (PST)	

Using the Import and Export Wizard

The best way to understand the import/export process is to go through the wizard and see the options. The following example shows how to import a file with comma separated values into the My Family and Friends folder in Outlook.

Importing Data Into Outlook

To use the Import and Export Wizard to import data into Outlook, do the following:

1. Open the Import and Export Wizard by selecting **File**, **Import and Export**. For this example, I'm choosing **Import from another program or file** from the available options, as shown in Figure 16.2. This is the default selection when you open the Import and Export Wizard.

FIGURE 16.2

The Import and Export Wizard opening screen opens with the option to import from another program or file selected.

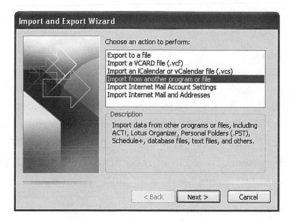

2. Select the file format you want to import or export and click **Next** to open the next wizard screen. For this example, I'm going to choose **Comma Separated Values (Windows)**. Figure 16.3 shows the Import a File screen of the wizard.

FIGURE 16.3

The Import a File screen enables you to select the file format to import.

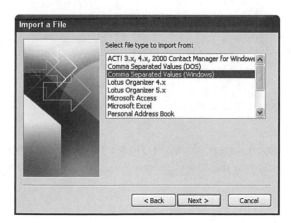

3. In the following screen, shown in Figure 16.4, select a file to import and click **Next** to proceed with the import.

FIGURE 16.4

Enter a filename or browse to the file you want to import and select options for dupli-cates created by importing.

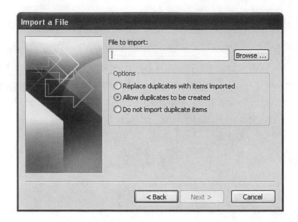

4. If you are importing data, you can choose to replace duplicate items with the imported items, allow duplicate items to be created, or not import duplicate items. Click **Next** to go to the next Import and Export Wizard screen.

5. Select the folder where you want to import the file. Figure 16.5 shows the folder selection screen. Click **Next** to go to the final Import and Export Wizard screen.

FIGURE 16.5

Select the folder where you want to import the file data in this wizard screen.

6. On the final import screen, shown in Figure 16.6, click the **Map Custom Fields** button to open the Map Custom Fields dialog.

FIGURE 16.6

FIGURE 16.6

The final wizard screen enables you to map custom fields, change the destination folder for the import, and finish the import process.

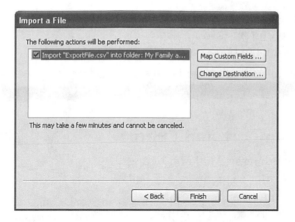

In the Map Custom Fields dialog, you can set how the fields in the imported data are imported into Outlook. Field names in the imported data may be different from Outlook field names, so you need to tell Outlook how to import the data. For example, if you import data that includes the field name Name1, and your equivalent Outlook field name is LastName, you need to map Name1 to LastName. That way, the LastName field is filled with the imported data in the Name1 field from the imported file.

To select how fields are mapped, do the following:

1. The Map Custom Fields dialog, shown in Figure 16.7, shows the fields in the imported data in the From pane and the Outlook fields the data will be mapped to in the To pane.

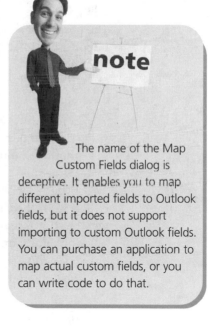

note

The name of the Map Custom Fields dialog is deceptive. It enables you to map different imported fields to Outlook fields, but it does not support importing to custom Outlook fields. You can purchase an application to map actual custom fields, or you can write code to do that.

FIGURE 16.7

The Map Custom Fields dialog.

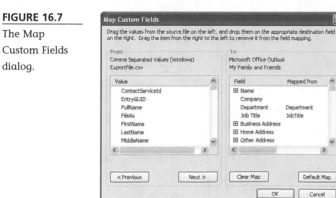

2. After mapping fields as needed, click **OK** to close the Map Custom Fields dialog and return to the final import or export screen.

3. Click **Finish** to close the wizard and start the import or export operation.

Final Thoughts About Import and Export

If you chose to import Internet Mail and Addresses, you can select to import mail, addresses, or both. If you select Outlook Express as the program to import from, you can also choose to import Outlook Express rules in addition to mail and addresses.

The process of exporting from Outlook to a file and importing using the other import choices is similar to importing from another program or a file. Select the type of import or export you want to perform and follow the steps in the wizard to complete other imports into Outlook or exports from Outlook.

Use a file you don't care about for a trial export into another program and create a new Outlook folder that you can easily delete later for a trial import into Outlook. After your trial import or export is finished, examine the results to learn whether they are satisfactory. You may have to do additional formatting of the new data or even try a different import or export format to achieve the results you want.

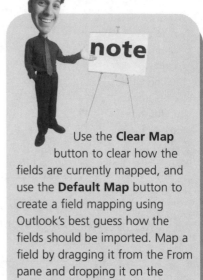

note

Use the **Clear Map** button to clear how the fields are currently mapped, and use the **Default Map** button to create a field mapping using Outlook's best guess how the fields should be imported. Map a field by dragging it from the From pane and dropping it on the Outlook field that will be mapped to the import field.

tip

Using Outlook Express to import from Outlook and to export to Outlook is often more successful than using Outlook for this purpose. To import or export from Outlook Express, open Outlook Express and select **File, Import** or **File**, **Export**. Follow the Outlook Express Import or Export Wizard steps to complete the import or export.

THE ABSOLUTE MINIMUM

In this chapter, you learned about importing and exporting Outlook items. To review, you now know how to

Identify the data formats supported for importing and exporting.

Use the Import and Export Wizard.

With the skills you acquired in this chapter, you now can import and export Outlook data. In the next chapter, you will learn how to perform mail merges of Outlook data to Word documents.

PART V

ADVANCED OUTLOOK TOPICS

IN THIS CHAPTER

- Understanding what mail merges are.
- Learning about setting up a mail merge from Outlook or from Word using Outlook contacts.
- Understanding how to create form letters for mail merges.
- Learning about merging to e-mail, labels, and envelopes.

17

SETTING UP A MAIL MERGE

You can use mail merges to send out form letters, e-mails, labels, and envelopes with information from one or more of your Outlook contacts inserted automatically in the merged documents. Among other things, you can use mail merges for mass mailings, holiday or other special occasion greetings, or anything else for which you want to use information from your contacts in the documents you are producing. In this chapter, you will learn how to set up and perform mail merges.

Understanding Mail Merges

Mail merges are used to create personalized documents that seem to have been written individually, even though copies of the document are generated for many different recipients. For example, Outlook can supply each recipient's first name or nickname for a greeting field in a merge document.

Mail merges are used to create documents that take information from a data source such as an Outlook address book, an Excel worksheet, or an Access database and place the information in a Word document. Of course, in this book the focus is on using Outlook information, so the Word instruction is limited to that context. In this chapter, the word *document* is used to refer to any type of output you generate, whether the output is a letter, an e-mail, a mailing label, or an envelope.

Mail merges use three ways of inserting Outlook information in a document:

- **Inserted directly in the document**—Information, such as names and mailing addresses, inserted this way is always in the document or copies of the document unless you delete it. An example of this is the way the Word Letter Wizard inserts information such as a mailing address. You will learn to use the Word Letter Wizard later in this chapter.

- **Inserting the information as Word AutoText entries**—The AutoText entry is always in the document or its copies. An example of this is the way the Word Letter Wizard inserts information such as a greeting like Dear Casey.

- **Using *merge fields* to know where to place information in a mail merge template**—Word supplies some mail merge templates, and you can create your own or modify the merge templates to fit your needs. Templates are used when a mail merge is being sent to more than one recipient. They also are used when you want to insert information that isn't available in the Letter Wizard, such as a fax number.

Mail merges can be simple merges using only contact name and mailing address information, or they can be more complex merges using any available contact field to merge information into a document. The easiest way to start a mail merge is to use the Letter Wizard, which you will learn to do in the next section.

Starting a Mail Merge Using the Letter Wizard

In this section, you will learn to use the Word Letter Wizard. The Word Letter Wizard produces a document that uses the first two methods mentioned in the section "Understanding Mail Merges" by inserting information directly in the document and inserting the information as Word AutoText entries.

In the next section, you will learn to start a mail merge using the Letter Wizard from Outlook.

Starting the Letter Wizard From Outlook

Documents produced using the Letter Wizard are intended for sending to only one recipient. You can start the Letter Wizard from Outlook when only one contact is selected. If more than one contact is selected, the New Letter to Contact menu command is disabled.

To start a Letter Wizard mail merge from Outlook, do the following:

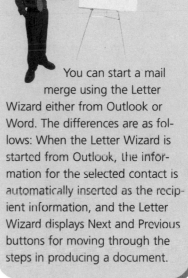

You can start a mail merge using the Letter Wizard either from Outlook or Word. The differences are as follows: When the Letter Wizard is started from Outlook, the information for the selected contact is automatically inserted as the recipient information, and the Letter Wizard displays Next and Previous buttons for moving through the steps in producing a document.

1. Navigate to a Contacts folder and select a contact whose information you want merged into a document.

2. Select **Actions**, **New Letter to Contact**, which opens Word and displays the Word Letter Wizard, which is shown in Figure 17.1. If the wizard isn't displayed, click on the Word document icon in the taskbar.

3. Select the letter format in Step 1 of the Letter Wizard, and click **Next** to go to Step 2. Another way to move between steps in the wizard is to select different tabs. For example, to go to Step 2, click the **Recipient Info** tab.

FIGURE 17.1

FIGURE 17.1

Step 1 in the Word Letter Wizard enables you to select the page design and letter style for mail merges.

The letter format consists of a page design such as plain or professional, a letter style such as full block, and settings for using a date line and preprinted letterhead paper. Some page designs also allow both a header and footer.

Many of the page designs show a preview of how they will look. You should use the previews and test mail merges to become familiar with all the types of documents you can generate.

The recipient information is already filled out on this tab; you just need to select a greeting style in the Salutation section. Figure 17.2 shows the Recipient Info tab of the Letter Wizard with all the information from the selected Outlook contact. The information for the selected contact is inserted into the document as a text insertion.

4. Click **Next** to go to Step 3 of the Letter Wizard. The Other Elements tab enables you to add the following elements to the merge document:

   ■ A reference line such as In regards to:

   ■ Mailing instructions such as VIA AIRMAIL

   ■ Attention line such as ATTN:

   ■ Subject line

   ■ Courtesy copies for additional recipients

The elements inserted in the Other Elements tab are inserted using Word AutoText entries.

FIGURE 17.2

The Recipient
Info tab of
Word's Letter
Wizard enables
you to select a
greeting style for
the merge
document.

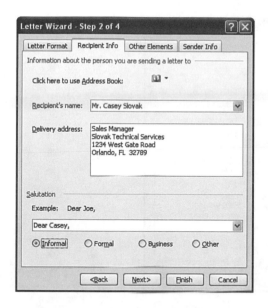

5. Click **Next** to go to Step 4 of the Letter Wizard.

    Set the sender information either by selecting
    the **Address Book** icon and selecting your
    information from the address book list or by
    typing in your sender information, as shown
    in Figure 17.3. You can include or omit a
    return address, a closing such as Best
    Wishes, your job title, your company name,
    and the initials of the writer or typist. You
    can also include or omit an enclosures line
    that tells how many enclosures are included
    with the merge document. Information
    added using the Sender Info tab is inserted
    as AutoText entries.

6. Click **Finish** to close the Letter Wizard and
    display the merged information in the docu-
    ment, as shown in Figure 17.4.

note

After you have per-
formed at least one merge
to a document, the sender information is already filled in for you
the next time you start a new
merge document using the Letter
Wizard.

FIGURE 17.3

The Sender Info tab of Word's Letter Wizard enables you to include information such as a return address.

FIGURE 17.4

The mail merge letter is ready for text.

Enter the text for the merge document in the highlighted area with the text "Type your text here."

As you can see, starting a mail merge from Outlook using the Letter Wizard with a selected contact is an easy process.

Starting the Letter Wizard from Word

To start the Letter Wizard from within Word, do the following:

1. Open Word and start the Letter Wizard by selecting **Tools**, **Letters and Mailings**, **Letter Wizard**.

2. When you start the Letter Wizard this way, it does not display the steps or Next and Previous buttons that it shows when you start it from Outlook. Select the **Letter Format**, **Recipient Info**, **Other Elements**, and **Sender Info** tabs and enter the required information.

3. To insert recipient information in the letter, click the **Address Book** icon on the Recipient Info tab. Then select a recipient from one of your Outlook address books in the resulting Select Name dialog, as shown in Figure 17.5. (When you start the Letter Wizard from Word, no contact is selected in Outlook, so you must select a contact using the Address Book icon.) Click **OK** to insert the contact information as the recipient information.

> **note**
>
> Although the usefulness of the Letter Wizard may seem limited, it does save you time and typing by entering the selected contact's information in the document. It also makes entering information such as salutations and other document elements easier by entering the information in the document for you.

FIGURE 17.5

The Select Name dialog of the Letter Wizard.

4. The recipient name in the Recipient Info tab is inserted based on how the contact is filed; for example, if your File As setting files the contacts by last name, first name, then the recipient name is inserted as Slovak, Katie. Edit the text in the **Recipient's Name** field in the Letter Wizard to change how the name is shown and how the salutation will appear in the finished letter.

5. Finish setting the Other Elements and Sender Information if needed and click **OK** to create the new merge letter.

After the merge information is added to the new document, enter the text for the document in the highlighted area with the text "Type your text here."

In the following sections of this chapter, you will learn how to perform more complex mail merges started from Outlook and from Word.

Using Merge Templates for Mail Merges

Merge templates used in mail merges have a number of advantages over mail merges using the Letter Wizard, and one major disadvantage:

- Mail merges using merge templates can be sent to more than one recipient.
- Merge templates can be saved for reuse in later mail merges. Once a merge template is designed and saved, it can be used with the same or different set of recipients as the original mail merge.
- Merge templates can use Outlook fields that aren't available in documents produced by the Letter Wizard, such as fax numbers and alternate mailing addresses.
- It's much easier to control the placement of merge fields in a document than it is to control where information or text inserted by the Letter Wizard is placed.
- The major disadvantage is it's more work to design and use a merge template than it is to use the Letter Wizard.

In the next section, you will learn to use a merge template to create a mail merge document that can be sent to more than one recipient.

Merging from Outlook

To start a mail merge from Outlook using a merge template, open a Contacts folder and select **Tools**, **Mail Merge** to open the Mail Merge Contacts

note

The Mail Merge menu command is not available in folders other than Contacts folders.

dialog, as shown in Figure 17.6. If you don't want to merge to all contacts in the current view, select one or more contacts before opening the Mail Merge Contacts dialog.

FIGURE 17.6

The Mail Merge Contacts dialog contains the options for setting up a mail merge using a template from within Outlook.

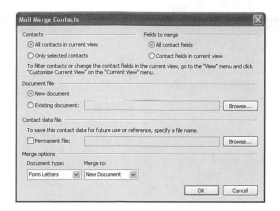

In this dialog, select the options you want to use for the mail merge. You can select contacts to use in the merge before you open the dialog, or you can use all the contacts in the current view. You can use all contact fields or just the ones shown in the current view. You can customize an Outlook view to show exactly what you want to merge and save that view to use again for mail merges if you want. You learned how to customize views in Chapter 14, "Outlook Views."

Select the document to use and the document type and destination. You can merge to a new Word document, to the printer, or to e-mails. If you have created and saved a merge document previously, you can use the existing merge document by selecting the **Existing document** option and browsing to that merge document. To save a merge document, select **File**, **Save** in Word before you merge any recipient information into the document. The merge document is saved with the merge fields and can be opened at a later time as a merge template. You can also save the set of contacts used in this merge for later use in this dialog. Click **OK** to open the merge document. If one or more distribution lists are among the selected contacts, a dialog opens informing you that distribution lists won't be used in the merge. Click **OK** to close that dialog if it appears.

When the merge document opens, the Mail Merge toolbar is visible. You can use it to insert merge fields from the contact fields, insert Word merge fields, merge to various destinations such as the printer or e-mail, and perform other mail merging tasks. Figure 17.7 shows the Mail Merge toolbar and the Insert Merge Field dialog displayed by selecting the **Insert Merge Fields** button.

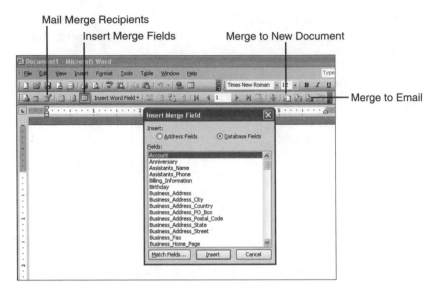

FIGURE 17.7

The Mail Merge toolbar and Insert Merge Field dialog enable you to insert Outlook data fields anywhere in a merge document and control the processing of the mail merge.

To insert Outlook contact fields in the merge document, select **Insert Merge Fields** and select the contact field you want to insert into the document. Select **Insert** to insert the field at the current cursor location in the document. If you insert multiple fields, they will be placed one after the other in the document. You can insert all the fields you want at one time and, after exiting the dialog, format space between the fields by adding spaces, tabs, new lines, or other formatting. You can also close the dialog after inserting each Outlook contact field, format the text, and open the dialog again to insert a new Outlook contact field. To close the dialog, click **Close**.

> **tip**
>
> You can use the **Mail Merge Recipients** button on the Mail Merge toolbar to select which Outlook contacts to use from the selected set of contacts. All contacts that are checked in the Mail Merge Recipients dialog are available for use in the mail merge.

Figure 17.8 shows a merge document containing merge fields with three Outlook contact fields inserted. Formatting has been added between the Outlook fields. The First_Name field has been inserted twice—first for the address block and again for the greeting.

FIGURE 17.8

A mail merge document can use both Outlook and Word merge fields to customize the document for each recipient.

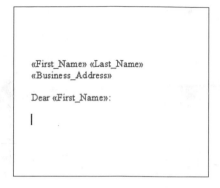

«First_Name» «Last_Name»
«Business_Address»

Dear «First_Name»:

tip

If you think you might want to use the merge document again in the future, save it now before you merge data into the document. You can then open the merge document at any time to be able to reuse the same formatted document.

To merge the selected recipients, select the **Merge to New Document** button in the Mail Merge toolbar to open the Merge to New Document dialog, as shown in Figure 17.9.

FIGURE 17.9

The Merge to New Document dialog enables you to select the range of Outlook contact records used in the mail merge.

When you are satisfied with the settings on this dialog, click **OK** to perform the mail merge. The resulting merge document is shown in Figure 17.10.

I recommend merging to a new document instead of merging directly to the printer or a fax driver. You can always print or fax the document later, and this way you have the opportunity to review the merge and make sure it looks good before it's sent out. You can also merge just one record to a new document and review it before merging directly to printer, e-mail, or fax. It's too late to make changes if you discover a problem with the merge after it has been sent out.

note

This chapter covers the basics of performing mail merges using Outlook data. Word has very sophisticated mail merge functions that are not covered in this book. *Sams Teach Yourself Microsoft Office Word 2003* from Sams Publishing has complete information about using Word for mail merging.

FIGURE 17.10

The final merged document includes the text you entered and the information merged from the selected Outlook contacts.

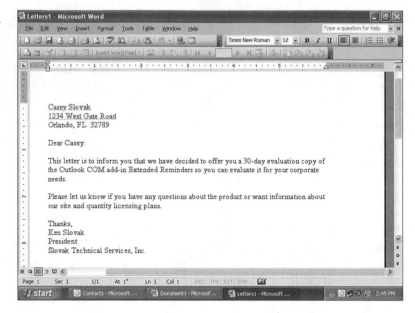

Merging to E-mail

Merging to e-mails is the same as merging to letters. The only difference is the destination of the merge.

You can merge to e-mail from Outlook by selecting **E-mail** as the **Merge to** destination in the Mail Merge Contacts dialog in Outlook. You learned about this dialog earlier in this chapter (see Figure 17.6). You can also merge to e-mail by selecting the **Merge to E-mail** icon from Word's Mail Merge toolbar.

THE ABSOLUTE MINIMUM

In this chapter, you learned about mail merging Outlook data into documents. To review, you now know how to

> Start a merge from Outlook and from Word.
>
> Perform merges using the Letter Wizard and the Word Mail Merge toolbar.
>
> Perform merges using the Mail Merge Contacts dialog in Outlook.
>
> Merge to an e-mail.

With the skills you acquired in this chapter, you can now merge Outlook data with Word documents. In the next chapter, you will learn how to use digitally signed and encrypted e-mails for secure e-mail.

IN THIS CHAPTER

- Understanding secure e-mail.
- Learning how e-mail security works.
- Knowing how to get a digital certificate.
- Learning how to change settings for secure e-mails
- Understanding how to send and receive secure e-mails.

18

SECURE E-MAIL

Most e-mail is sent using normal text, which anyone can intercept and read. Received e-mails are trusted based on who seems to have sent them, but the identity of the sender usually can't be proved. Secure e-mail, which you will learn about in this chapter, is used to provide a solution to both problems.

Is Your E-mail Secure?

E-mails sent over the Internet aren't really secure. People can use various tools to read your e-mails as they are passed along from server to server on the Internet. This risk isn't very big usually, but it is a risk. Being aware of this risk can be important particularly for business e-mails that contain confidential information, or for other e-mails in which security is important. Using *digital encryption* of e-mails so only the intended recipient can read them is a good way to solve this problem.

Another security problem that can be solved by using secure e-mail is verification of the person who sent you the e-mail. It's possible for someone, or for a computer virus, to pretend to be someone else. A digital signature is used to verify the sender of an e-mail.

Digital certificates, which you will learn about in the next section, are used both for encrypting e-mail and for digitally signing e-mails.

How E-Mail Security Works

Secure e-mails rely on digital certificates to establish a trust relationship between two computers. Digital certificates are issued by certification authorities, which can be trusted third parties or certificate servers set up by your company.

A digital certificate consists of two parts: a private key and a public key. E-mails are encrypted using a public key that is available to anyone, but they can be decrypted only by using the private key. A copy of the private key is sent when you establish trust with another computer, and the digital certificate with that private key is stored in the contact record for the person with whom you are establishing trust.

Figure 18.1 shows a digital e-mail certificate.

Details about the certificate and a path tracing from the original certification authority to the certificate are available on the Details and Certification Path tabs of the digital certificate. In the next section, you will learn how to get a digital certificate.

> **note**
>
> Some well-known certificate authorities include VeriSign and Thawte. You will learn how to get a free e-mail signing certificate later in this chapter, in the section "Getting a Digital Certificate."

FIGURE 18.1

Digital e-mail
certificate.

Getting a Digital Certificate

Microsoft provides links to various certificate authorities so you can get a digital certificate. To go to the Web page with these links, select **Tools**, **Options** and then select the **Security** tab. At the bottom of the Security tab on the Options dialog, shown in Figure 18.2, select the **Get a Digital ID** button.

The Get a Digital ID button opens your Web browser and connects to a Microsoft Web site with links to various certification authorities. Some of the certification authorities offer free trial e-mail signing certificates, and others offer free certificates valid for a year. You can also purchase a certificate for use with additional features or identity verification. Thawte, a certification authority listed on the certificate Web page, offers free one-year e-mail signing certificates.

To get a certificate, select one of the certification authorities on this Web page and follow the instructions on the certification authority's Web site to complete enroll-ment for a digital certificate. After you are issued the certificate, you will also receive instructions for installing it on your computer. The certificate will be linked to the e-mail address you gave when obtaining it.

You can export your certificate to another computer, but that computer must have an Outlook profile set up to use the e-mail address that is already linked to the certificate.

FIGURE 18.2

Security tab in
Outlook Options.

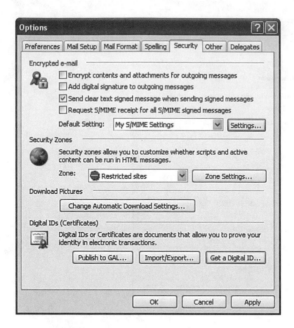

Exporting a Certificate

To export a certificate to another computer, or to save the certificate as a file for
backup, follow these steps:

1. Select **Tools**, **Options** and select the **Security** tab.

2. Select the **Import/Export** button to open the dialog shown in Figure 18.3.

3. Select the **Export** option and click the **Select** button to select a digital certificate to export.

4. Click **OK** to use the selected certificate and return to the Import/Export
Digital ID dialog.

5. Choose a filename and location to save the certificate, and enter and confirm
the password for the certificate you used when you obtained the certificate.

6. If you are using a version of Internet Explorer later than version 4, leave the
Internet Explorer 4.0 Compatible checkbox unchecked. Select **Delete
Digital ID from System** if you want to delete the certificate from the com-
puter from which you are exporting the certificate.

7. Click **OK** to export the certificate. If you receive a message that an application
is requesting access to a protected item, click **OK** to continue the export. The
certificate will be exported and saved to the file system with a .pfx extension.

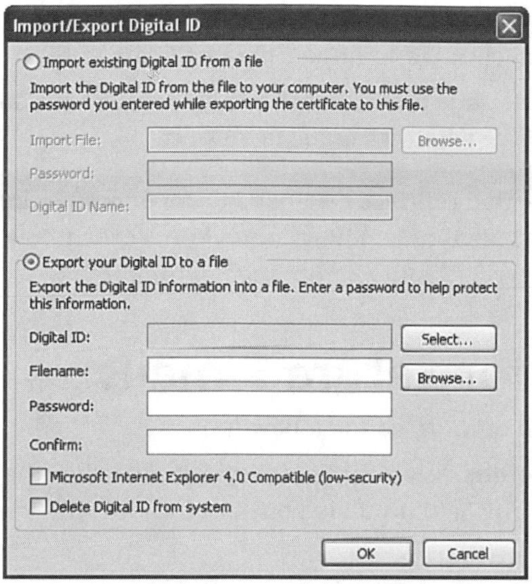

FIGURE 18.3

The Import/
Export Digital
ID dialog shown
after the Export
option has been
selected.

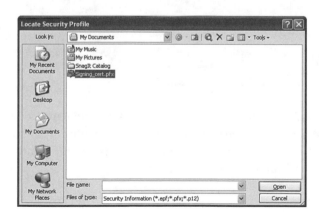

Importing a Certificate

To import a certificate to a different computer, do the following:

1. Select **Tools**, **Options** and select the **Security** tab.

2. Select the **Import/Export** button to open the Import/Export Digital ID dialog.

3. Select the **Import** option and locate the .pfx file to which you exported the certificate, as shown in Figure 18.4.

FIGURE 18.4

Importing a
.pfx file.

4. Enter the password and digital ID name you were issued when you received the certificate and click **OK** to import the certificate to the computer.

5. If you receive a message that an application is creating a protected item, click **OK** to continue with the certificate import.

Remember that the imported certificate is linked to an e-mail address, so your Outlook profile must include that e-mail account. You learned how to set up an Outlook profile in Chapter 2, "Outlook from the Beginning."

Changing Settings for Secure E-mails

To set your secure e-mail settings, do the following:

1. Select **Tools**, **Options**, select the **Security** tab, and click the **Settings** button. The Change Security Settings dialog opens, as shown in Figure 18.5.

FIGURE 18.5

The Change Security Settings dialog.

2. Enter a name for the settings you are creating and leave the **Cryptography Format** setting as **S/MIME**. S/MIME (Secure Multipurpose Internet Mail Extension) is a widely supported Internet standard for secure e-mail and is the protocol Outlook uses for secure e-mail.

3. Check the **Default Security Setting for this cryptographic message format** checkbox.

4. Check the **Default Security Setting for all cryptographic messages** checkbox unless you intend to create other settings for different cryptographic message formats.

5. Click the **Choose** button and select your certificate. Click **OK** to use that certificate.

6. Check the **Send these certificates with signed messages** checkbox.

7. For most purposes, leave the default **Hash Algorithm** of **SHA1** and the default **Encryption Algorithm** of **3DES** unless you need to use other hash or encryption algorithms.

The various hash and encryption algorithms aren't covered in this book. The default hash and encryption algorithms will work in almost all cases, unless you are instructed to use other algorithms by either the certificate authority who issued the certificate or a recipient who requests you use different hash and encryption algorithms for him or her.

The settings related to secure e-mails on the Security tab of the Outlook Options dialog, shown in Figure 18.2, are for your secure e-mail defaults. You can send signed e-mails to people who do not use e-mail clients that support secure e-mail or who do not have a copy of your certificate. Encrypted e-mails can be sent only to recipients who use e-mail clients that support secure e-mail and who have exchanged certificates with you.

Table 18.1 shows the effect of the secure e-mail settings.

Table 18.1   Outlook Secure E-mail Settings

Setting	Effect
Encrypt Contents and Attachments	Encrypts all outgoing messages and attachments.
Add Digital Signature	Adds your digital signature to all outgoing messages so the recipients can verify they came from you and were not altered.

A *signed* e-mail uses the certificate to sign the e-mail when it is sent out. Any alteration of the e-mail or an invalid certificate is shown when you receive the e-mail. An *encrypted* e-mail is coded and can be read only by someone who has the key needed to decrypt the e-mail.

Table 18.1 (continued)

Setting	Effect
Send Clear Text Signed Message	Sends a plain text message that can be read without verification of your digital signature to recipients with e-mail clients that don't support S/MIME. An e-mail message with this setting can be read by anyone, but any alteration to the message would invalidate the digital signature.
Request S/MIME Receipt	Requests a receipt for all signed messages to ensure all signed messages are received with no alterations and are secure.

tip

Unless you intend to send e-mail only to other people with digital certificates, I recommend checking only the **Send Clear Text Signed Message** setting and leaving the other settings unchecked. When you want to send a signed or encrypted e-mail, you can turn those settings on for that e-mail message.

Sending and Receiving Secure E-mails

As soon as you have installed your digital certificate and set up your secure e-mail settings, you can send digitally signed messages to people. Sending a digitally signed message is a required first step for exchanging encrypted e-mails with them.

To send someone a signed e-mail message, open a new e-mail message and select the **Digitally Sign** icon on the toolbar. The Digitally Sign and Encrypt Message icons are automatically added to your toolbar in e-mails after you have configured secure e-mail settings. The Digitally Sign icon is an envelope with a red ribbon, and the Encrypt Message icon is an envelope with a blue padlock, as shown in Figure 18.6.

You can also sign or encrypt an e-mail by selecting the **Options** icon on the toolbar in an open e-mail, selecting the **Security Settings** button in the Message Options dialog, and setting secure e-mail options in the Security Properties dialog.

caution

Do not encrypt an e-mail at this stage; just digitally sign the message. If you send an encrypted e-mail to someone at this stage, that person will not be able to read it.

FIGURE 18.6

Digitally Sign and Encrypt Message icons.

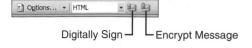

Digitally Sign ⏌ ⎿Encrypt Message

The e-mail recipient should also send you a signed, nonencrypted e-mail if you want to exchange encrypted e-mails with him or her.

If you click in the red ribbon icon in the e-mail in the Reading Pane, a dialog will open showing the signature is valid and trusted, unless there are problems with the signature or the certificate authority that issued the certificate isn't already trusted. The Digital Signature: Valid dialog is shown in Figure 18.7.

FIGURE 18.7

The Digital Signature: Valid dialog shows that the certificate is valid.

If the certificate authority isn't trusted, you can choose to trust the signature and the certificate authority if you are positive the signature and certificate are valid. (You will learn how to trust a signature and certificate authority later in this section.) Click **Details** to view more information about the digital certificate.

When you receive a signed e-mail, open it and right-click the **From** address shown in the open e-mail. Select **Add to Outlook Contacts** from the context menu and select the **Certificates** tab to verify the certificate is included in the contact item, as shown in Figure 18.8.

Save and close the contact. If the contact already exists in one of your Contacts folders, you will be given an option to merge the information with the existing contact. Click **OK** to install the certificate used by that contact for signing and encrypting e-mails. After you both have exchanged certificates and installed them on your systems, you are ready to exchange encrypted e-mails with that contact.

FIGURE 18.8

A digital certificate in the Certificates tab in a contact.

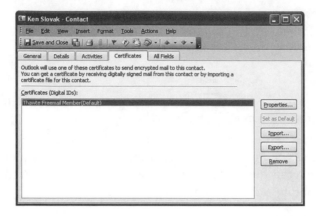

Open a new e-mail message and select both the **Digitally Sign** and **Encrypt Message** icons on the e-mail's toolbar. When you receive an encrypted e-mail, it has the blue padlock icon and cannot be read in the Reading Pane, as shown in Figure 18.9.

FIGURE 18.9

Digitally encrypted e-mail cannot be read in the Reading Pane and can be read only by someone with whom you have exchanged encryption keys.

Open the e-mail to read it, and you'll notice the digital signature and encryption icons at the right side of the e-mail, as shown in Figure 18.10. Click in the blue padlock icon of encrypted e-mails to view information about the signing and encrypting certificate.

If the certificate authority that issued the certificate is not already trusted, the e-mail will appear with red lines above and below the signature icon, as shown in Figure 18.11.

FIGURE 18.11

Untrusted signatures show red lines above and below the signature and indicate a problem with the signature.

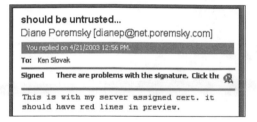

Click the **red signature ribbon** icon to open the Digital Signature: Invalid dialog; then select the **Details** button to show the Message Security Properties dialog. Select the **Trust Certificate Authority** button and then **Trust** if you want to always trust certificates issued by this certificate authority.

Select the **Edit Trust** button and make sure the Edit Trust setting is either **Inherit Trust from Issuer** if you have trusted this certificate authority, or **Explicitly Trust This Certificate** if you want to trust only this one certificate and not all certificates issued by this certificate authority. Click **OK** to close the Edit Trust dialog and **Close** to close the Message Security Properties dialog.

The Digital Signature: Invalid dialog title will change to Digital Signature: Valid, indicating the signature is now trusted. You can now proceed, as outlined earlier in the section, to install the certificate and exchange encrypted e-mails with the owner of this digital signature.

THE ABSOLUTE MINIMUM

In this chapter, you learned about secure Outlook e-mail. To review, you now know

- Whether or not the e-mail you send is secure and how to go about making sure your e-mail is read only by the intended recipient.
- How to get a digital certificate for signing and encrypting e-mails.
- How to export and import a certificate.
- How to set secure e-mail settings.
- How to send and receive secure e-mails.

With the skills you acquired in this chapter, you can now make sure that your e-mail is secure. In the next chapter, you will learn how to organize e-mail with rules.

In this chapter

- Understanding how rules work.
- Learning how to create rules.
- Knowing how to run rules.

19

Organizing E-mail with Rules

In Outlook rules are used to perform actions either when new messages arrive in your Inbox or when you send a message. Rules can also be run manually at any time you want. Actions that rules can take include moving, deleting, and flagging items; playing a sound when certain items arrive in your Inbox; and sending alerts to mobile devices. Rules are used to help automatically organize the way items are filed and to take specific actions when e-mails of interest are sent or received.

How Rules Work

Rules can examine who messages are from or to and take action based on that information. They can also search for specific words in the subject or text of an e-mail, or the sender's or recipient's address, among many other conditions.

Here are some examples of rules you can create:

- Move messages from a certain person to a specified folder when they arrive in the Inbox.
- Flag messages from a certain person with a flag.
- Send a message to a cell phone or pager when a message from a certain person arrives in the Inbox.
- Assign a category to a message if it has an attachment when it is sent and flag the message for follow-up in seven days.

Rules follow a series of steps, with each rule you have being processed in the order you set. Rules work only with e-mail messages and are applied after an e-mail is received or sent, unless you run the rule manually.

Each rule consists of one or more conditions, such as checking an e-mail for a flag, importance level, presence of attachments, or being sent by a specific person. A rule also has zero or more exceptions, which are used to stop the rule if any exception is true. Some examples of exceptions are when the e-mail was sent using a specific e-mail account or if the e-mail has specific words in the text of the message.

The following steps describe how rules for received e-mails work; the same steps are followed for rules for sent e-mails:

1. An e-mail message is delivered to the Inbox.
2. The first rule for received e-mails is started.
3. Any conditions for the rule are checked—for example, a message from a certain person.
4. If every rule condition is true, any exceptions to the rule are checked to see whether they are true. If the condition tests fail, or any exceptions are true, the rule is ended and processing starts with the next rule at step 3. If there are no more rules, rule processing stops.
5. All actions for the rule are taken, such as moving the e-mail message to a folder.
6. If the rule was true and the stop processing more rules action was set, no more rules are checked for that message; otherwise, the next rule is started at step 3.

Rules are generally run in Outlook, although if you are using Exchange server, some rules can be run on the server. Rules that run in Outlook are referred to as *client-side* rules and require that Outlook is running for the rules to work. *Server-side* rules are those that run on Exchange Server; Outlook doesn't have to be running for server-side rules to run.

Now that you know how rules work you will learn how rules are designed.

How Rules Are Designed

You can design rules using the Rules Wizard, which provides some predefined rule templates and also enables you to create rules from a blank rule template. The Rules Wizard is started when you create a new rule or edit an existing rule using the Rules and Alerts dialog.

The following predefined rule templates are supplied in the Rules Wizard:

- Move messages from someone to a folder
- Move messages with specific words in the subject to a folder
- Move messages sent to a distribution list to a folder
- Delete a conversation
- Flag messages from someone with a colored flag
- Display mail from someone in the New Item Alert Window
- Play a sound when I get messages from someone
- Send an alert to my mobile device when I get messages from someone

You can create many additional rules using a blank rule template.

There is no specific limit to the number of rules you can have; the limit is based on how much space your rules take up. Each rule takes a certain amount of space, with each condition and exception adding to the space the rule takes. You can have a maximum of 32KB's worth of rules. Only active rules are counted toward the 32KB limit. Rules that have been turned off and are inactive aren't counted toward the 32KB limit for rules.

note

You can create simple rules without using the Rules Wizard by using the Create Rule option. You will learn about this option in the "Creating a Rule" section of this chapter.

caution

Rules are stored inside Outlook 2003, so knowing how much space your rules take up can be difficult. You won't know you are running up against the 32KB limit for all rules until you receive an error when you try to create a new rule.

The Rules and Alerts Dialog

Rules are managed using the Rules and Alerts dialog, shown in Figure 19.1. You open the dialog by selecting **Tools**, **Rules and Alerts**.

The following commands are available in the Rules and Alerts dialog:

- **New Rule** starts the Rules Wizard to create a new rule.

- **Change Rule** opens a menu, shown in Figure 19.2, which has commands that enable you to **Edit Rule Settings** in the Rules Wizard, **Rename Rule**, and add actions to an existing rule.

- **Copy** makes a copy of an existing rule, which enables you to modify a rule without changing the original rule.

Alerts are used primarily to notify you of changes in shared workspaces on Microsoft Windows SharePoint Services or Microsoft SharePoint Portal Server. Both of these topics are beyond the scope of this book.

- **Delete** deletes the selected rule.

- The up- and down-arrow buttons move the selected rule up or down in the list of rules. Rules are run in the order they appear in the list.

- **Run Rules Now** enables you to select one or more rules to run immediately. You specify the folder where the rule will run and if the rule is to be applied to All Messages, Unread Messages, or Read Messages.

- **Options** opens the Options dialog, where you can export rules to an .rwz file that is compatible with earlier versions of Outlook, import rules from an .rwz file from an earlier version of Outlook, and upgrade imported rules for better performance when executing imported rules.

If you have a previous version of Outlook and want to use rules you have already defined, you must import the rules and convert them to use with Outlook 2003. To import rules, follow these steps:

1. Select **Options**, **Import Rules** in the Rules and Alerts dialog.
2. Navigate to the .rwz file used by the previous version of Outlook and select **Open**.
3. If the **Upgrade Now** button becomes enabled, click it to upgrade the rules to increase their performance in Outlook 2003.

You learned earlier in this chapter that there is a 32KB limit for all active rules and that rules are stored inside Outlook 2003, so it's hard to know how much space your rules take up.

FIGURE 19.1

The Rules and Alerts dialog enables you to create rules, edit existing rules, set the order in which rules run, and import and export rules.

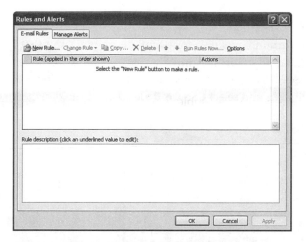

FIGURE 19.2

The Change Rule menu enables you to add additional actions to a rule as well as edit or rename the rule.

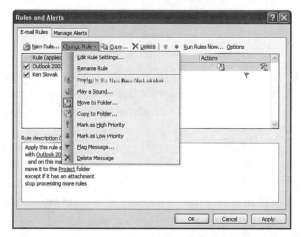

To get an idea of how much space your rules take, select **Options**, **Export Rules.** Navigate to the place where you want to save your exported rules, name the export file, and select **Save** to export your rules to the file. View the file in Windows Explorer using the Details view to see its size and the approximate space your rules take.

Creating a Rule

Rules can be created in two ways. Simple rules for a specific e-mail can be created using the Create Rule option; more general or more complex rules are created using the Rules Wizard. You will learn how to create rules using both methods in the following sections.

Using the Create Rule Command

Create Rule is a command available for e-mail items; you can use it to create a simple rule to display an e-mail in an Alert window, play a sound, or move an e-mail to another folder based on the conditions you select. To use the Create Rule dialog, right-click on an e-mail item and select **Create Rule** to open the dialog shown in Figure 19.3.

FIGURE 19.3

The Create Rule dialog enables you to create a rule that shows an e-mail in an Alert window, play a sound, or move the e-mail when it arrives.

Create Rule
When I get e-mail with all of the selected conditions
☐ From Ken Slovak
☐ Subject contains   Rule creation
☐ Sent to   me only
Do the following
☐ Display in the New Item Alert window
☐ Play a selected sound: Windows XP Notify.w   ▶ ■   Browse...
☐ Move e-mail to folder: Select Folder   Select Folder...
OK   Cancel   Advanced Options...

The checkboxes at the top of the Create Rule dialog set the conditions the incoming e-mail must meet to take the actions selected in the bottom portion of the dialog. You can check one or more of the available conditions; all checked conditions must be met for the rule to activate.

The From condition always uses the identity of the person who sent the selected e-mail. The Subject condition defaults to the subject of the selected e-mail, but you can change the subject text by typing the desired subject in the Subject text entry area. The Sent to condition is me only if the selected e-mail was sent only to you. If the e-mail was sent to more than one person, their names or e-mail addresses as well as the me only selection are shown in the Sent to drop-down. If you want the new rule to apply only when an e-mail is addressed to you, make sure the Sent to condition is me only.

Every checked action in the Create Rule dialog box will be taken when the rule conditions are met. To display the e-mail in the New Item Alert window, check that option. To choose a sound to play when the e-mail arrives, select **Browse** and then select the desired .wav file. The Play and Stop buttons that resemble controls on a tape recorder are used to test the selected sound. To move the incoming e-mail to a folder, click the **Select Folder** button to open the Select Folder dialog. Select the folder to move the e-mail to and click **OK** to save the folder selection.

To open the Rules Wizard from the Create Rule dialog, select **Advanced Options**. You will learn about the Rules Wizard in the next section.

When you are satisfied with the rule conditions and actions, click **OK** to create the new rule. If rule creation is successful, a Success dialog is displayed. Check the checkbox to run the rule now if you need to run the rule immediately. Click **OK** to close the Success dialog.

Using the Rules Wizard

Using the Rules Wizard, you can create rules that are more general than the Create Rule option enables you to create. To open the Rules Wizard, select **Tools**, **Rules and Alerts** to open the Rules and Alerts dialog and then select **New Rule** to open the Rules Wizard, shown in Figure 19.4. The Rules Wizard starting screen enables you to create a rule from a template or from a blank rule. You also can open the Rules Wizard to edit an existing rule by selecting **Change Rule**, **Edit Rule Settings**.

FIGURE 19.4

The Rules Wizard steps you through creating a rule from a predefined template or a blank rule template.

Creating Rules Using a Template

The first rule you create will use a predefined template to add a green flag to all e-mails sent to you by a selected person:

1. Open the Rules and Alerts dialog if it is not already open and select **New Rule**.
2. Select **Start creating a rule from a template**.
3. In the Step 1 section of the first Rules Wizard screen, select **Flag messages from someone with a colored flag**.
4. In the Step 2 section, select the **people or distribution list** link to open the Rule Address dialog.

5. Highlight an entry from the Contacts list in the Rule Address dialog and click **OK**.

6. Select the **a colored flag** link.

7. In the Select Flag Color dialog, select **Green Flag** in the flag color drop-down and click **OK**.

8. Select **Finish** to proceed to the final wizard screen.

9. If you are using Outlook with an Exchange Server mailbox, click **OK** on the message that the rule is a client-only rule and will process only when Outlook is running.

The new rule you created is now shown in the Rules and Alerts dialog and is ready to run the next time the person you chose sends you an e-mail.

Creating Modified Rules Using a Template

The next rule you will learn how to create is one that moves all messages related to a business project you are working on to a Project folder. In creating this rule, you will proceed through each wizard screen instead of creating the rule in the first screen. This method enables you to modify the predefined rule by adding conditions or exceptions and shows the structure of the Rules Wizard:

1. Open the Rules and Alerts dialog if it is not already open and select **New Rule**.

2. Select **Start creating a rule from a template**.

3. Select **Move messages with specific words in the subject to a folder**.

4. Select **Next** to move to the next wizard screen, shown in Figure 19.5, to select the conditions for the rule.

5. Click **specific words** in the edit box at the bottom of the wizard screen.

6. In the Search Text dialog, shown in Figure 19.6, type the words Outlook 2003 project into the text box and click **Add**.

7. When you are finished adding words and phrases, click **OK** to close the Search Text dialog. The words Outlook 2003 project replace the term specific words in the rule conditions.

8. Select **Next** to move to the next wizard screen, shown in Figure 19.7, to select the actions for the rule.

9. Select **specified** in the edit area to open the folder selection dialog. Select the folder you want the rule to move messages to, as shown in Figure 19.8, and then click **OK**.

FIGURE 19.5

The conditions for the rule are already selected when you create a rule from a predefined template.

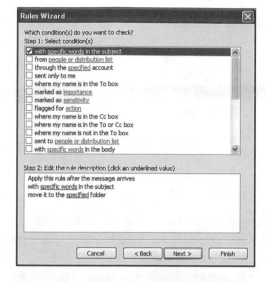

FIGURE 19.6

You can search for more than one word or phrase in a rule by separately adding each word or phrase you want to search on.

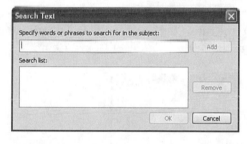

FIGURE 19.7

You can take more than one action in a rule by checking as many actions as you want and specifying the actions if needed.

FIGURE 19.8

Select the folder to move the messages to if the rule condition is met.

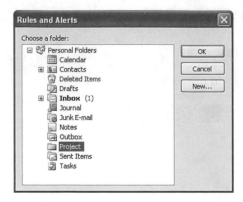

10. Select **Next** to move to the next wizard screen, where you can select any exceptions to the rule. Exceptions are used to prevent the rule from being applied when one or more conditions are met.

11. If you always want to leave messages that have attachments in your Inbox even if they have the words Outlook 2003 project in the subject, you need to add an exception to the rule. Check **except if it has an attachment** to add this exception to the rule, as shown in Figure 19.9.

FIGURE 19.9

Exceptions help fine-tune a rule, and you can add multiple exceptions to a rule.

12. Select **Next** to move to the final Rules Wizard screen, shown in Figure 19.10.

13. The rule has already been named based on the search words Outlook 2003 project and is enabled to run automatically. You can rename the rule if you

want, disable it from running, or run it now on existing items in the Inbox. Select **Finish** when you are done changing the rule.

Both of the rules you defined are now shown in the Rules and Alerts dialog, with the most recently defined rule shown above earlier rules, as you can see in Figure 19.11.

FIGURE 19.10

The final Rules Wizard screen enables you to rename the rule, disable or enable it, and run it immediately.

FIGURE 19.11

Rules are run in order, with the most recently defined rule running first.

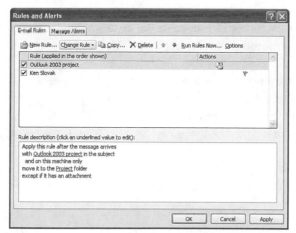

Creating Rules Using a Blank Rule

Creating a rule from a blank rule template is almost the same as creating a predefined rule. The first steps are to select **Start from a blank rule** and then whether the rule is for arriving messages or for outgoing messages. After that, the steps are the same as steps 4 to 12 in the preceding section, except no condition or action has been previously selected. Check as many conditions, actions, and exceptions as you want for the rule and customize each condition, action, or exception as needed, as in the preceding example.

Ordering Your Rules

Rules run in order, one after another, from top to bottom as shown in the Rules and Alerts dialog. To change the order in which the rules run, highlight a rule and select the down arrow to move the rule down one place or select the up arrow to move the rule up one place.

The order your rules are in is important because a message might meet the conditions for more than one rule. This wouldn't matter if one rule sets a flag on the message and a second rule moves the message to another folder. However, if the first rule moves the message, and the second rule tries to set a flag on the message, you will get an error because the message has already been moved by the time the second rule runs.

An example of this is the two rules that were defined earlier in this chapter. The first rule that runs is the Outlook 2003 project rule, which moves messages with the words `Outlook 2003 project` to the Project folder. The second rule flags messages from someone with a green flag. If a message arrives that meets the conditions in both rules, the message will have been moved by the time the second rule is applied, and you will get an error.

You can fix this situation in two possible ways. One is to move the green flag rule above the Outlook 2003 project rule so that it runs first, and the message is flagged in green before it is moved to the Project folder. The second way to fix the situation leaves the rule order alone and adds a stop processing action to the Outlook 2003 project rule. You would use this method if you want messages from the person in the green flag rule moved to the Project folder but not flagged green.

The stop processing action is used to stop processing all subsequent rules. Here's how it works.

When a rule is processed the conditions in the rule are evaluated. If the conditions for the rule are met, and there are no exceptions that stop the rule, the actions for the rule are taken. After any other actions in the rule are taken, the stop processing action is taken, and no subsequent rules are

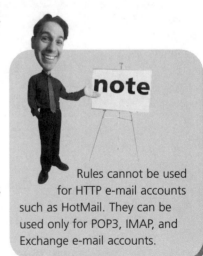

note

Rules cannot be used for HTTP e-mail accounts such as HotMail. They can be used only for POP3, IMAP, and Exchange e-mail accounts.

processed for that message. If the conditions for a rule aren't met, no actions are taken, including the stop processing action, and subsequent rules are processed.

To add a stop processing action to the Outlook 2003 project rule, follow these steps:

1. Select the Outlook 2003 project rule in the Rules and Alerts dialog.
2. Select **Change Rule**, **Edit Rule Settings**.
3. Select **Next** to move to the Select Actions screen of the Rules Wizard.
4. Scroll down the list of actions and check **stop processing more rules**, as shown in Figure 19.12.
5. Select **Finish** to complete your edit of the rule.

FIGURE 19.12

The stop processing more rules action provides a way to prevent subsequent rules from running.

tip

Unless you plan on having some rules that cascade processing from one rule to the next, it is a good idea to add a stop processing action to most of your rules. If you do this, you don't have to be so concerned with the order in which your rules run.

Running a Rule

Rules run automatically for the most part, but sometimes you will want to run rules manually. You can manually run a newly created rule to clean up e-mail that was in your Inbox or some other folder before the rule was defined. If you have a rule that you don't want to run automatically, you can choose to only run it manually.

To run one or more rules manually, select **Run Rules Now** in the Rules and Alerts dialog to open the Run Rules Now dialog, shown in Figure 19.14.

To run one or more rules manually, do the following:

1. Check any rules you want to run.
2. If you want to run the rules in a folder other than the Inbox, select **Browse**, highlight the folder in which you want to run the rule from the Select Folder

dialog, and click **OK**. If you want the rule to run in all folders, select **Personal Folders** (or **Mailbox** if you are running an Exchange Server mailbox).

3. If you want the rule to also run in subfolders of the selected folder, check the **Include subfolders** checkbox.

4. In the **Apply rules to** drop-down, select whether to apply the rule to All Messages, Unread Messages, or Read Messages.

5. Select **Run Now** to run the selected rules in the selected folders.

FIGURE 19.14

Running rules manually enables you to run rules when you want and in folders other than the Inbox.

tip

To prevent a rule from running automatically, uncheck it. This makes the rule inactive, which also prevents the rule from counting against the 32KB limit for all active rules.

Running rules manually enables you to control when and where your rules run and to run rules that aren't enabled for automatic processing, thus allowing you the maximum control over your rules.

THE ABSOLUTE MINIMUM

In this chapter, you learned about Outlook rules. To review, you now know

What rules can do.

How to create or edit a rule.

Why the order of rules in the Rules and Alerts dialog is important and how to change their order.

How to run rules manually.

Using rules is one of the easiest ways to customize the way Outlook handles incoming messages. In the next chapter, you will learn how to customize Outlook forms.

IN THIS CHAPTER

- Learning how to design Outlook custom forms using modified standard forms.

- Understanding the basics of Outlook forms design.

20

CUSTOMIZING OUTLOOK FORMS

When you find yourself repeatedly adding the same text or attachments to e-mail, such as text saying the e-mail contains confidential information, you are a candidate for a custom Outlook form. A custom e-mail form with disclaimer text saying the e-mail is confidential has the text in the e-mail when it is created, so you don't have to manually type the disclaimer in every e-mail. This saves time and ensures that the e-mail has the correct disclaimer, with no typos, spelling errors, or missing information. In this chapter, you will learn how to use the basics of Outlook form design to produce customized forms that can be reused over and over again.

Introducing Custom Forms

Outlook *custom forms* are based on one of the standard Outlook forms (e-mails, tasks, and so on). You are already familiar with Outlook forms, even if you don't realize it. Every time you create a new e-mail, you are working with an e-mail form. Every other Outlook item you open such as a task, contact, appointment, or Journal entry is shown as an Outlook form.

Every Outlook form has a name that describes what the form is used for. For example, an e-mail form is named IPM.Note. The first part of a form name is *IPM*, which stands for *InterPersonal Message*. All Outlook forms you will work with have names that start with IPM. The second part of the form name describes the type of form. Table 20.1 shows the names for the standard Outlook forms.

Table 20.1   Outlook Form Names

Form Type	Name
E-mail	IPM.Note
Task	IPM.Task
Appointment	IPM.Appointment
Contact	IPM.Contact
Journal Entry	IPM.Activity
Post	IPM.Post

Outlook's Notes cannot be customized at all and aren't included in this table, although their form name is IPM.StickyNote.

When you customize a form, a third part is added to its name, a part that describes the custom form and indicates that it is a custom form. For an e-mail disclaimer form such as the one mentioned earlier in this chapter, you might describe it as "Disclaimer." In that case, the form's complete name would become IPM.Note.Disclaimer.

Outlook forms can be customized in two ways: from an open Outlook item or from a special form template. When you customize an open Outlook e-mail item, you can't use Word as your e-mail editor.

In this chapter's example, you will create a custom e-mail form with a disclaimer. So, the first thing you need to do to follow along is to stop using

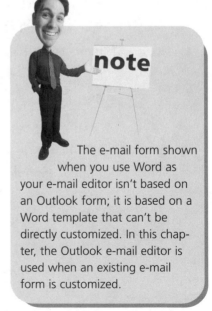

note

The e-mail form shown when you use Word as your e-mail editor isn't based on an Outlook form; it is based on a Word template that can't be directly customized. In this chapter, the Outlook e-mail editor is used when an existing e-mail form is customized.

Word as your e-mail editor. You can return to using Word as your e-mail editor when you are finished customizing the e-mail disclaimer form.

To stop using Word as your e-mail editor so that you can customize an open Outlook e-mail form, select **Tools**, **Options**, select the **Mail Format** tab, and uncheck the **Use Microsoft Office Word 2003 to edit e-mail messages** checkbox. Click **OK** to save the change.

Creating a Simple Custom Form

The disclaimer form is a standard e-mail form that is customized with a disclaimer message. To create this form, do the following:

1. Make sure you have disabled Word as your e-mail editor, as described in the preceding section, and select the Inbox as your current folder in the Navigation Pane.

2. Select **Actions**, **New Mail Message** to open a new Outlook e-mail form.

3. Click in the text area of the e-mail message and press **Enter** twice to create two blank lines in the message.

4. Enter your disclaimer text or the following text in the text area of the e-mail message:

    `This email may contain confidential material.`
    `If you were not an intended recipient, please notify`
    `the sender and delete all copies.`

    If you want a dividing line before the disclaimer text, create the dividing line now. The custom form should look something like the one shown in Figure 20.1.

FIGURE 20.1

The custom disclaimer form enables you to open an e-mail with your disclaimer text already entered.

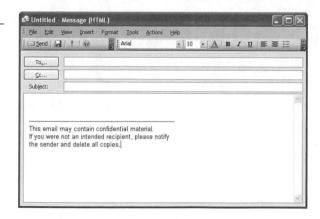

5. Select **Tools**, **Forms**, **Design This Form** to open the form in design mode. The form should now look like the one in Figure 20.2. Close the Field Chooser window; you don't need it for this form, and it gets in the way of viewing the form.

FIGURE 20.2

Design mode enables you to add controls and create new tabs that are shown as part of the customized forms.

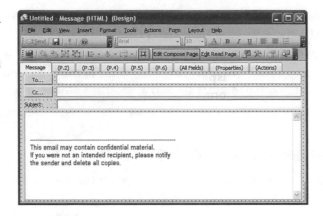

6. Select the **Properties** tab of the form.

7. In the **Version** field, enter 1.0 as the version, and enter a form number for this form, if you want.

8. All custom forms show the icon of a Post form unless you change the form icon. To change the large icon for the form, select **Change Large Icon**. In the File Open dialog, navigate to the C:\Program Files\Microsoft Office\OFFICE11\FORMS\1033\ folder and select **NOTEL.ICO**. If you are not using U.S. English as your Office language, some number other than 1033 will be used as the name for your language folder. Select **Open** to use the large e-mail icon for the custom form.

9. Select **Change Small Icon**, navigate to the same folder as in step 8, select **NOTES.ICO**, and then click **Open** to select the small e-mail icon. The Properties tab of the form should now look like the one shown in Figure 20.3.

FIGURE 20.3

The Properties tab enables you to set the form's version, icons, and other properties and to password-protect the design of the form.

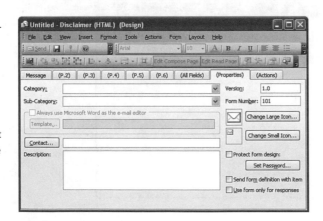

10. Select **Tools**, **Forms**, **Publish Form** to open the Publish Form As dialog.

11. In the **Look In** drop-down, select **Inbox** to make the form available from the Actions menu in the Inbox.

12. Type `Disclaimer` in the **Display Name** field and select **Publish** to publish the form. The form name is now `IPM.Note.Disclaimer`.

13. Select **No** in the publishing dialog to prevent the Save Form Definition checkbox from being checked.

14. Close the form and select **No** in the dialog asking you to save changes.

Now you can navigate to the Inbox and select **Actions**, **New Disclaimer** to open the new disclaimer form you just created. This custom form is available whenever you want to use it; you never have to enter the disclaimer text because it's already in the form.

If you want to return to using Word as your e-mail editor, now you can. To do so, select **Tools**, **Options**, select the **Mail Format** tab, and check the **Use Microsoft Office Word 2003 to edit e-mail messages** checkbox. Click **OK** to save the change.

> **caution**
>
> When you send the form definition with the form, the form becomes much larger in size due to the inclusion of the form definition with the item. In addition, existing instances of the form will not be changed if you revise the form because the existing forms contain the earlier form definition. This condition is known as a *one-offed form* and should be avoided wherever possible.

Reviewing Custom Form Basics

The custom disclaimer form is very simple and doesn't have any custom fields, but it introduces a number of the issues you will also be concerned with for all custom forms:

- **Version**—When you open a custom form, Outlook caches the form design (saves it locally on your hard drive) so it will open more quickly after the first time the form is opened. If you change the design of the form and publish it with the new design and the same name, Outlook can become confused and open a previous version of the form. To prevent this from happening, always use a version number for your forms and change the version each time you publish a new version of the form.

- **Icons**—Outlook custom forms always use the icon for the Post form by default. To have a custom form use the standard icon for that type of Outlook item, or to use a special icon that you have designed, you must set the large and small icons for the form.

- **Properties of existing forms**—In the disclaimer form, you entered the disclaimer text in the e-mail message and then placed the form into design mode. Any text, signature, recipients, attachments, or other settings or properties present in the form when it is placed in design mode will be present in the custom form.

- **The form definition sent with the item**—The form definition consists of all the customizations you have made to a standard form. In the disclaimer form, the only customizations were the disclaimer text and the properties such as Version that you set on the Properties tab of the form. More complex custom forms might include custom controls such as drop-downs and checkboxes, programming code that the form runs when opened or saved, and many other customizations. When you publish a form, as you did the Disclaimer form, the form definition is stored in Outlook, so you don't need to save it in your form. In most cases, you shouldn't ever save the form definition with the form; the form becomes much larger when the form definition is included. There are other disadvantages to saving the form definition with the form, so the rule of thumb is never to do so.

- **Publishing location**—When you publish a form, you must select where to publish it. The default location is the Personal Forms Library. Publishing in this location makes the form available for your use; you can access it by selecting **Tools**, **Forms**, **Choose Form** and selecting a custom form from this library. If you select a specific Outlook folder as the location to publish the form, the form is available from the **Actions** menu when you are in that folder. In the case of the Disclaimer form, you published it in the Inbox, so the form is available in the Actions menu when you are in the Inbox.

> **caution**
>
> Never publish a custom form in more than one location. Doing so corrupts the forms cache that Outlook maintains for custom forms and might result in your opening an incorrect version of the form. If different versions are published in different locations, the problem only gets worse, and you can end up losing your custom form completely.

Design Mode

All Outlook forms have two modes: run mode and design mode. Run mode is the normal mode for forms; every time you create and open a new contact, it opens in run mode. Design mode is used only when you are designing custom forms. In the Disclaimer example, you placed a form that was in run mode into design mode when you selected the **Tools**, **Forms**, **Design This Form** command.

Design mode enables you to perform such design functions as adding controls and fields to forms, showing additional tabs in forms to provide space in the form for your customizations, and adding programming code to forms. Design mode also enables you to set the custom form's version, icons, and other properties that you set in the Disclaimer example.

Outlook Controls and Fields

All Outlook forms consist of controls and fields. *Controls* are the visible components of forms, and *fields* are used to contain the data that is shown in data controls.

When you view contacts in a Contacts folder, you see data in fields such as first name, last name, and company. If you open one of your contacts, you are opening a contact form, and the data you see is shown in the controls on the form. The controls and fields are linked. If you change the contact's name in the Full Name text control, the Full Name field is changed when the contact is saved.

Figure 20.4 shows the Full Name text control selected behind the Properties for that control. The Field property shows that the Full Name text control is linked to the Full Name field.

FIGURE 20.4

The Full Name control is linked to the Full Name field, so information entered in the control is saved in the field.

The text area of an e-mail message is another example of this concept; it is a text control, and it is linked to the Message field. All the text in the e-mail is contained in the Message field, which is also referred to as the *Body* of the e-mail, and the Message control displays the text that is in the Message field.

Controls display data, but they can't save data. If you place a control such as a textbox on a form, you can enter data in the textbox when the form is opened, but the data can't be saved unless a field is used to save the data. Fields, on the other hand, can save data but can't display the data in a form. It's only when a control and a field are linked that data can be both saved and displayed in a form.

The fields that are standard in forms are referred to as *standard fields*, and the fields that you create in a custom form are referred to as *user-defined fields (UDFs)*. Most standard fields in forms are linked to controls on the forms so the data in the fields can be displayed and easily changed. A user-defined field isn't linked to a control unless you add a control and link it to the field.

One other concept is important in understanding Outlook fields: the question of where the fields are located. Fields can be located in Outlook items or in Outlook folders or in both locations.

Fields that are in Outlook items are available only in the items that have those fields. Fields that are in Outlook folders are available for use in defining custom views. Fields that are in both locations are available in the individual items in addition to being available for use in folder views. You learned about displaying different fields in views in Chapter 14, "Outlook Views."

When you design a custom form, it is important to plan out the form ahead of time and decide what controls you want to add, which controls will be linked to Outlook fields, and where those fields will be located.

Outlook Form Tabs

All Outlook forms have *form tabs*, also referred to as *pages*. For example, the Contact form contains five tabs: General, Details, Activities, Certificates, and All Fields. The Properties and Actions tabs are shown in a form only when the form is in design mode. In addition to those named tabs, each form has tabs that normally are invisible, named P.2, P.3, P.4, P.5, and P.6. Tabs that aren't shown when the form is in run mode are shown in design mode with their names enclosed in parentheses. Figure 20.5 shows a contact form in design mode with the available form tabs.

FIGURE 20.5

The unused tabs of a form are shown in design mode with parentheses, such as (P.2).

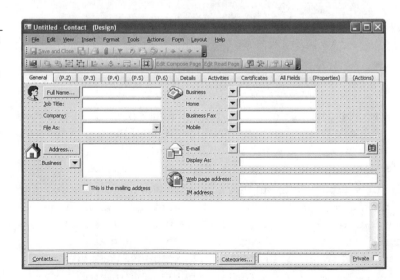

Some of the named tabs can be customized. You can also show and customize any of the P.2 to P.6 tabs. You can't add additional tabs to Outlook forms, however; you must work with the available tabs. Table 20.2 lists the tabs for each type of Outlook form and indicates which of those tabs can be customized. Tabs P.2 to P.6 aren't listed in this table because they are customizable in all types of Outlook forms. The All Fields, Properties, and Actions tabs aren't listed because they aren't customizable in any type of Outlook form.

Table 20.2   Outlook Form Tabs

Form Type	Customizable	Not Customizable
E-mail	Message	
Task		Task, Details
Appointment		Appointment, Scheduling
Contact	General	Details, Activities, Certificates
Journal Entry		General
Post	Message	

To display a tab in the custom form, select the tab when in design mode and then select **Form**, **Display This Page**. This menu item is a toggle and alternates between checked and unchecked states each time it is selected. Alternatively, you can place a control on the tab, and the **Display This Page** toggle is checked automatically to display the tab when the form is in run mode.

Compose and Read Pages

In addition to tabs, Outlook forms also have different Compose and Read pages. For example, the Compose page is shown when you create a new e-mail item. Figure 20.6 shows the Compose page of a form in design mode, which displays the To button and text control.

FIGURE 20.6

The Compose page is shown when you create a new item.

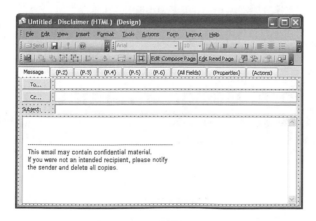

The Read page is shown when you open an existing e-mail item. The e-mail item that you read doesn't have the Send button and displays the To and From fields differently than when you compose the e-mail. Figure 20.7 shows the Read page of a form in design mode.

FIGURE 20.7

The Read page is shown when you open an existing item.

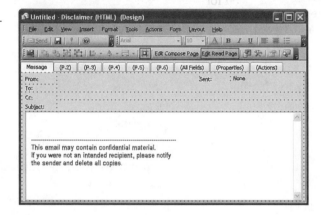

You can design a form to use separate layouts for the Compose and Read pages, or you can use one layout for both composing and reading. Each form tab can be set individually to use separate Compose and Read pages or one layout for both composing and reading:

- To change from editing the Compose page or the Read page to editing the other page, select either **Edit Compose Page** or **Edit Read Page** on the design toolbar.

- To use one layout for both the Compose and Read pages, select **Form**, **Separate Read Layout**. This menu item is a toggle and changes from using a separate layout to the same layout and back.

caution

When you switch from using separate page layouts to one page layout for both the Compose and Read pages, the layout for the current page is used, and the other page layout is discarded. Make sure you are using the layout you want preserved when you switch to one page layout, or if you intend to use only one, switch before you start designing the page.

Locating More Form Design Information

Many chapters have been devoted to Outlook form design in Outlook programming books, so you can't learn everything there is to know about designing Outlook forms in just one small chapter in this book.

For more information about designing Outlook forms, see *Special Edition Using Outlook 2003* by Patricia Cardoza. You can also find a wealth of information about designing Outlook forms at the Slipstick Web site at `http://www.slipstick.com/dev/forms.htm`.

Many sample forms supplied by Microsoft and others can be downloaded and used as is, or they can be customized for your requirements. Examining sample forms is one of the best ways to learn about customizing Outlook forms.

Microsoft sample forms are available from the Templates link on the Office Online Web site. Each template indicates what Office application the template is for, using an icon that represents the Office application.

The easiest way to find Outlook-specific templates supplied by Microsoft is to look on the `http://www.slipstick.com/addins/mssampleapps.htm` Web page. Sample forms are categorized there by the uses for the forms.

Many other sample custom forms supplied by others are available for download from links at `http://www.slipstick.com/dev/forms.htm#samples`.

THE ABSOLUTE MINIMUM

In this chapter, you learned the basics of customizing Outlook forms. To review, you now know

> What sorts of things you can do with custom Outlook forms.
>
> How to create a custom Outlook form from a modified standard Outlook form.
>
> Where to find more information about customizing Outlook forms and where to locate sample custom forms.

Now that you know about custom Outlook forms, you will learn about using Outlook to collaborate with other people in the next chapter.

IN THIS CHAPTER

- Learning how to use Outlook to share scheduling information with other people.

- Understanding how to plan meetings with other people.

- Learning how to use Microsoft Exchange server's collaborative features.

21

COLLABORATING WITH OUTLOOK AND EXCHANGE

In this chapter, you will learn how to use Outlook to work collaboratively with other people. You will learn about sharing your schedule information so other people can see when you are free and when you are busy while they are planning meetings. You will also learn how to share your Outlook folders with other people if you are using Microsoft Exchange server and how to keep private items you don't want other people to see. Finally, you will learn how to use Exchange server public folders.

Sharing Free/Busy Information

The most difficult part of planning a meeting is finding a free time and date for the attendees and resources when the meeting can take place. Outlook can publish information from your schedule so other people can see when you are free and when you are busy. Figure 21.1 shows how Outlook displays free/busy information that is used for scheduling meetings.

FIGURE 21.1

Free/busy information shows whether people's time is free, busy, tentative, out of office, or not available.

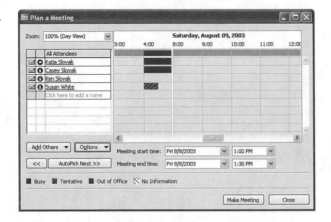

Free/busy information is automatically available, if you are using Microsoft Exchange server, for everyone else on the same Exchange server. For planning meetings with people in other organizations or people not using Microsoft Exchange server, Outlook can publish your free/busy information on a Free/Busy Server on the Internet. Microsoft provides an Internet Free/Busy Service that can be used for this purpose and is free for anyone to use. You will learn to use free/busy information in the section "Using the Meeting Planner" later in this chapter.

By default, free/busy information is published every 15 minutes to the Free/Busy Server and covers a period of two months. Both of these settings can be changed if meetings are planned more than two months in the future, or if you need more frequently updated free/busy information.

To change your free/busy settings, do the following:

1. Select **Tools**, **Options.** Click the **Preferences** tab and select the **Calendar Options** button.

2. Select **Free/Busy Options** to open the dialog shown in Figure 21.2.

3. To change how often free/busy information is published and for how many months, type your desired changes in the **Options** section of the dialog.

FIGURE 21.2

In the Free/Busy
Options dialog,
you can change
settings for
where and how
often free/busy
information is
published.

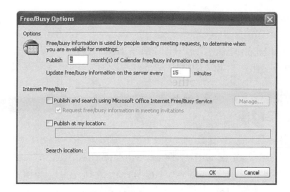

4. Check the **Publish and search using Microsoft Office Internet Free/Busy Service** checkbox if you want to use Microsoft's free Internet service.

5. Check the **Request free/busy information in meeting invitations** checkbox to include text in a meeting invitation inviting the person to authorize you to access his or her free/busy information on the Internet Free/Busy Service.

6. Select **Manage** to go to the home page of the Microsoft Office Internet Free/Busy Service. You must be online so that you can log in to the service using Microsoft Passport. Follow the instructions on the Web site to add names of people who can view your free/busy information from the service. Everyone sharing Internet free/busy information must be enrolled in the service.

   If your Passport uses a different e-mail address than your Outlook profile, the sign-in screen will remind you to use the correct Passport sign-in e-mail address and password. After setting up your free/busy information on the Microsoft Office Internet Free/Busy Service, log out of the server and close Internet Explorer; then return to Outlook to continue with step 7.

7. If you are using a free/busy service other than Microsoft, check the **Publish at my location** checkbox and enter the Web address of the service. Configuration and sign-in information for the free/busy service will be supplied by the service or your administrator. You can use both the Microsoft service and another free/busy service at the same time.

8. To specify a default server for storing free/busy information, type the URL of the server in the **Search location** area. The file extension for free/busy files is .VFB.

9. Click **OK** three times to save the free/busy settings and exit the Options dialog.

When you plan a meeting, Outlook requests free/busy information for attendees and resources from any configured free/busy services as well as from Microsoft Exchange server if you are using Exchange. You will learn how to work with free/busy information in the following sections.

Scheduling Meetings

Meetings must be scheduled, and finding a time and date when everyone attending a meeting is free can be a lot of work. If you are the meeting organizer, you often have to e-mail or call every attendee repeatedly until a time and date are finally arranged, or you can use Outlook to make planning a meeting easier.

Outlook has built-in meeting planning features for setting up meeting rosters, checking attendees' schedules, issuing invitations, and tracking invitation responses. Events for more than one person are planned the same way meetings are planned.

Outlook's meeting planning features make it easy to find a time and date when all attendees are free. The meeting planner can autopick suggested times for meetings based on the free/busy information for each attendee, or you can manually search for appropriate times for meetings.

You can also set up group schedules that always include the same group of people and resources. You can plan meetings for the group or include the group in meetings that include other people outside the group.

The differences between the meeting planner and group schedules are as follows:

- Meeting Planner attendees must be added to the meeting roster each time you use the meeting planner.

- Group Schedules always include the same people and resources. When you use a group schedule, you don't have to select the attendees each time.

When you use the meeting planner to view free/busy information, you can show calendar details in addition to information about a person's free/busy status such as free, busy, or no information. Calendar details show the specifics of any appointments, meetings, or events for a person—for example, busy at 4:00 PM with a sales meeting in the office that is scheduled to last until 5:00 PM. Calendar details can be shown in the meeting planner grid, when you hover your mouse over an allocated block of time, or both. Private calendar items never show any details, just the free/busy status.

Figure 21.3 shows pop-up calendar details for a block of time when using the meeting planner in a group schedule.

FIGURE 21.3

Pop-up details show how, where, and when a person's time is allocated.

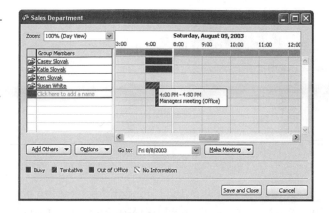

Configuring Meeting Planning Options

To configure how your meeting planning options work, follow these steps:

1. Select **Tools**, **Options**, click the **Preferences** tab, and select **Calendar Options** to open the dialog shown in Figure 21.4.

2. Check or uncheck the **Allow attendees to propose new times for meetings you organize** checkbox depending on how you want to organize meetings. If this setting is checked, people invited to meetings can suggest alternate meeting times when they respond to a meeting invitation. If this setting is not checked, people invited to a meeting can only accept or decline the invitation.

FIGURE 21.4

The Calendar Options dialog enables you to configure meeting planning and free/busy options.

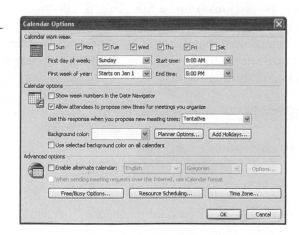

3. Select a response to use for proposed meetings. The default response is Tentative, and the choices are Tentative, Accept, and Decline.

4. Select **Planner Options** to open the Planner Options dialog, as shown in Figure 21.5.

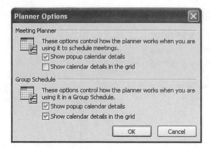

FIGURE 21.5

In the Planner Options dialog, you can set how you want free/busy information to appear when you plan meetings and use group schedules.

5. Check the checkboxes for showing calendar details using pop-ups when you hover the mouse over an allocated block of time, in the free/busy grid, or both depending on how you want to see the details, if you do at all. Separate checkboxes are available for details in the meeting planner and the meeting planner used in group schedules.

6. Click **OK** on the Planner Options dialog and then **OK** two more times to save the settings for the meeting planner.

Using the Meeting Planner

You can display the meeting planner in a number of ways. The meeting planner is displayed in the Scheduling tab of appointments, all-day events, and meeting requests; when you select **Actions**, **Plan a Meeting** in a Calendar folder; or when you work with Group Schedules. The only difference in the meeting planners displayed in these different ways is that the meeting planner opened from the Plan a Meeting menu command has two additional buttons: Make Meeting and Close. This meeting planner is shown in Figure 21.6.

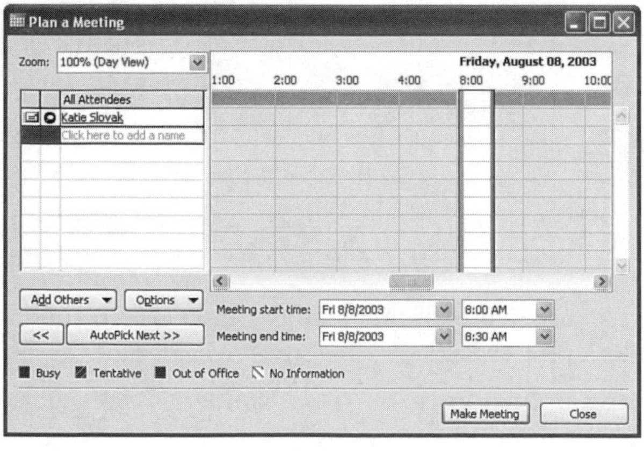

FIGURE 21.6

The meeting planner enables you to select free times for all attendees of a meeting and issue invitations to the meeting.

The meeting organizer is always included in the meeting as a required attendee. Additional attendees can be added as required, optional, or resource attendees.

To use the meeting planner to plan a meeting, follow these steps:

1. Open the meeting planner by selecting **Actions**, **Plan a Meeting** in a Calendar folder or select the **Scheduling** tab in an open appointment, all-day event, or meeting request. Your name appears as a required attendee for the meeting.

2. To add additional attendees to the meeting, either enter names in the All Attendees list or select attendees from an address book or Exchange Public Folder by selecting **Add Others**. Names you enter directly must be in one of your address books so their e-mail addresses can be found. You can also enter an e-mail address instead of a name.

3. If you use **Add Others**, **Add from Address Book** to select attendees, highlight each attendee and select one of the buttons for **Required**, **Optional**, or **Resources** to add that attendee to the meeting roster. When you are finished adding attendees from an address book, click **OK** to return to the meeting planner.

4. To change an attendee's status, select the icon to the left of the attendee name in the All Attendees list and select a new status from the drop-down list. The selections are Required Attendee, Optional Attendee, or Resource (Room or Equipment). The status of the meeting organizer cannot be changed; the organizer is always a required attendee.

5. Select the meeting start and end times in the **Meeting Start Time** and **Meeting End Time** date and time drop-downs. These start and end times are used as the starting point for picking a date and time for the meeting. The start and end times can be changed when you select a final time and date.

6. If you want to display only meeting times that occur during the attendees' working hours, select the **Options**, **Show Only Working Hours** toggle.

7. Other options you can select are **Show Calendar Details**, **AutoPick**, and **Refresh Free/Busy**. AutoPick enables you to select from the following options:

   ■ **All People and Resources** picks free time for all attendees; required, optional, and resource attendees' free time is used.

   ■ **All People and One Resource** picks free time for all required and optional attendees. Free time for the first resource in the attendees list is used.

   ■ **Required People** picks free time for all required attendees.

   ■ **Required People and One Resource** picks free time for all required attendees. Free time for the first resource in the attendees list is used.

8. If the initial suggested date and time for the meeting conflict with the sched-ules of any of the meeting attendees, select **<<** to autopick an earlier date and time or select **AutoPick Next >>** to select a later date and time for the meeting.

9. When you find a meeting date and time free for all attendees, select **Make Meeting** to open a Meeting Request form. The meeting planner displays a meeting and free/busy times for attendees, as shown in Figure 21.7.

10. Select **File**, **Send** to send out the meeting request as an invitation to the meeting attendees. Responses to the meeting invitation are tallied as they are received on a **Tracking** tab in the meeting request.

11. Click **Close** to close the meeting planner.

FIGURE 21.7

The meeting planner shows the free/busy information for all meeting attendees when it is available.

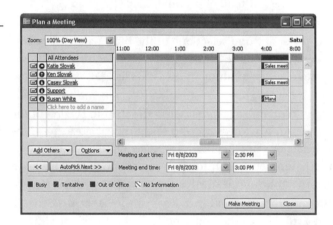

In the meeting invitation, you can include any information that will be helpful to the meeting attendees. This information can include attachments of agendas, travel direc-tions, or anything else that will help the attendees. Information can also be included in the text of a meeting invitation. You can also use a meeting workspace as a reposi-tory for documents and agendas related to the meeting. A meeting workspace is located on a server and usually is a Windows Sharepoint Services Web site created by an administrator. If you are using a meeting workspace, select **Meeting Workspace** in the meeting invitation to open the Meeting Workspace task pane, where you can select an existing meeting workspace or create a new meeting workspace.

Inviting Resources

Resources are things such as conference rooms, slide projectors, caterers, and com-puters. Inviting a resource to a meeting is a way of reserving the resource for the meeting. If the resource accepts the meeting invitation, its time is listed as Busy for the duration of the meeting.

Resources are assigned mailboxes on a Microsoft Exchange server or on a computer running Outlook. Invitations to meetings are e-mailed to resources the same way they are e-mailed to people attending the meetings.

One or more people are assigned to be the resource manager and accept or decline meeting invitations for the resource. Resource managers are usually granted Owner permissions for the resource mailbox, so they have full permissions for the folder. Custom programs can also run in the resource folder and accept or decline invitations for the resource. The person or people assigned as resource manager are responsible for ensuring the resource is present at the meeting.

Settings for resource scheduling are available to automatically accept meeting requests, decline conflicting meeting requests, and decline recurring meeting requests. To view or set the resource scheduling settings, select **Tools**, **Options**, **Preferences**, **Calendar Options**, **Resource Scheduling**.

Using Group Schedules

Group Schedules are useful when the same group of people and resources are meeting attendees over and over, such as departmental meetings at work. Instead of adding the same people and resources again and again, you can create a Group Schedule that includes the attendees and use the Group Schedule either as the attendee list for a meeting or as the starting point for an attendee list.

To view or create Group Schedules, select **Actions**, **View Group Schedules**. To view an existing Group Schedule, highlight the group and select **Open**. To remove a group, select **Delete**.

To create a new group, select **New**. Enter a name for the group and click **OK** to open a meeting planner where you can add group members by entering names or using **Add Others,** as you learned to do earlier in the "Using the Meeting Planner" section. When you are finished adding members to the group, you can select **Save and Close** to save the new group, or you can start using the Group Schedule immediately.

To use a Group Schedule, open it if it is not already open and select **Make Meeting** to show the available meeting choices:

- **New Meeting** opens a new Meeting Request form addressed to all the group members except the meeting organizer.
- **New Meeting with All** opens a new Meeting Request form addressed to all the group members.
- **New Meeting as Resource** opens a Meeting Request form for scheduling a resource. The resource must be a mailbox, and you must have been granted permission to schedule that resource.

- **New <u>M</u>ail Message** opens an e-mail addressed to all the group members except the meeting organizer.
- **New Mail Me<u>s</u>sage with All** opens an e-mail addressed to all the group members.

Figure 21.8 shows an example of a Group Schedule.

FIGURE 21.8

Group Schedules make it easy to repeatedly invite the same group of people and resources to meetings.

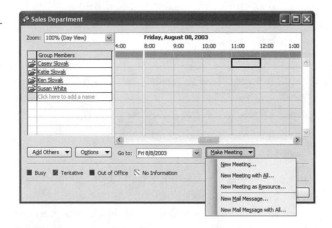

Using Exchange Public Folders

Public Folders are available when you are using Microsoft Exchange server. Public Folders are folders that are available within an Exchange organization on a shared basis. Various permissions determine who can view, create, edit, and delete items in each Public Folder, which you will learn about in the section "Folder Permissions" later in this chapter.

Public Folders are visible in a separate group of folders than your Exchange mailbox. To view Public Folders, display the Folder List in the Navigation Pane. Under the Public Folders folder are two main folders—Favorites and All Public Folders—as shown in Figure 21.9.

Public Folders Favorites

Public Folders Favorites is a special folder that is used to determine which Public Folders are available when you are working offline. Making a folder available in offline mode requires a few steps because you not only have to make the folder available, but you also have to update the offline folder so it has current data.

FIGURE 21.9

Public Folders are displayed in their own group of folders apart from your Exchange mailbox.

To make a Public Folder available when you are working offline, follow these steps:

1. Right-click the desired folder in the Folder List and select **Add to Favorites**.

2. In the Add to Favorites dialog, change the offline name of the folder if you want. If you want to automatically add subfolders of the current folder to Favorites, select **Options** and select the desired subfolder options.

3. Select **Add** to add the folder with any selected subfolder options to Favorites. The folder is added to Favorites but is empty until it is synchronized with its online counterpart.

A folder can be updated or synchronized for offline use automatically, or it can be performed manually in one of two ways. All methods of synchronization have advantages and disadvantages, so you will have to decide which to use based on how you work with Outlook.

Synchronizing folders in Outlook means keeping the data in the online and offline folders identical. Each item in a folder that is being synchronized is checked for the date and time the item was created or modified, and compared to the same item in the other folder. Items in both folders are updated so the item with the most recent timestamp is retained.

Automatic synchronization occurs when the Public Folder is set for synchronization during send/receive operations that occur automatically at a preset interval of time. If you also set a send/receive operation to occur when you exit Outlook, you are always assured of having your offline Public Folders up to date.

You can perform manual synchronization by selecting **Tools**, **Send/Receive** and then selecting either **Send/Receive All** or selecting the send/receive group that is used to synchronize the offline folders. Another method of manual synchronization for only one folder is to select the offline folder you want to synchronize in the Public Folders Favorites group. When the folder is viewed as the current folder, it is immediately synchronized.

Selecting a folder in the Public Folders Favorites group synchronizes only that one folder for offline use. This method provides control over which folders are synchronized and when. If you use many offline folders, either a manual or automatic send/receive operation is an easier method of offline synchronization.

To add Public Folders Favorites folders to a send/receive group, do the following:

1. Select **Tools**, **Send/Receive**, **Send/Receive Settings**, **Define Send/Receive Groups** to open the Send/Receive Groups dialog, as shown in Figure 21.10. You can also open the dialog by pressing the keyboard shortcut **Ctrl+Alt+S**.

FIGURE 21.10

The Send/Receive Groups dialog enables you to configure when folders are synchronized.

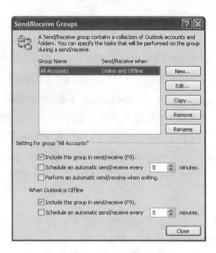

2. Select the send/receive group to which you want to add the offline folders and select **Edit** to open the Send/Receive Settings dialog.

3. Scroll down the list of folders in the Send/Receive Settings dialog and expand the Public Folders and Favorites groups. Check the folders you want synchronized for offline use, as shown in Figure 21.11, and click **OK** to return to the Send/Receive Groups dialog. If you don't see the Public Folders and Favorites groups in the list of folders, see the section "Making Public Folders Favorites Available Offline" located immediately after these steps.

FIGURE 21.11

Each Public Folder that is checked is included as part of the send/ receive group.

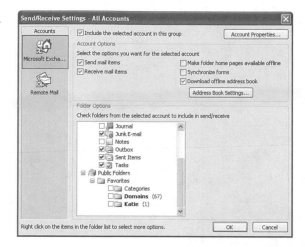

4. If you want to automatically synchronize offline folders, check the **Schedule an automatic send/receive every** checkbox, and select a time interval in the up-down control in both the **Setting for group** and **When Outlook is Offline** areas. Figure 21.12 shows these options in the Send/Receive Groups dialog.

5. To automatically synchronize offline folders when you exit Outlook, check the **Perform an automatic send/receive when exiting** checkbox.

6. Make sure **Include this group in send/ receive (F9)** is checked in both the **Setting for group** and **When Outlook is Offline** areas to ensure the offline folders send/ receive group is automatically synchronized.

7. Click **Close**.

Making Public Folders Favorites Available Offline

If you don't see the Public Folders and Favorites groups in the list of folders to include in send/receive operations for a Send/Receive Group:

1. Select the Microsoft Exchange e-mail account and click **Account Properties** in the Send/Receive Settings dialog, as shown in Figure 21.11, to open the Exchange e-mail account properties dialog.

2. Select the Advanced tab, as shown in Figure 21.12.

3. Check the **Download Public Folder Favorites** checkbox. Public Folder Favorites are not available for selection for offline use unless this checkbox is checked. You will have to exit and restart Outlook to make the change in this setting work.

FIGURE 21.12

Download Public Folder Favorites must be checked for public folders to be available for synchronizing and working with when offline.

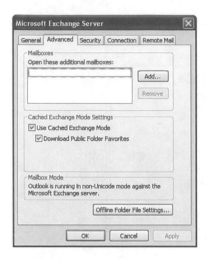

4. Click **OK** twice and then click **Close**.

5. Exit and restart Outlook.

All Public Folders

Public folders are located under the All Public Folders folder. A public folder can be any type of Outlook folder, such as a Contacts or Calendar folder.

Sharing Contacts folders for workgroups or departments is one of the most common uses for public folders. A public Contacts folder can be enabled for use as an Outlook address book and can be used anywhere any other address book can be used.

Some other common uses for public folders are

- Calendar folders used for departmental or workgroup calendars
- E-mail folders used to post messages for bulletin boards or discussions, moderated or unmoderated
- E-mail folders that can receive e-mail used for Help desk and support functions
- E-mail folders used to receive mailing lists that groups of people can access as needed
- Shared Tasks, Journal, and Notes folders for group use
- Folders used for Exchange server collaborative, routing, and workflow applications
- Secure folders that contain confidential items visible only to certain people or groups

Posting to a Public Folder

To post a message to a public folder, select the folder and then select **File**, **New**, **Post in This Folder**. After you finish composing the post message, select the **Post** icon on the Standard toolbar to post the message.

To reply to a message posted in a folder, select the message, right-click, and select **Post Reply to Folder**. A Post message opens already addressed to the folder and with the same conversation topic as the original message. Select the **Post** icon on the Standard toolbar to post the reply.

If you select **Reply** when you right-click on a message posted in a folder instead of **Post Reply to Folder**, a new e-mail message opens already addressed to the person who posted the message to the folder. This message is sent directly to the original poster and is not posted to the folder.

tip

Even if a folder is hidden from the GAL, it still can receive e-mail if you know its e-mail address. The e-mail address of a public folder is the folder name followed by the domain name of the Exchange server. If your Exchange domain name is outlook2003.com, the e-mail address of a public Categories folder would be categories@outlook2003.com.

Posts with the same conversation topics and an Arrange By Conversation view of a folder enable viewing discussions or bulletin board postings grouped by topic.

Public folders have e-mail addresses, and you can send e-mail to a public folder. By default, all public folder e-mail addresses are hidden from the Exchange Global Address List (GAL), but the Exchange administrator can show or hide any public folder in the GAL. If a public folder is visible in the GAL, you can select it as an e-mail address the same way you would select any other recipient in the GAL.

Working with Other People's Folders

Users of Microsoft Exchange server can, with the appropriate permissions, open and work with other people's folders. Permissions can also be granted to allow other people to send items on your behalf. Folder permissions also are set by the owners of Exchange public folders to control access to public folders. You will learn about folder permissions in the next section.

Folder Permissions

All folders have access permissions, which are used when you share one of your own folders or when you access an Exchange Public Folder. You don't have to worry about permissions when you access one of your own folders because you are the owner of all the folders in your Outlook data file. Permissions determine what you can do in a folder, and even if the folder is visible at all.

Outlook provides the permissions listed in Table 21.1 for working with folders.

Table 21.1   Outlook Folder Permissions

Permission Level	Permissions
None	No permissions for items; folder invisible
Contributor	Create items; folder visible
Reviewer	Read items; folder visible
Nonediting Author	Create, read, delete own items; folder visible
Author	Create, read, edit own items; delete own items; folder visible
Publishing Author	Create, read, edit own items; delete own items; create subfolders; folder visible
Editor	Create, read, edit all items; delete all items; folder visible
Publishing Editor	Create, read, edit all items; delete all items; create subfolders; folder visible
Owner	Create, read, edit all items; delete all items; create subfolders; folder visible; assign permissions; assign delegates

In addition to the standard permissions, you can change any of the available permissions to create custom permissions assignments. When you access a shared folder or an Exchange Public Folder, you can perform only the functions allowed by your assigned permissions.

Sharing Folders with Other People

To make an Exchange mailbox folder available to other people, follow these steps:

1. Select the folder and select **File**, **Folder**, **Sharing**. If you have a group selected in the Navigation Pane, such as Calendar, you can select **Share My Calendar** in the Navigation Pane. The Permissions tab of the folder Properties opens, as shown in Figure 21.13. The **Share My Folder** command in the Navigation Pane is available for the Calendar, Contacts, Tasks, Notes, and Journal groups.

2. Select **Add**. Then select one or more people from the Global Address List and click **Add** and then **OK** to add those people to the permissions list for the folder.

FIGURE 21.13

Folder permissions can use predefined roles or can be customized to fine-tune the access granted to the folder.

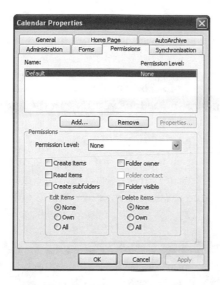

3. The people added usually have no permissions on the folder until you select each person and assign a permission from the **Permission Level** drop-down. When you select a permission level from the drop-down, the appropriate permission checkboxes and options are set based on that permission level.

4. Alternatively, you can check permission checkboxes and set options, and the equivalent permission level is automatically assigned. If permissions are granted that are normally not available for a standard permission level, the permission level is changed to Custom.

5. Click **OK** to save the permissions assigned for the folder.

Opening Other People's Folders

There are two ways to open folders in another person's Exchange mailbox:

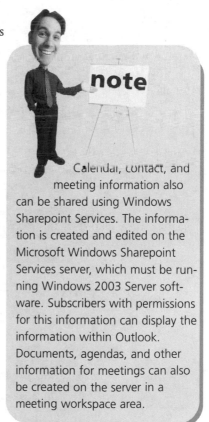

note

Calendar, contact, and meeting information also can be shared using Windows Sharepoint Services. The information is created and edited on the Microsoft Windows Sharepoint Services server, which must be running Windows 2003 Server software. Subscribers with permissions for this information can display the information within Outlook. Documents, agendas, and other information for meetings can also be created on the server in a meeting workspace area.

- Permanently opening the mailbox as part of your profile
- Permanently or temporarily opening folders in the mailbox in the current Outlook session

Before you can open another person's mailbox or folders, that person must grant you permissions on the folder and for the actions you take in the folder.

Opening a Mailbox as Part of Your Profile

When a mailbox is opened as part of your profile, it is available automatically when you start Outlook. The mailbox and any folders you have permission to access are displayed in the Navigation Pane the same ways as any of your own folders, as shown in Figure 21.14.

FIGURE 21.14

Shared folders are accessible the same ways your own folders are when they are part of your profile.

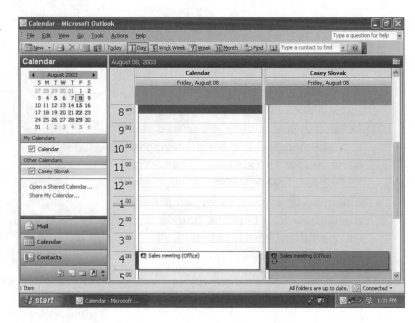

To open another person's mailbox as part of your profile, do the following:

1. Select **Tools**, **E-mail Accounts**.
2. Select the **View or Change Existing E-mail Accounts** option and **Next** to open the E-mail Accounts dialog, as shown in Figure 21.15.
3. Select the Microsoft Exchange server e-mail account and select **Change**.
4. Select **More Settings** and then click the **Advanced** tab.
5. Select **Add** to open the Add Mailbox dialog, as shown in Figure 21.16.

FIGURE 21.15

Select your Exchange server e-mail account to be able to change its properties.

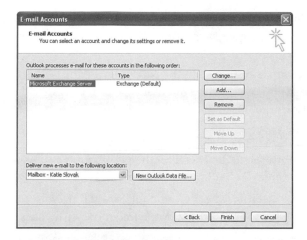

FIGURE 21.16

The Add Mailbox dialog enables you to add a mailbox to your profile if the mailbox owner has given you permissions to open the mailbox.

6. Enter the name of the mailbox you want to open and click **OK**.

7. Click **OK**, **Next**, and then **Finish** to open the mailbox.

After the mailbox is added to your profile, it and the folders for which you have permissions are available every time you start Outlook, until the mailbox is removed from your profile, or the mailbox owner revokes your permissions to the mailbox.

To remove a mailbox from your profile, follow steps 1 to 4 shown previously for adding the profile; then select the mailbox and select **Remove**. Choose **Yes** in the dialog that asks whether you are sure you want to remove the mailbox and then follow steps 6 and 7 to complete removal of the mailbox from your profile.

Opening a Folder Permanently

To open a single folder in another person's mailbox and have it available each time you open Outlook, do the following:

1. Select the folder type you want to open from among the Calendar, Contacts, Tasks, Notes, or Journal groups in the Navigation Pane. This example uses the Calendar group.

2. When the group is displayed in the Navigation Pane, select **Open Shared Calendar**. If you are opening another type of folder, substitute that folder name for Calendar.

3. Select **Name**, select a name from the Global Address List, and click **OK** twice.

You can now work with the folder based on the permissions you were granted by the folder owner.

After the folder is opened this way, it is available every time you start Outlook until you remove it from your shared folders, or the folder owner revokes your permissions for the folder.

Opening a Folder Temporarily

Folders that are opened temporarily must be re-opened each time you want to work with them, unlike folders in mailboxes opened as part of your profile, or folders opened permanently. After a folder is opened, you can work with it just like you would any of your own folders during that Outlook session. Calendar, Contacts, Tasks, Notes, and Journal folders are shown in the appropriate Navigation Pane group.

To temporarily open a folder in another person's mailbox for only the current Outlook session, follow these steps:

1. Select **File**, **Open**, **Other User's Folder**.

2. In the Open Other User's Folder dialog, select **Name** to open the address book or enter the name of the mailbox. If you open the address book, select the mailbox from the Global Address List and click **OK**.

note

The exception to showing the folder in the appropriate Navigation Pane group is the Inbox, which is not shown in the Mail group. If you switch away from viewing the Inbox in another person's mailbox, you have to re-open it to view it again.

3. In the Open Other User's Folder dialog, select the folder you want to open in the **Folder** drop-down. You can open the default Calendar, Contacts, Inbox, Journal, Notes, or Tasks folder.

4. Click **OK** to open the other person's folder.

You can now work with the folder based on the permissions you were granted by the folder owner.

Setting Up Delegates

When you make someone your delegate, that person is granted access to your folders based on permissions you grant. In addition to having access to your folders, delegates also can send items on your behalf. A common scenario is a secretary or assistant who is a delegate for someone. This assistant sends and answers e-mails, responds to meeting and event invitations, and performs other chores on behalf of another person.

To view another person's folders, the delegate must open the folders by either of the methods covered in the preceding section of this chapter.

To grant someone delegate permissions for your mailbox, follow these steps:

1. Select **Tools**, **Options** and then click the **Delegates** tab.
2. Select **Add** to open the Add Users dialog.
3. Select one or more users from the Global Address List and click **OK** to open the Delegate Permissions dialog, as shown in Figure 21.17.

FIGURE 21.17
You can set the permissions for each folder you want the delegate to be able to access.

4. Assign the permissions you want to grant for each folder.
5. Checkboxes are available for sending a summary of the permissions granted to the delegate and for allowing the delegate to see private items. Select the appropriate checkboxes.
6. Click **OK** twice to add the delegate.

Privacy

Sharing folders has privacy implications because you may have e-mails, appointments, contacts, or other items that you don't want anyone else to see, such as medical appointments or e-mails about that new job for which you're interviewing. Instead of moving those items to folders that aren't shared, you can mark the items as private.

Calendar, Contacts, Tasks, and Journal items can be marked as private items on the General tab of their forms. To mark a Calendar, Contacts, Tasks, or Journal item private, open it and check the **Private** checkbox. Select **File**, **Save** to save the change.

To mark an e-mail item private, select **Options** in the E-mail toolbar of an open e-mail. Set the Sensitivity to **Private** and select **Close**. E-mail items can be marked private only before they are sent.

To mark a post item private, open it and select **File, Properties** if you are using the Outlook editor. Set the Sensitivity to **Private** and click **OK**. Post items can be marked private only before they are posted. If you are using Word as your editor, you can't set the Sensitivity of a Post item.

Private items can be seen only by folder owners and delegates with permission to view private items.

tip

You can make all new e-mails you create private by using a global e-mail option. Select **Tools**, **Options**, **Preferences**, **E-mail Options**, **Advanced E-mail Options** and then set the Sensitivity to **Private** in the **Set sensitivity** drop-down.

Click **OK** three times to save the setting and exit the Options dialog. All new e-mails you create after this will have a sensitivity of Private.

The Absolute Minimum

In this chapter, you learned how to use Outlook to collaborate with other people. To review, you now know how to

- Publish your calendar free/busy information.
- Plan meetings using the meeting planner and free/busy information.
- Work with Microsoft Exchange server Public Folders.
- Open other people's data files and assign delegates when using Microsoft Exchange server.

With the knowledge you acquired in this chapter, you now know about Outlook's collaboration features. The appendixes that follow this chapter will teach you how to install Outlook and its optional features, how to find support and resources for Outlook, and how to solve common Outlook problems.

APPENDIXES

Found on the Web at www.quepublishing.com

Index

How can we make this index more useful? Email us at indexes@quepublishing.com

How can we make this index more useful? Email us at indexes@quepublishing.com

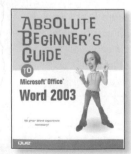
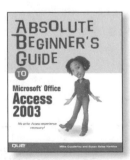